COLORADO TRAILS
CENTRAL REGION

Cover photos
Clockwise from bottom left: Medano Pass and Great Sand Dunes Trail, Baldwin Lakes Trail, Schofield Pass and Devil's Punchbowl Trail

Back cover photos
From left: Waldorf and Santiago Ghost Town Trail, Red Cone Peak Trail

COLORADO TRAILS

CENTRAL REGION

PETER MASSEY
ANGELA TITUS
JEANNE WILSON

ADLER
PUBLISHING

Contents

Before You Go

Why a 4WD Does It Better

The design and engineering of 4WD sport utility vehicles provide them with many advantages over normal cars when you head off the paved road:

- improved distribution of power to all four wheels;
- a transmission transfer case, which provides low-range gear selection for greater pulling power and for crawling over difficult terrain;
- high ground clearance;
- less overhang of the vehicle's body past the wheels, which provides better front- and rear-clearance when crossing gullies and ridges;
- large-lug, wide-tread tires;
- rugged construction (including underbody skid plates on many models).

If you plan to do off-highway touring, all of these considerations are important whether you are evaluating the capabilities of your current sport utility vehicle (SUV) or are looking to buy one; each is considered in detail in this chapter.

To explore the most difficult trails described in this book, you will need a SUV that is well rated in each of the above features. If you own a 2WD sport utility vehicle, a lighter car-type SUV, or a low-clearance 2WD pickup truck, your ability to explore the more difficult trails will depend on conditions and your level of experience.

A word of caution: Whatever type of 4WD vehicle you drive, understand that it is not invincible or indestructible. Nor can it go everywhere. A SUV has a much higher center of gravity and weighs more than a car, and so has its own consequent limitations.

Experience is the only way to learn what your vehicle can and cannot do. Therefore, if you are inexperienced, we strongly recommend that you start with trails that have lower difficulty ratings. As you develop an understanding of your vehicle and of your own taste for adventure, you can safely tackle the more challenging trails.

One way to beef up your knowledge quickly, while avoiding the costly and sometimes dangerous lessons learned from on-the-road mistakes, is to undertake a 4WD driving course taught by a professional. Look in the Yellow Pages for courses in your area.

Using This Book

Route Planning

The regional map at the beginning of this book provides a convenient overview of the trails in the Central Region of Colorado. Each trail is highlighted in a different color, and major highways and towns are indicated, to help you plan various routes by connecting a series of trails and paved roads.

As you plan your overall route, you will probably want to utilize as many backroads and 4x4 trails as possible. However, check the difficulty rating and time required for each trail before finalizing your plans. You don't want to be stuck 50 miles from the highway—at sunset and without camping gear, since your trip was supposed to be over hours ago—when you discover that your vehicle can't handle a certain difficult passage.

Using Route Directions

Most of the trails can be started from either end, and the route directions include both directions of travel; reverse directions are printed in red below the main directions. When traveling in reverse, read from the end of the route directions for that trail and work up.

For every trail, we describe and pinpoint (by odometer reading) nearly every significant feature along the route—such as intersections, streams, washes, gates, cattle guards, and so on—and provide directions from these landmarks. Odometer readings will vary from vehicle to vehicle, so you should allow for slight variations. Be aware that trail conditions can quickly change. A new trail may be cut around a washout, a faint trail can be graded by the county, or a well-used trail may fall into disuse. All these factors will affect the accuracy of the given directions.

If you diverge from the route, zero your trip meter upon your return and continue along the route, making the necessary adjustment to the point-to-point odometer readings. In the directions, we regularly reset the odometer readings—at significant landmarks or popular lookouts and spur trails—so that you won't have to recalculate for too long.

Route directions include cross-references whenever two trails included in this book connect; these cross-references allow for an easy change of route or destination.

Each trail includes periodic latitude and longitude readings to facilitate using a global positioning system (GPS) receiver. These readings may also assist you in finding your location on the maps. The GPS coordinates were taken using the WGS 84 datum and are in the format dd°mm.mm'. To save time when loading coordinates into your GPS receiver, you may wish to include only one decimal place, since in Colorado, the first decimal place equals about 165 yards and the second only about 16 yards.

Difficulty Ratings

We utilize a point system to rate the difficulty of each backroad and 4x4 trail. Any such system is subjective, and your experience of the trails will vary depending on your skill and the road conditions at the time. Indeed, any amount of rain may make the trails much more difficult, if not completely impassable.

We have rated the trails on a scale of 1 to 10—1 being passable for a normal passenger vehicle in good conditions and 10 requiring a heavily modified vehicle and an experienced driver who expects to encounter vehicle damage. Because this book is designed for owners of unmodified, high-clearance 4WD vehicles—who we assume do not want to damage their vehicles—most of the trails are rated 5 or lower. A few trails are included that rate as high as 7, while those rated 8 to 10 are beyond the scope of this book.

This is not to say that the moderate-rated trails are easy. We strongly recommend that inexperienced drivers not tackle trails rated at 4 or higher until they have undertaken a number of the lower-rated ones, so that they can gauge their skill level and prepare for the difficulty of the higher-rated trails.

In assessing the backroads and 4x4 trails, we have always assumed good road conditions (dry road surface, good visibility, and so on). The factors influencing our ratings are as follows:

■ obstacles such as rocks, mud, ruts, sand, slickrock, and stream crossings;
■ the stability of the road surface;
■ the width of the road and the vehicle clearance between trees or rocks;
■ the steepness of the road;
■ the margin for driver error (for example, a very high, open shelf road would be rated more difficult even if it was not very steep and had a stable surface).

The following is a guide to the ratings.

Rating 1: The trail is graded dirt but suitable for a normal passenger vehicle. It usually has gentle grades, is fairly wide, and has very shallow water crossings (if any).

Rating 2: High-clearance vehicles are preferred but not necessary. These trails are dirt roads, but they may have rocks, grades, water crossings, or ruts that make clearance a concern in a normal passenger vehicle. The trails are fairly wide, making passing possible at almost any point along the trail. Mud is not a concern under normal weather conditions.

Rating 3: High-clearance 4WDs are preferred, but any high-clearance vehicle is acceptable. Expect a rough road surface; mud and sand are possible but will be easily passable. You may encounter rocks up to 6 inches in diameter, a loose road surface, and shelf roads, though these will be wide enough for passing or will have adequate pull-offs.

Rating 4: High-clearance is required, 4WD is preferred, though some stock SUVs are acceptable. Expect a rough road surface with rocks larger than 6 inches, but there will be a reasonable driving line available. Patches of mud are possible but can be readily negotiated; sand may be deep and require lower tire pressures. There may be stream crossings up to 12 inches deep, substantial sections of single-lane shelf road, moderate grades, and sections of moderately loose road surface.

Rating 5: High-clearance 4WDs are required. These trails have either a rough, rutted surface, rocks up to 9 inches, mud and deep sand that may be impassable for inexperienced drivers, or stream crossings up to 18 inches deep. Certain sections may be steep enough to cause traction problems, and you may encounter very narrow shelf roads with steep drop-offs and tight clearance between rocks or trees.

Rating 6: These trails are for experienced four-wheel drivers only. They are potentially dangerous, with large rocks, ruts, or terraces that may need to be negotiated. They may also have stream crossings at least 18 inches deep, involve rapid currents, unstable stream bottoms, or difficult access; steep slopes, loose surfaces, and narrow clearances; or very narrow sections of shelf road with steep drop-offs and possibly challenging road surfaces.

Rating 7: Skilled, experienced four-wheel drivers only. These trails include very challenging sections with extremely steep grades, loose surfaces, large rocks, deep ruts, and/or tight clearances. Mud or sand may necessitate winching.

Rating 8 and above: Stock vehicles are likely to be damaged and may find the trail impassable. Highly skilled, experienced four-wheel drivers only.

Scenic Ratings

If rating the degree of difficulty is subjective, rating scenic beauty is guaranteed to lead to arguments. Despite the subjectivity of attempting a comparative rating of diverse scenery, we have tried to provide a guide to the relative scenic quality of the various trails. The ratings are based on a scale of 1 to 10, with 10 being the most attractive.

Estimated Driving Times

In calculating driving times, we have not allowed for stops. Your actual travel time may be considerably longer depending on the number and duration of the stops you make. Add more time for stops and if you prefer to drive more slowly than good conditions allow.

Current Road Information

All the 4WD trails described in this book may become impassable in poor weather conditions. Storms can alter roads, remove tracks, and create impassable washes. Most of the trails described, even easy backroads, can quickly become impassable even to 4WD vehicles after only a small amount of rain. For each trail, we have provided a phone number for obtaining current information about conditions.

Abbreviations

The route directions for the 4WD trails use a series of abbreviations as follows:

SO	CONTINUE STRAIGHT ON
TL	TURN LEFT
TR	TURN RIGHT
BL	BEAR LEFT
BR	BEAR RIGHT
UT	U-TURN

Map References

We recommend that you supplement the information in this book with more-detailed maps. For each trail, we list the sheet maps and road atlases that provide the best detail for the area. Typically, the following references are given:

- Bureau of Land Management Maps
- U.S. Forest Service Maps

- *Colorado Road & Recreation Atlas*, 1st ed. (Medford, Oregon: Benchmark Maps, 2007)—Scale 1:280,000
- *Colorado Atlas & Gazetteer*, 7th ed. (Yarmouth, Maine: DeLorme Mapping, 2007)—Scale 1:250,000
- *The Roads of Colorado*, (Addison, Texas: Mapsco, Inc., 2007)—Scale 1:160,000
- Maptech-Terrain Navigator Topo Maps—Scale 1:100,000 and 1:24,000

We recommend Benchmark's *Road & Recreation Atlas* series. The maps provide excellent overall coverage with page-to-page overlap, large type, topographical relief, and they are field checked for accuracy. These atlases provide United States, regional, and state maps for orientation, as well as enlarged "Metro Maps" for navigating urban areas. The Recreation Guide section, which provides information on local attractions and recreation, is also handy for trip planning. It is particularly useful if you wish to explore the hundreds of side roads that you will encounter when driving the backroads and 4x4 trails in this book.

The DeLorme *Colorado Atlas & Gazetteer* is useful and provides you with maps of the entire state at a reasonable price.

U.S. Forest Service maps lack the topographic detail of the other sheet maps and, in our experience, are occasionally out of date. They have the advantage of covering a broad area and are useful in identifying land use and travel restrictions. These maps are most useful for the longer trails.

The Terrain Navigator series of maps published on CD by Maptech are also very useful. These CDs contain an amazing level of detail because they include the entire set of U.S. Geological Survey topographical maps of Colorado at both the 1:24,000 scale and the 1:100,000 scale. These maps offer many advantages over normal maps:

- GPS coordinates for any location can be found and loaded into your GPS receiver. Conversely, if you have your GPS coordinates, your location on the map can be pinpointed instantly.

- Towns, rivers, passes, mountains, and many other sites are indexed by name so that they can be located quickly.

- 4WD trails can be marked and profiled for elevation changes and distances from point to point.

- Customized maps can be printed out.

- The CDs can be used with a laptop computer and a GPS receiver in your vehicle to monitor your location on the map and navigate directly from the display.

All these maps should be available through good map stores.

Backcountry Driving

Rules and Permits

Four-wheel driving involves special techniques and road rules. This section outlines information all backcountry drivers should know.

4WD Road Rules

To help ensure that these trails remain open and available for all four-wheel drivers to enjoy, it is important to minimize your impact on the environment and not be a safety risk to yourself or anyone else. Remember that the 4WD clubs fight a constant battle with the government and various lobby groups to retain the access that currently exists.

The fundamental rule when traversing the backroads and 4x4 trails described in this book is to use common sense. In addition, special road rules for 4x4 trails apply:

- Vehicles traveling uphill have the right of way.

- If you are moving more slowly than the vehicle behind you, pull over to let the other vehicle by.

- Park out of the way in a safe place. Blocking a track may restrict access for emergency vehicles as well as for other recreationalists. Set the parking brake—don't rely on leaving the transmission in park. Manual transmissions should be left in the lowest gear.

Tread Lightly!

Remember the rules of the Tread Lightly! program:

■ Be informed. Obtain maps, regulations, and other information from the forest service or from other public land agencies. Learn the rules and follow them.

■ Resist the urge to pioneer a new road or trail or to cut across a switchback. Stay on constructed tracks and avoid running over young trees, shrubs, and grasses, damaging or killing them. Don't drive across alpine tundra; this fragile environment can take years to recover.

■ Stay off soft, wet backroads and 4x4 trails readily torn up by vehicles. Repairing the damage is expensive, and quite often authorities find it easier to close the road rather than repair it.

■ Travel around meadows, steep hillsides, stream banks, and lake shores that are easily scarred by churning wheels.

■ Stay away from wild animals that are rearing young or suffering from a food shortage. Do not camp close to the water sources of domestic or wild animals.

■ Obey gate closures and regulatory signs.

■ Preserve America's heritage by not disturbing old mining camps, ghost towns, or other historical features. Leave historic sites, Native American rock art, ruins, and artifacts in place and untouched.

■ Carry out all your trash, and even that of others.

■ Stay out of designated wilderness areas. They are closed to all vehicles. It is your responsibility to know where the boundaries are.

■ Get permission to cross private land. Leave livestock alone. Respect landowners' rights.

Report violations of these rules to help keep these trails open and to ensure that others will have the opportunity to visit these backcountry sites. Many groups are actively seeking to close these public lands to vehicles, thereby denying access to those who are unable, or perhaps merely unwilling, to hike long distances. This magnificent countryside is owned by, and should be available to, all Americans.

Assessing Your Vehicle's Off-Road Ability

Many issues come into play when evaluating your SUV, although all of the high-clearance 4WDs with high- and low-range gearing are suitable for even the roughest trails described in this book. Engine power will be adequate in even the least-powerful modern vehicle. However, some vehicles are less suited to off-highway driving than others, and some of the newest, carlike sport utility vehicles simply are not designed for off-highway touring. The following information should allow you to identify the good, the bad, and the ugly.

Differing 4WD Systems

All 4WD systems have one thing in common: The engine provides power to all four wheels rather than to only two, as is typical in most standard cars. However, there are a number of differences in the way power is applied to the wheels.

The other feature that distinguishes nearly all 4WDs from normal passenger vehicles is that the gearboxes have high and low ratios that effectively double the number of gears. The high range is comparable to the range on a passenger car. The low range provides lower speed and more power, which is useful when towing heavy loads, driving up steep hills, or crawling over rocks. When driving downhill, the 4WD's low range increases engine braking.

Various makes and models of SUVs offer different drive systems, but these differences center on two issues: the way power is applied to the other wheels if one or more wheels slip, and the ability to select between 2WD and 4WD.

Normal driving requires that all four wheels be able to turn at different speeds; this allows the vehicle to turn without scrubbing its tires. In a 2WD vehicle, the front wheels (or rear wheels in a front-wheel-drive vehicle) are not powered by the engine and thus are free to turn individually at any speed. The rear wheels, powered by the engine, are only able to turn at different speeds because of the differential, which applies power to the faster-turning wheel.

This standard method of applying traction has certain weaknesses. First, when power is applied to only one set of wheels, the other set cannot help the vehicle gain traction. Second, when one powered wheel loses traction, it spins, but the other powered wheel doesn't turn. This happens because the differential applies all the engine power to the faster-turning wheel and no power to the other wheels, which still have traction. All 4WD systems are designed to overcome these two weaknesses. However, different 4WDs address this common objective in different ways.

Full-Time 4WD

For a vehicle to remain in 4WD all the time without scrubbing the tires, all the wheels must be able to rotate at different speeds. A full-time 4WD system allows this to happen by using three differentials. One is located between the rear wheels, as in a normal passenger car, to allow the rear wheels to rotate at different speeds. The second is located between the front wheels in exactly the same way. The third differential is located between the front and rear wheels to allow different rotational speeds between the front and rear sets of wheels. In nearly all vehicles with full-time 4WD, the center differential operates only in high range. In low range, it is completely locked. This is not a disadvantage because when using low range the additional traction is normally desired and the deterioration of steering response will be less noticeable due to the vehicle traveling at a slower speed.

Part-Time 4WD

A part-time 4WD system does not have the center differential located between the front and rear wheels. Consequently, the front and rear drive shafts are both driven at the same speed and with the same power at all times when in 4WD.

This system provides improved traction because when one or both of the front or rear wheels slips, the engine continues to provide power to the other set. However, because such a system doesn't allow a difference in speed between the front and rear sets of wheels, the tires scrub when turning, placing additional strain on the whole drive system. Therefore, such a system can be used only in slippery conditions; otherwise, the ability to steer the vehicle will deteriorate and the tires will quickly wear out.

Some vehicles offer both full-time and part-time 4WD in high range.

Limiting Wheel Slippage

All 4WDs employ various systems to limit wheel slippage and transfer power to the wheels that still have traction. These systems may completely lock the differentials or they may allow limited slippage before transferring power back to the wheels that retain traction.

Lockers completely eliminate the operation of one or more differentials. Some SUVs offer the option of having manual lockers on all three differentials, while others offer manual lockers on the center and rear differential. Manual lockers are the most controllable and effective devices for ensuring that power is provided to the wheels with traction. However, because they allow absolutely no slippage, they must be used only on slippery surfaces.

An alternative method for getting power to the wheels that have traction is to allow limited wheel slippage. Systems that work this way may be called limited-slip differentials, posi-traction systems, or in the center differential, viscous couplings. The advantage of these systems is that the limited difference they allow in rotational speed between wheels enables such systems to be used when driving on a dry surface. All full-time 4WD systems allow limited slippage in the center differential.

For off-highway use, a manually locking

differential is the best of the above systems, but it is the most expensive. Limited-slip differentials are the cheapest but also the least satisfactory, as they require one wheel to be slipping at 2 to 3 mph before power is transferred to the other wheel. For the center differential, the best system combines a locking differential and, to enable full-time use, a viscous coupling.

Tires

The tires that came with your vehicle may be satisfactory, but many SUVs are factory-fitted with passenger-car tires. These are unlikely to be the best choice because they are less rugged and more likely to puncture on rocky trails. They are particularly prone to sidewall damage as well. Passenger vehicle tires also have a less aggressive tread pattern than specialized off road tires, providing less traction in mud.

For information on purchasing tires better suited to off-highway conditions, see Special Equipment below.

Clearance

Road clearances vary considerably among different SUVs—from less than 7 inches to more than 10 inches. Special vehicles may have far greater clearance. For instance, the first consumer Hummer, modelled on the military vehicle, had a 16-inch ground clearance. High ground clearance is particularly advantageous on the rockier or more rutted 4x4 trails in this book.

When evaluating the ground clearance of your vehicle, you need to take into account the clearance of the bodywork between the wheels on each side of the vehicle. This is particularly relevant for crawling over larger rocks. Vehicles with sidesteps have significantly lower clearance than those without.

Another factor affecting clearance is the approach and departure angles of your vehicle—that is, the maximum angle the ground can slope without the front of the vehicle hitting the ridge on approach or the rear of the vehicle hitting on departure. Mounting a winch or tow hitch to your ve-

hicle is likely to reduce your angle of approach or departure.

If you do a lot of driving on rocky trails, you will inevitably hit the bottom of the vehicle. When this happens, you will be far less likely to damage vulnerable areas such as the oil pan and gas tank if your vehicle is fitted with skid plates. Most manufacturers offer skid plates as an option. They are worth every penny.

Maneuverability

When you tackle tight switchbacks, you will quickly appreciate that maneuverability is an important criterion when assessing SUVs. Where a full-size vehicle may be forced to go back and forth a number of times to get around a sharp turn, a small SUV might go straight around. This is not only easier, it's safer.

If you have a full-size vehicle, all is not lost. We have traveled hundreds of trails in a Suburban. That is not to say that some of these trails wouldn't have been easier to negotiate in a smaller vehicle! We have noted in the route descriptions if a trail is not suitable for larger vehicles.

In Summary

Using the criteria above, you can evaluate how well your SUV will handle off-road touring, and if you haven't yet purchased your vehicle, you can use these criteria to help select one. Choosing the best 4WD system is, at least partly, subjective. It is also a matter of your budget. However, for the type of off-highway driving covered in this book, we make the following recommendations:

■ Select a 4WD system that offers low range and, at a minimum, has some form of limited slip differential on the rear axle.

■ Use light truck, all-terrain tires as the standard tires on your vehicle. For sand and slickrock, these will be the ideal choice. If conditions are likely to be muddy, or traction will be improved by a tread pattern that will give more bite, consider an additional set of mud tires.

■ For maximum clearance, select a vehicle with 16-inch wheels or at least choose the tallest tires that your vehicle can accommodate. Note that if you install tires with a diameter greater than standard, the speedometer and odometer will undercalculate speed and the distance you have traveled. Your engine braking and gear ratios will also be affected.

■ If you are going to try the rockier 4x4 trails, don't install a sidestep or low-hanging front bar. If you have the option, have underbody skid plates mounted.

■ Remember that many of the obstacles you encounter on backcountry trails are more difficult to navigate in a full-size vehicle than in a compact SUV.

Four-Wheel Driving Techniques

Safe four-wheel driving requires that you observe certain golden rules:

■ Size up the situation in advance.

■ Be careful and take your time.

■ Maintain smooth, steady power and momentum.

■ Engage 4WD and low-range gears before you get into a tight situation.

■ Steer toward high spots, trying to put the wheel over large rocks.

■ Straddle ruts.

■ Use gears and not just the brakes to hold the vehicle when driving downhill. On very steep slopes, chock the wheels if you park your vehicle.

■ Watch for logging and mining trucks and smaller recreational vehicles, such as all-terrain vehicles (ATVs).

■ Wear your seat belt and secure all luggage, especially heavy items such as tool boxes or coolers. Heavy items should be secured by ratchet tie-down straps rather than elastic-type straps, which are not strong enough to hold heavy items if the vehicle rolls.

Colorado's backroads and 4x4 trails have a number of common obstacles, and the following provides an introduction to the techniques required to surmount them.

Rocks

Tire selection is important in negotiating rocks. Select a multiple ply, tough sidewall, light-truck tire with a large-lug tread.

As you approach a rocky stretch, get into 4WD low range to give yourself maximum slow-speed control. Speed is rarely necessary, since traction on a rocky surface is usually good. Plan ahead and select the line you wish to take. If a rock appears to be larger than the clearance of your vehicle, don't try to straddle it. Check to see that it is not higher than the frame of your vehicle once you get a wheel over it. Put a wheel up on the rock and slowly climb it, then gently drop over the other side using the brake to ensure a smooth landing. Bouncing the car over rocks increases the likelihood of damage, as the body's clearance is reduced by the suspension compressing. Running boards also significantly reduce your clearance in this respect. It is often helpful to use a "spotter" outside the vehicle to assist you with the best wheel placement.

Steep Uphill Grades

Consider walking the trail to ensure that the steep hill before you is passable, especially if it is clear that backtracking is going to be a problem.

Select 4WD low range to ensure that you have adequate power to pull up the hill. If the wheels begin to lose traction, turn the steering wheel gently from side to side to give the wheels a chance to regain traction.

If you lose momentum, but the car is not in danger of sliding, use the foot brake, switch off the ignition, leave the vehicle in gear (if manual transmission) or park (if automatic), engage the parking brake, and get out to examine the situation. See if you can remove any obstacles, and figure out the line you need to take. Reversing a couple of yards and starting again may allow you to get better traction and momentum.

If halfway up, you decide a stretch of road is impassably steep, back down the trail. Trying to turn the vehicle around on a steep hill is extremely dangerous; you will very likely cause it to roll over.

Steep Downhill Grades

Again, consider walking the trail to ensure that a steep downhill is passable, especially if it is clear that backtracking uphill is going to be a problem.

Select 4WD low range and use first gear to maximize braking assistance from the engine. If the surface is loose and you are losing traction, change up to second or third gear. Do not use the brakes if you can avoid it, but don't let the vehicle's speed get out of control. Feather (lightly pump) the brakes if you slip under braking. For vehicles fitted with ABS, apply even pressure if you start to slip; the ABS helps keep vehicles on line.

Travel very slowly over rock ledges or ruts. Attempt to tackle these diagonally, letting one wheel down at a time.

If the back of the vehicle begins to slide around, gently apply the throttle and correct the steering. If the rear of the vehicle starts to slide sideways, do not apply the brakes.

Sand

As with most off-highway situations, your tires are the key to your ability to cross sand. It is difficult to tell how well a particular tire will handle in sand just by looking at it, so be guided by the manufacturer and your dealer.

The key to driving in soft sand is floatation, which is achieved by a combination of low tire pressure and momentum. Before crossing a stretch of sand, reduce your tire pressure to between 15 and 20 pounds. If necessary, you can safely go to as low as 12 pounds. As you cross, maintain momentum so that your vehicle rides on the top of the soft sand without digging in or stalling. This may require plenty of engine power. Avoid using the brakes if possible; removing your foot from the accelerator alone is normally enough to slow or stop. Using the brakes digs the vehicle deep in the sand.

Air the tires back up as soon as you are out of the sand to avoid damage to the tires and the rims. Airing back up requires a high-quality air compressor. Even then, it is a slow process.

Slickrock

When you encounter slickrock, first assess the correct direction of the trail. It is easy to lose sight of the trail on slickrock, as there are seldom any developed edges. Often the way is marked with small cairns, which are simply rocks stacked high enough to make a landmark.

All-terrain tires with tighter tread are more suited to slickrock than the more open, luggier type tires. As with rocks, a multiple-ply sidewall is important. In dry conditions, slickrock offers pavement-type grip. In rain or snow, you will soon learn how it got its name. Even the best tires may not get an adequate grip. Walk steep sections first; if you are slipping on foot, chances are your vehicle will slip too.

Slickrock is characterized by ledges and long sections of "pavement." Follow the guidelines for travel over rocks. Refrain from speeding over flat-looking sections, as you may hit an unexpected crevice or water pocket, and vehicles bend easier than slickrock! Turns and ledges can be tight, and vehicles with smaller overhangs and better maneuverability are at a distinct advantage—hence the popularity of the compacts in the slickrock mecca of Moab, Utah.

On the steepest sections, engage low range and pick a straight line up or down the slope. Do not attempt to traverse a steep slope sideways.

Mud

Muddy trails are easily damaged, so they should be avoided if possible. But if you must traverse a section of mud, your success will depend heavily on whether you have open-lugged mud tires or chains. Thick mud fills the tighter tread on normal tires, leaving the tire with no more grip than if it were bald. If the muddy stretch is only a few yards long, the momentum of your vehicle may allow you to get through regardless.

If the muddy track is very steep, uphill or downhill, or off camber, do not attempt it. Your vehicle is likely to skid in such conditions, and you may roll or slip off the edge of the road. Also, check to see that the mud has a reasonably firm base. Tackling deep mud is definitely not recommended unless you have a vehicle-mounted winch—and even then, be cautious, because the winch may not get you out. Finally, check to see that no ruts are too deep for the ground clearance of your vehicle.

When you decide you can get through and have selected the best route, use the following techniques to cross through the mud:

■ Avoid making detours off existing tracks to minimize environmental damage.

■ Select 4WD low range and a suitable gear; momentum is the key to success, so use a high enough gear to build up sufficient speed.

■ Avoid accelerating heavily, so as to minimize wheel spinning and to provide maximum traction.

■ Follow existing wheel ruts, unless they are too deep for the clearance of your vehicle.

■ To correct slides, turn the steering wheel in the direction that the rear wheels are skidding, but don't be too aggressive or you'll overcorrect and lose control again.

■ If the vehicle comes to a stop, don't continue to accelerate, as you will only spin your wheels and dig yourself into a rut. Try backing out and having another go.

■ Be prepared to turn back before reaching the point of no return.

Stream Crossings

By crossing a stream that is too deep, drivers risk far more than water flowing in and ruining the interior of their vehicles. Water sucked into the engine's air intake will seriously damage the engine. Likewise, water that seeps into the air vent on the transmission or differential will mix with the lubricant and may lead to serious problems in due course.

Even worse, if the water is deep or fast flowing, it could easily carry your vehicle downstream, endangering the lives of everyone in the vehicle.

Some SUV user manuals tell you what fording depth the vehicle can negotiate

safely. If your vehicle's owner's manual does not include this information, your local dealer may be able to assist. If you don't know, then avoid crossing through water that is more than a foot or so deep.

The first rule for crossing a stream is to know what you are getting into. You need to ascertain how deep the water is, whether there are any large rocks or holes, if the bottom is solid enough to avoid bogging down the vehicle, and whether the entry and exit points are negotiable. This may take some time and involve getting wet, but you take a great risk by crossing a stream without first properly assessing the situation.

The secret to water crossings is to keep moving, but not too fast. If you go too fast, you may drown the electrics, causing the vehicle to stall midstream. In shallow water (where the surface of the water is below the bumper), your primary concern is to safely negotiate the bottom of the stream, avoiding any rock damage and maintaining momentum if there is a danger of getting stuck or of slipping on the exit.

In deeper water (between 18 and 30 inches), the objective is to create a small bow wave in front of the moving vehicle. This requires a speed that is approximately walking pace. The bow wave reduces the depth of the water around the engine compartment. If the water's surface reaches your tailpipe, select a gear that will maintain moderate engine revs to avoid water backing up into the exhaust; and do not change gears midstream.

Crossing water deeper than 25 to 30 inches requires more extensive preparation of the vehicle and should be attempted only by experienced drivers.

Snow

The trails in this book that receive heavy snowfall are closed in winter. Therefore, the snow conditions that you are most likely to encounter are an occasional snowdrift that has not yet melted or fresh snow from an unexpected storm. Getting through such conditions depends on the depth of the snow, its consistency, the stability of the underlying surface, and your vehicle.

If the snow is no deeper than about 9 inches and there is solid ground beneath it, crossing the snow should not be a problem. In deeper snow that seems solid enough to support your vehicle, be extremely cautious: If you break through a drift, you are likely to be stuck, and if conditions are bad, you may have a long wait.

The tires you use for off-highway driving, with a wide tread pattern, are probably suitable for these snow conditions. Nonetheless, it is wise to carry chains (preferably for all four wheels), and if you have a vehicle-mounted winch, even better.

Vehicle Recovery Methods

If you do enough four-wheel driving, you are sure to get stuck sooner or later. The following techniques will help you get back on the go. The most suitable method will depend on the equipment available and the situation you are in—whether you are stuck in sand, mud, or snow, or are high-centered or unable to negotiate a hill.

Towing

Use a nylon yank strap of the type discussed in the Special 4WD Equipment section below. This type of strap will stretch 15 to 25 percent, and the elasticity will assist in extracting the vehicle.

Attach the strap only to a frame-mounted tow point. Ensure that the driver of the stuck vehicle is ready, take up all but about 6 feet of slack, then move the towing vehicle away at a moderate speed (in most circumstances this means using 4WD low range in second gear) so that the elasticity of the strap is employed in the way it is meant to be. Don't take off like a bat out of hell or you risk breaking the strap or damaging a vehicle.

Never join two yank straps together with a shackle. If one strap breaks, the shackle will become a lethal missile aimed at one of the vehicles (and anyone inside). For the same reason, never attach a yank strap to the tow ball on either vehicle.

Jacking

Jacking the vehicle allows you to pack under the wheel (with rocks, dirt, or logs) or use your shovel to remove an obstacle. However, the standard vehicle jack is unlikely to be of as much assistance as a high-lift jack. We highly recommend purchasing a good high-lift jack as a basic accessory if you decide that you are going to do a lot of serious, off-highway four-wheel driving. Remember a high-lift jack is of limited use if your vehicle does not have an appropriate jacking point. Some brush bars have two built-in forward jacking points.

Tire Chains

Tire chains can be of assistance in both mud and snow. Cable-type chains provide much less grip than link-type chains. There are also dedicated mud chains with larger, heavier links than on normal snow chains. It is best to have chains fitted to all four wheels.

Once you are bogged down is not the best time to try to fit the chains; if at all possible, try to predict their need and have them on the tires before trouble arises. An easy way to affix chains is to place two small cubes of wood under the center of the stretched-out chain. When you drive your tires up on the blocks of wood, it is easier to stretch the chains over the tires because the pressure is off.

Winching

Most recreational four-wheel drivers do not have a winch. But if you get serious about four-wheel driving, this is probably the first major accessory you should consider buying.

Under normal circumstances, a winch would be warranted only for the more difficult 4x4 trails in this book. Having a winch is certainly comforting when you see a difficult section of road ahead and have to decide whether to risk it or turn back. Also, major obstacles can appear when you least expect them, even on trails that are otherwise easy.

Owning a winch is not a panacea to all

your recovery problems. Winching depends on the availability of a good anchor point, and electric winches may not work if they are submerged in a stream. Despite these constraints, no accessory is more useful than a high-quality, powerful winch when you get into a difficult situation.

If you acquire a winch, learn to use it properly; take the time to study your owner's manual. Incorrect operation can be extremely dangerous and may cause damage to the winch or to your anchor points, which are usually trees.

Navigation by the Global Positioning System (GPS)

Although this book is designed so that each trail can be navigated simply by following the detailed directions provided, nothing makes navigation easier than a GPS receiver.

The global positioning system (GPS) consists of a network of 24 active satellites, nearly 13,000 miles in space, in six different orbital paths. The satellites are constantly moving at about 8,500 miles per hour, making two complete orbits around the earth every 24 hours.

Each satellite is constantly transmitting data, including its identification number, its operational health, and the date and time. It also transmits its location and the location of every other satellite in the network.

By comparing the time the signal was transmitted to the time it is received, a GPS receiver calculates how far away each satellite is. With a sufficient number of signals, the receiver can then triangulate its location. With three or more satellites, the receiver can determine latitude and longitude coordinates. With four or more, it can calculate altitude. By constantly making these calculations, it can determine speed and direction. To facilitate these calculations, the time data broadcast by GPS is accurate to within 40 billionths of a second.

The U.S. military uses the system to provide positions accurate to within half an inch. When the system was first established, civilian receivers were deliberately fed slightly erroneous information in order to effectively deny military applications to hostile countries or terrorists—a practice called selective availability (SA). However on May 1, 2000, in response to the growing importance of the system for civilian applications, the U.S. government stopped intentionally downgrading GPS data. The military gave its support to this change once new technology made it possible to selectively degrade the system within any defined geographical area on demand. This new feature of the system has made it safe to have higher-quality signals available for civilian use. Now, instead of the civilian-use signal having a margin of error being between 20 and 70 yards, it is only about one-tenth of that.

A GPS receiver offers the four-wheeler numerous benefits:

■ You can track to any point for which you know the longitude and latitude coordinates with no chance of heading in the wrong direction or getting lost. Most receivers provide an extremely easy-to-understand graphic display to keep you on track.

■ It works in all weather conditions.

■ It automatically records your route for easy backtracking.

■ You can record and name any location, so that you can relocate it with ease. This may include your campsite, a fishing spot, or even a silver mine you discover!

■ It displays your position, allowing you to pinpoint your location on a map.

■ By interfacing the GPS receiver directly to a portable computer, you can monitor and record your location as you travel (using the appropriate map software) or print the route you took.

However, remember that GPS units can fail, batteries can go flat, and tree cover and narrow canyons can block the signals. Never rely entirely on GPS for navigation. Always carry a compass for backup.

Special 4WD Equipment

Tires

When 4WD touring, you will likely encounter a wide variety of terrain: rocks, mud, talus, slickrock, sand, gravel, dirt, and bitumen. The immense variety of tires on the market includes many specifically targeted at one or another of these types of terrain, as well as tires designed to adequately handle a range of terrain.

Every four-wheel driver seems to have a preference when it comes to tire selection, but most people undertaking the backroads and 4x4 trails in this book will need tires that can handle all of the above types of terrain adequately.

The first requirement is to select rugged, light-truck tires rather than passenger-vehicle tires. Check the size data on the sidewall: it should have "LT" rather than "P" before the number. Among light-truck tires, you must choose between tires that are designated "all-terrain" and more-aggressive, wider-tread mud tires. Either type will be adequate, especially on rocks, gravel, talus, or dirt. Although mud tires have an advantage in muddy conditions and soft snow, all-terrain tires perform better on slickrock, in sand, and particularly on ice and paved roads.

When selecting tires, remember that they affect not just traction but also cornering ability, braking distances, fuel consumption, and noise levels. It pays to get good advice before making your decision.

Yank Straps

Yank straps are industrial-strength versions of the flimsy tow straps carried by the local discount store. They are 20 to 30 feet long and 2 to 3 inches wide, made of heavy nylon, rated to at least 20,000 pounds, and have looped ends.

Do not use tow straps with metal hooks in the ends (the hooks can become missiles in the event the strap breaks free). Likewise, never join two yank straps together using a shackle.

Cell Phones and CB Radios

Each year the reception of cell phones in remote areas becomes better. Many times we have found we have cell phone reception in locations where we would never have expected it. However, the difference between cell phone companies can be considerable and one company can be superior in one location and not in another. The topography is also a major contributor to variances in reception. We highly recommend you take your cell phone with you; better yet take two if you have them and they have different service providers.

A citizen's band (CB) radio can also be invaluable. CB radios are relatively inexpensive and do not require an FCC license. Their range is limited, especially in very hilly country, as their transmission patterns basically follow lines of sight. Range can be improved using single sideband (SSB) transmission, an option on more expensive units. Range is even better on vehicle-mounted units that have been professionally fitted to ensure that the antenna and cabling are matched appropriately.

Winches

There are three main options when it comes to winches: manual winches, removable electric winches, and vehicle-mounted electric winches.

If you have a full-size SUV—which can weigh in excess of 7,000 pounds when loaded—a manual winch is of limited use without a lot of effort and considerable time. However, a manual winch is a very handy and inexpensive accessory if you have a small SUV. Typically, manual winches are rated to pull about 5,500 pounds.

Electric winches can be mounted to your vehicle's trailer hitch to enable them to be removed, relocated to the front of your vehicle (if you have a hitch installed), or moved to another vehicle. Although this is a very useful feature, a winch is heavy, so relocating one can be a two-person job. Consider that 5,000-pound-rated winches weigh only about 55 pounds, while 12,000-pound-rated models weigh around

140 pounds. Therefore, the larger models are best permanently front-mounted. Unfortunately, this position limits their ability to winch the vehicle backward.

When choosing between electric winches, be aware that they are rated for their maximum capacity on the first wind of the cable around the drum. As layers of cable wind onto the drum, they increase its diameter and thus decrease the maximum load the winch can handle. This decrease is significant: A winch rated to pull 8,000 pounds on a bare drum may only handle 6,500 pounds on the second layer, 5,750 pounds on the third layer, and 5,000 pounds on the fourth. Electric winches also draw a high level of current and may necessitate upgrading the battery in your 4WD or adding a second battery.

There is a wide range of mounting options—from a simple, body-mounted frame that holds the winch to heavy-duty winch bars that replace the original bumper and incorporate brush bars and mounts for auxiliary lights.

If you buy a winch, either electric or manual, you will also need quite a range of additional equipment so that you can operate it correctly:

- at least one choker chain with hooks on each end,
  - winch extension straps or cables,
  - shackles,
  - a receiver shackle,
  - a snatch block,
  - a tree protector,
  - gloves.

Grill/Brush Bars and Winch Bars

Brush bars protect the front of the vehicle from scratches and minor bumps; they also provide a solid mount for auxiliary lights and offer high-lift jacking points. The level of protection they provide depends on how solid they are and whether they are securely mounted onto the frame of the vehicle. Lighter models attach in front of the standard bumper, but the more substantial units replace the bumper. Prices range from about $150 to $450.

Winch bars replace the bumper and usually integrate a solid brush bar with a heavy-duty winch mount. Some have the brush bar as an optional extra to the winch bar component. Manufacturers such as Warn, ARB, and TJM offer a wide range of integrated winch bars. These are significantly more expensive, starting at about $650.

Portable Air Compressors

Many portable air compressors on the market are flimsy models that plug into the cigarette lighter and are sold at the local discount store. These are of very limited use for four-wheel driving. They are very slow to inflate the large tires of a SUV vehicle; for instance, to reinflate from 15 to 35 pounds typically takes about 10 minutes for each tire. They are also unlikely to be rated for continuous use, which means that they will overheat and cut off before completing the job. If you're lucky, they will start up again when they have cooled down, but this means that you are unlikely to reinflate your tires in less than an hour.

The easiest way to identify a useful air compressor is by the price—good ones cost $200 or more. All such pumps draw between 15 and 20 amps and thus should not be plugged into the cigarette lighter socket but attached to the vehicle's battery with clips. Some units can be permanently mounted under the hood.

Auxiliary Driving Lights

There is a vast array of auxiliary lights on the market today, and selecting the best lights for your purpose can be a confusing process.

Auxiliary lights greatly improve visibility in adverse weather conditions. Rear-mounted auxiliary lights provide greatly improved visibility for backing up.

For off-highway use, you will need quality lights with strong mounting brackets. Some high-powered off-highway lights are not approved by the Department of Transportation for use on public roads.

Roof Racks

Roof racks can be excellent for storing gear, as well as providing easy access for certain weatherproof items. However, they raise the center of gravity on the vehicle, which can substantially alter the rollover angle. A roof rack is best used for lightweight objects that are well strapped down. Heavy recovery gear and other bulky items should be packed low in the vehicle's interior to lower the center of gravity and stabilize the vehicle.

A roof rack should allow for safe and secure packing of items and be sturdy enough to withstand knocks.

Packing Checklist

Before embarking on any 4WD adventure, whether a lazy Sunday drive on an easy trail or a challenging climb over rugged terrain, be prepared. The following checklist may help you gather the items you need.

Essential

- ❑ Rain gear
- ❑ Small shovel or multipurpose ax, pick, and sledgehammer
- ❑ Heavy-duty yank strap
- ❑ Spare tire that matches the other tires on the vehicle
- ❑ Working jack and base plate for soft ground
- ❑ Maps
- ❑ Emergency medical kit, including sun protection and insect repellent
- ❑ Bottled water
- ❑ Blankets or space blankets
- ❑ Parka, gloves, and boots
- ❑ Spare vehicle key
- ❑ Jumper leads
- ❑ Heavy-duty flashlight
- ❑ Multipurpose tool, such as a Leatherman
- ❑ Emergency food—high-energy bars or similar

Worth Considering

- ❑ GPS receiver
- ❑ Cell phone
- ❑ A set of light-truck, off-highway tires and matching spare
- ❑ High-lift jack
- ❑ Additional tool kit
- ❑ CB radio
- ❑ Portable air compressor
- ❑ Tire gauge
- ❑ Tire-sealing kit
- ❑ Tire chains
- ❑ Handsaw
- ❑ Binoculars
- ❑ Firearms
- ❑ Whistle
- ❑ Flares
- ❑ Vehicle fire extinguisher
- ❑ Gasoline, engine oil, and other vehicle fluids
- ❑ Portable hand winch
- ❑ Electric cooler

If Your Credit Cards Aren't Maxed Out

- ❑ Electric, vehicle-mounted winch and associated recovery straps, shackles, and snatch blocks
- ❑ Auxiliary lights
- ❑ Locking differential(s)

Saxon Mountain Road

STARTING POINT Clear Creek Road, 1.4 miles from I-70

FINISHING POINT Colorado 103, 4.9 miles south of I-70

TOTAL MILEAGE 13.1 miles

UNPAVED MILEAGE 13.1 miles

DRIVING TIME 2 hours

ROUTE ELEVATION 8,405 to 11,140 feet

USUALLY OPEN Late May to October

DIFFICULTY RATING 4

SCENIC RATING 8

Special Attractions

- Excellent views over Georgetown and Georgetown Lake.
- Trail links with a large network of side roads.
- Area is rich in mining history.
- Accessible to snowmobiles in winter.

History

Mining began in the area of Lamartine around 1887. Four men from Idaho Springs, Colorado, discovered a large vein of silver while following Trail Creek. Together, the four staked a claim and named it Lamartine. When one of the partners died not long after staking the claim, Peter Himrod bought a quarter interest in the claim from the partner's widow for $250. When none of the remaining partners seemed interested in developing the claim, he bought them out.

The Lamartine was first seriously worked in 1887. Although Himrod poured thousands of dollars into the mine, he received little return on his investment. When Himrod died, he passed the mine on to his son, who continued to finance its development. Himrod's son became frustrated with the lack of results and sold the mine for $360. The new owners quickly found the rich ore sought after by Himrod and his son.

With this discovery in the late 1880s, the town of Lamartine was established. The town flourished in the 1890s and early 1900s, as the Lamartine Mine produced millions of dollars' worth of gold, silver,

One of the trail's many switchbacks

View back down over the trail's switchbacks with Georgetown below

and lead. Yet even at the peak of the town's mining production, the population of Lamartine never exceeded 500. In 1905, the Lamartine Mine was leased out and eventually abandoned.

A couple of miles down the mountain from Lamartine was the town of Freeland. The town was established around 1880 and grew rapidly after the discovery of the Freeland lode in 1877. In 1878, a reporter from the *Georgetown Miner* wrote that 17 houses had been built in Freeland in the prior year. Just a week later, another reporter claimed that 34 houses were occupied in the town. Undisputedly, a number of businesses were flourishing in Freeland.

The town boasted a meat market, grocery store, assay office, and blacksmith shop. A post office, as well as a public school, opened in 1879. A teacher at the school, Bernice Poppen, reported that many of the pupils were older than herself. That same year the town blacksmith helped organize a Presbyterian church. He was described by a fellow resident as one who "points out the error of their ways to perishing sinners on Sundays." Freeland had a reputation of being a severely moral town, with little of the rough activities typical of many western mining towns. A visitor to

the town reported that one could hear "no enticing jingle of beer glasses at Freeland."

The prosperity of the town was largely dependent upon the production of the Freeland Mine. The Freeland turned out large quantities of ore, which contained mainly silver as well as some gold and copper. The mine had its own sawmill to provide lumber for homes, heating, and supports within the mines. At the time of the mine's peak production, the majority of trees surrounding Freeland were cut.

Freeland was a bustling place during the boom years and even merited inclusion in the *Colorado Business Directory* from 1893 to 1905. Around the turn of the century, however, production at the Freeland Mine began to decline, and the town's fortunes followed. By 1901, only 100 people resided in Freeland. The post office closed in 1908, and the town became abandoned.

Description

Saxon Mountain Road begins on the northeastern edge of Georgetown and immediately begins its long ascent up a shelf road along the northwestern flank of Saxon Mountain. The road switchbacks a number of times during the climb, revealing better and better views over Georgetown and

Georgetown Lake. The road surface is very rocky; however, the rocks are small and easily negotiated by high-clearance vehicles. The surface is loose enough to make four-wheel drive preferable but not absolutely necessary.

The road flattens out and enters the forest on top of the mountain. At the first zero point, FR 712.2C continues ahead and climbs toward the top of Saxon Mountain. Navigation thus far has been very simple. However, once on the mountain, numerous side roads (marked and unmarked) can easily lead to confusion. The main trail is not always the correct one as far as the route described below goes. A GPS unit is a big help in staying on track. Although the many side tracks make for difficult navigation, they are also a lot of fun to explore.

The trail standard remains relatively consistent for the entire trip. There are many rocks scattered about the trail; a few ruts also make the driving more interesting.

The trail passes a few indications of the region's mining history. A few crumbling cabins can be found along the trail. Additional remains can be found along trails branching off of the main route. The trail also passes right through the once-bustling town of Lamartine, now little more than an empty lot. At press time, the forest service reports that a condominium complex may be built in the vicinity of Lamartine. Currently, only some land has been cleared. Finally, there are some large tailings piles passed along the trail, as well as an old boiler that was shipped all the way across the country from Coatesville, Pennsylvania.

The trail widens as it joins graded dirt Ute Creek Road. The final descent along Ute Creek passes private property. Stay on the main trail here and do not explore the private side roads. The trail ends on Colorado 103, a few miles south of Idaho

Old cabin and campsite beside the trail

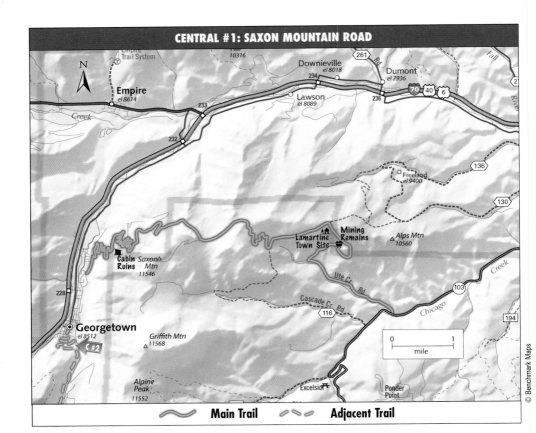

~~ Main Trail   ~~ Adjacent Trail

© Benchmark Maps

Springs. A good side trip from the end of the trail is to take Colorado 103 south to the Mount Evans Scenic Byway, a paved road that takes you to the top of the 14,264-foot mountain.

Current Road Information
Arapaho & Roosevelt National Forests
Clear Creek Ranger District
101 Chicago Creek Road
Idaho Springs, CO 80452
(303) 567-3000

Map References
USFS   Arapaho & Roosevelt National
       Forests
Maptech CD:
       Denver/Steamboat Springs/North
       Central
Benchmark's *Colorado Road & Recreation
       Atlas*, p. 74
Colorado Atlas & Gazetteer, p. 39
The Roads of Colorado, p. 79
Trails Illustrated, #104

Route Directions

▼0.0   From the Georgetown exit (#228) of
            I-70, zero trip meter and head east
            toward town. At 0.1 miles, make your
            first right onto Argentine Road. At 0.8
            miles, turn right onto 22nd Street. At
            0.9 miles, turn right onto Clear Creek
            Road. At 1.4 miles, zero trip meter
            and turn right (east) onto Saxon
            Mountain Road (not labeled at time of
            research).
5.8▲   Trail ends on Clear Creek Road. Turn
            right and follow above directions in
            reverse for I-70 and
            Georgetown.
            GPS: N39°43.15' W105°41.44'

▼0.2   BR   Private driveways on left and old
            building on right. Follow sign to
            Saxon Mountain summit.
5.6▲   SO   Private driveways on right and old
            building on left.

▼1.0   SO   Seasonal closure gate.
4.8▲   SO   Seasonal closure gate.

▼1.4   SO   Track on left.
4.4▲   SO   Track on sharp right rejoins.

▼1.5   SO   Track on left rejoins.
4.3▲   SO   Track on right.

▼1.8   SO   Cabin remains on right; then campsite on left.
4.0▲   BR   Campsite on right; then cabin remains on left.
        GPS: N39°43.51′ W105°40.99′

▼2.1   BR   Track down hill on left.
3.7▲   SO   Track on sharp right.
        GPS: N39°43.72′ W105°40.94′

▼2.5   SO   Track on left on right-hand switchback.
3.3▲   BL   Track straight ahead on left-hand switchback.

▼2.7   BR   Track on left on right-hand switchback goes past campsite to mining remains.
3.1▲   BL   Track straight ahead on left-hand switchback goes past campsite to mining remains.
        GPS: N39°43.68′ W105°40.80′

▼3.5   SO   Cabin remains on right.
2.3▲   SO   Cabin remains on left.

▼4.3   BR   Track on left.
1.5▲   SO   Track on sharp right.
        GPS: N39°43.78′ W105°40.36′

▼5.0   SO   Cabin remains and campsite on right.
0.8▲   SO   Cabin remains and campsite on left.

▼5.8   TL   FR 712.2C continues straight ahead. Turn left onto FR 712.2, following sign to Cascade Creek. Zero trip meter.
0.0▲   Continue to the north.
        GPS: N39°43.67′ W105°39.36′

▼0.0   Continue to the east.

Difficult section near the top of the switchbacks

3.3▲	**TR**	T-intersection. Track on left is FR 712.2C. Remain on FR 712.2, following sign to Georgetown. Zero trip meter.	▼3.2	**SO**	Track on left is FR 712.2E.
			0.1▲	**SO**	Track on right is FR 712.2E.

▼3.2 **SO** Track on left is FR 712.2E.
0.1▲ **SO** Track on right is FR 712.2E.

▼0.1 **BR/TL** Bear right at fork in road with FR 710.1 signed to Griffith Mountain on right and FR 712.2 on left.Then turn left at 4-way intersection with FR 712.2 signed to Lamartime on left and 710.1 signed to Highland Parkon right. Proceed onto FR 712.2 following sign to Lamartine.

3.2▲ **TR** 4-way intersection with FR 710.1 on right signed to Georgetown; then track on sharp right is FR 712.2 rejoining.
GPS: N39°43.63′ W105°39.30′

▼0.2 **SO** Narrow track on sharp left is FR 712.2 rejoining.
3.1▲ **BL** Track on right is FR 712.2.

▼0.7 **SO** Track on right; then track on left.
2.6▲ **SO** Track on right; then track on left.

▼1.0 **SO** Track on left; then faint track on right.
2.3▲ **SO** Faint track on left; then track on right.
GPS: N39°43.92′ W105°38.49′

▼1.5 **SO** Track on right is FR 712.21.
1.8▲ **BR** Track straight ahead is FR 712.21.
GPS: N39°43.59′ W105°38.37′

▼1.8 **TR** 4-way intersection. FR 712.2G on left. Unmarked track ahead goes to cabin remains.
1.5▲ **TL** 4-way intersection. FR 712.2G straight ahead. Unmarked track on right goes to cabin remains.
GPS: N39°43.75′ W105°38.20′

▼2.2 **SO** Track on sharp right is FR 712.2B.
1.1▲ **BR** Track on left is FR 712.2B.

▼2.4 **SO** Track on sharp left is FR 712.2F.
0.9▲ **BL** Track on right is FR 712.2F.

▼2.9 **SO** Track on right goes to camping area.
0.4▲ **SO** Track on left goes to camping area.

▼3.3 **TR** Track on left is FR 727.1B; then Lamartine town site. Camping area on left. Track straight ahead is FR 712.1. Zero trip meter.
0.0▲ Continue west on FR 712.2.
GPS: N39°43.90′ W105°37.07′

▼0.0 Continue southeast on FR 712.2A, following sign to Ute Creek. Track on right is FR 727.1B.
4.0▲ **TL** T-intersection at Lamartine town site. Camping area straight ahead. Track on right is FR 712.1. Zero trip meter.

▼0.5 **SO** Private property on left. Many tracks on right and left lead to private property for the next 3.5 miles.
3.5▲ **SO** Private property on right.

▼1.1 **SO** Tailings piles and mining remains on left and right; then track on left and campsite and pylon on right.
2.9▲ **SO** Campsite and pylon on left and track on right; then tailings piles and mining remains on left and right.
GPS: N39°43.55′ W105°36.84′

▼1.7 **TL** T-intersection. Track on right is private. Turn left onto FR 118.0.
2.3▲ **TR** Track ahead is private. Follow homemade sign for Lamartine and Cascade.
GPS: N39°43.33′ W105°37.39′

▼4.0 Trail ends at T-intersection with Colorado 103. Turn left for Idaho Springs; turn right for Mount Evans.
0.0▲ Trail starts on Colorado 103, 4.9 miles south of I-70, just south of mile marker 5. Turn north onto graded dirt Ute Creek Road and zero trip meter. Many tracks on right and left lead to private property for the next 3.5 miles.
GPS: N39°42.52′ W105°35.83′

Guanella Pass Trail

STARTING POINT Grant, at intersection of US 285 and CR 62

FINISHING POINT Georgetown, at Old Georgetown Railway Station

TOTAL MILEAGE 24.2 miles

UNPAVED MILEAGE 10.5 miles

DRIVING TIME 1 hour

ROUTE ELEVATION 8,600 to 11,669 feet

USUALLY OPEN Year-round

DIFFICULTY RATING 1

SCENIC RATING 9

Special Attractions

- Attractive scenery with expansive views from the pass.
- An accessible backcountry route, which can be undertaken by passenger vehicles.
- Fall viewing of the aspens.
- Abundant wildlife.

History

This pass is named for Byron Guanella, a Clear Creek commissioner who was a supporter of building a road over the pass.

Buffalo used to graze their way across this pass, and the Indians used the pass as

Commemorative plaque at the pass

they followed the migration of the buffalo herds. Early prospectors seeking to use the pass were always on guard against being attacked by the Indians. In 1861, Captain Edward Berthoud and Jim Bridger crossed the pass when surveying potential routes for a railroad west.

The route starts in the town of Grant,

Clear Lake USFS Campground

View of the northern end of the trail

which was established in 1870 and originally named Grantville, in honor of President Ulysses S. Grant. Its population peaked at about 200 in 1887.

The route ends in Georgetown, which began as a gold settlement in 1859, when George Griffith from Kentucky found gold there. He brought his wife, his brother, their father, and a couple of prospectors to the area. They called it George's Town, in honor of George Griffith. The group worked hard to live on the modest amounts of gold they found despite the large amounts of seemingly worthless silver-bearing ore in their lode.

In 1864, plentiful veins of quartz were discovered, creating a boom that brought prospectors pouring into the area. The resulting settlement was called Elizabethtown in honor of George's wife, Elizabeth. Before long, George's Town and Elizabethtown combined under the name Georgetown, and a post office was established in 1866.

The following year brought the silver explosion. Houses and businesses were erected at a dizzying rate, the streets buzzed with activity, merchants did brisk business, and lots of people were on the verge of becoming very wealthy. Georgetown was known as the Silver Queen of the Rockies. As it grew, the town acquired an attractive mix of Victorian cottages and a substantial brick business district. Georgetown became the home of many rich men with rich tastes. Large, ornate residences grew in size and ostentation as their owners prospered.

Although Georgetown had a wild side—with more than thirty saloons and plenty of red-light houses and gambling dens—it was also a mining town with culture and refinement. Citizens enjoyed two opera houses, met in public halls and a Masonic lodge, and attended society events. In contrast to most other mining camps, families were an integral part of Georgetown. Schools and churches were constructed from the early days, and homes were built with an air of permanence.

Georgetown is home to many interesting old and historic buildings. The Hotel de Paris (now a museum operated by the National Society of Colonial Dames) was a luxurious French inn of outstanding quality that used to accommodate businessmen from the East and Europe while they speculated over mining investments. President Ulysses S. Grant stayed there and was very fond of it. The Hotel de Paris was richly

Grant in 1938, shortly before the tracks were removed

furnished and served exotic foods. The owners bottled their own wine and kept an extensive wine cellar. Fish were kept in an indoor fountain so they could be selected by and prepared for the guests. The Hammill House (now a museum at Argentine and Third Streets) was once a modest home built by mining investor and politician William A. Hammill. As Hammill grew wealthier, his house became more opulent. He added bay windows, a solarium with curved glass panels, a stable, an office, and a six-seat outhouse (with three walnut seats for the family and three pine ones for the servants). The Maxwell House is another immaculately kept Victorian home that was quite modest in its original state and took on a much more lavish appearance as the owner prospered.

In 1884, railroad workers accomplished a true feat of engineering when they completed the Georgetown Loop narrow gauge between Georgetown and Silver Plume (2 miles west of Georgetown). A series of curves constructed in a spiral fashion helped trains gain momentum for the steep grades on the straightaways; in one spot, the railroad actually crossed over itself on a 300-foot trestle. The journey, popular with tourists who wanted to observe the beautiful scenery and experience the thrill, was similar to a roller-coaster ride.

After the silver crash of 1893, Georgetown became a sleepy mountain town, although it continued to produce gold and other metals. The railroad was abandoned in 1939; the trestle was dismantled, and the rails were scrapped. However, the entire narrow gauge railway route between Georgetown and Silver Plume has been reconstructed. During Colorado's milder months, thousands of tourists ride the Georgetown Loop Railroad across the 95-foot Devil's Gate High Bridge between Silver Plume and Georgetown.

Georgetown today is a charming community with interesting architecture and a fascinating history. The town has been a National Historic Landmark since 1966. In 1970, residents formed the Georgetown Society, which has made an ongoing effort to restore and preserve many of Georgetown's Victorian buildings (including the Hammill House) to their original states.

Guanella Pass summit

Description

Today, this very popular route is used year-round for picnicking, camping, and cross-country skiing. The easy 2WD route is very scenic and provides good fall viewing of the aspens.

The route starts at the tiny township of Grant and heads north on FR 118 beside Geneva Creek, traveling through a wooded valley with scenic rock formations along the road. The land surrounding the road alternates between private property and national forest.

After about 4 miles, the road starts its climb toward the pass and leaves the creek behind. It continues above timberline, with the scenery becoming considerably more rugged. The summit offers expansive views of Mount Bierstadt, Mount Evans, and the Sawtooth Range to the east and the Continental Divide to the west.

The descent to Georgetown follows Clear Creek past a number of lakes and reservoirs, as well as the Cabin Creek hydroelectric plant. The paved road switchbacks down into the town of Georgetown.

The route offers access to four forest service campgrounds and numerous hiking trails. It is especially scenic in fall when the vast aspen stands turn bright yellow and blanket the surrounding mountains.

Current Road Information

Arapaho & Roosevelt National Forests
Clear Creek Ranger District
101 Chicago Creek Road
Idaho Springs, CO 80452
(303) 567-3000

Georgetown Visitor Information Center
1491 Argentine
Georgetown, CO 80444
(303) 569-2405

Map References

USFS   Arapaho & Roosevelt National
    Forests
Maptech CD:
    Colorado Springs/Ski Areas/Central;
    Denver/Steamboat Springs/North
    Central

Benchmark's *Colorado Road & Recreation*
    Atlas, p. 74
Colorado Atlas & Gazetteer, pp. 39, 49
The Roads of Colorado, p. 79
Trails Illustrated, #104 (incomplete)

Route Directions

▼0.0   At intersection of US 285 and CR 62 in Grant, zero trip meter and turn onto Guanella Pass Road toward Georgetown.

12.9▲   End at intersection with US 285 in Grant.
    GPS: N 39°27.61' W 105°39.75'

▼0.4   **SO** Unpaved.

Geneva Creek alongside Guanella Pass Trail

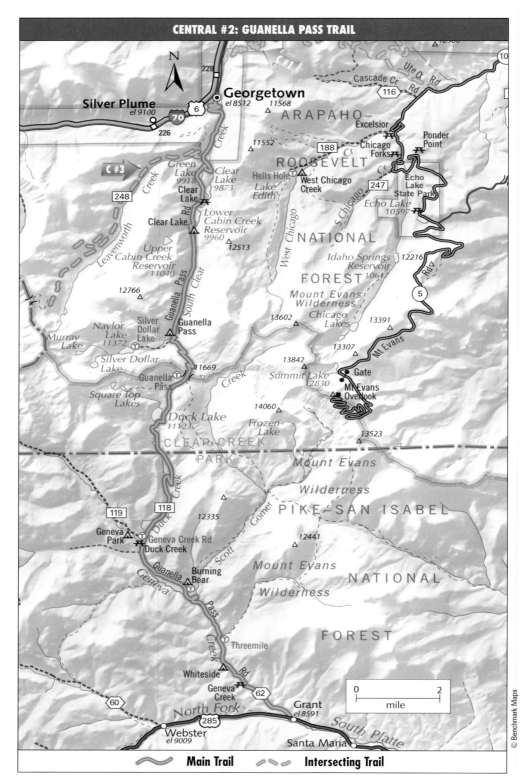

Main Trail   **Intersecting Trail**

© Benchmark Maps

12.5▲	**SO**	Paved.

▼1.5	**SO**	Enter National Forest.
11.4▲	**SO**	Leave National Forest.

▼1.7	**SO**	Geneva Creek Picnic Grounds.
11.2▲	**SO**	Geneva Creek Picnic Grounds.

▼2.3	**SO**	USFS Whiteside Campground.
10.6▲	**SO**	USFS Whiteside Campground.

▼4.0	**SO**	Pavement begins.
8.9▲	**SO**	Pavement ends.

▼5.0	**SO**	Burning Bear Trailhead on left.
7.9▲	**SO**	Burning Bear Trailhead on right.

▼5.1	**SO**	Cattle guard.
7.8▲	**SO**	Cattle guard.

▼5.2	**SO**	USFS Burning Bear Campground.
7.6▲	**SO**	USFS Burning Bear Campground.

▼6.8	**SO**	Track to Geneva City town site at Duck Creek Picnic Ground on left.
6.1▲	**SO**	Track to Geneva City town site at Duck Creek Picnic Ground on right.

▼10.4	**SO**	Track on left to Geneva Creek (FR 119).
2.5▲	**SO**	Track on right to Geneva Creek (FR 119).

▼11.2	**SO**	Unpaved.
1.7▲	**SO**	Paved.

▼12.9	**SO**	Summit of Guanella Pass. Zero trip meter.
0.0▲		Continue toward Grant.
		GPS: N 39°35.72′ W 105°42.61′

▼0.0		Continue toward Georgetown.
8.1▲	**SO**	Summit of Guanella Pass. Zero trip meter.

▼1.9	**SO**	Silver Dollar Lake Trail (1 mile) on left.
6.2▲	**SO**	Silver Dollar Lake Trail (1 mile) on right.

▼2.1	**SO**	USFS Guanella Campground on left.
6.0▲	**SO**	USFS Guanella Campground on right.

▼4.2	**SO**	Cross over South Clear Creek.
3.9▲	**SO**	Cross over South Clear Creek.

▼5.0	**SO**	USFS Clear Lake Campground on left.
3.1▲	**SO**	USFS Clear Lake Campground on right.

▼5.2	**SO**	Paved.
2.9▲	**SO**	Unpaved.

▼6.2	**SO**	Road to Clear Lake on right.
1.9▲	**SO**	Road to Clear Lake on left.

▼6.9	**SO**	Green Lake on right.
1.2▲	**SO**	Green Lake on left.

▼8.1	**SO**	Intersection with Central #3: Waldorf and Santiago Ghost Town Trail (FR 248.1) on left. Zero trip meter.
0.0▲		Proceed south on Guanella Pass Road.
		GPS: N39°40.99′ W105°42.17′

▼0.0		Proceed north on Guanella Pass Road.
3.2▲	**SO**	Intersection with Central #3: Waldorf and Santiago Ghost Town Trail (FR 248.1) on right. Zero trip meter.

▼0.8	**SO**	Georgetown water supply reservoir on right.
2.4▲	**SO**	Georgetown water supply reservoir on left.

▼2.5	**SO**	Enter Georgetown, remaining on the paved road. As it comes into town, the name becomes Rose Street.
0.8▲	**SO**	Leave Georgetown on Guanella Pass Road toward Guanella Pass.

▼3.2		End at Royal Gorge Route Railroad offices on the corner of Rose and 11th Streets.
0.0▲		From the Royal Gorge Route Railroad offices at the corner of Rose and 11th Streets in Georgetown, zero trip meter and proceed south along Rose Street.
		GPS: N 39°42.69′ W 105°41.69′

Waldorf and Santiago Ghost Town Trail

STARTING POINT Central #2: Guanella Pass Trail, 2.5 miles south of Georgetown

FINISHING POINT Argentine Pass

TOTAL MILEAGE 13.6 miles, including spur (one-way)

UNPAVED MILEAGE 13.6 miles, including spur

DRIVING TIME 2 hours, including spur (one-way)

ROUTE ELEVATION 9,580 to 13,265 feet

USUALLY OPEN June to September

DIFFICULTY RATING 5

SCENIC RATING 10

Special Attractions

- Waldorf town site and Santiago ghost town.
- Rocky climb up to Argentine Pass.
- Excellent side route from any trip over Guanella Pass.

History

Part of the East Argentine Mining District, the Waldorf mines were discovered and worked early in Colorado mining history. A large silver deposit was discovered in 1864, and the town of Waldorf was established three years later. Methodist minister Edward John Wilcox encouraged the development of the Waldorf mines, founding the Waldorf Milling and Mining Company and investing money in building the Argentine Central Railroad.

The Argentine Central originated in Silver Plume, traveled through Waldorf, and ended at the summit of Mount McClellan. When the railroad line was completed in 1906, it was the highest steam railroad route in the world. In addition to hauling ore, the railroad transported tourists to Waldorf and Mount McClellan. Soon revenue from tourists outnumbered that from transporting freight roughly 10:1. Of great interest to sightseers was the Ice Palace, an old mine covered in ice formations. The

A rocky and eroded section of the trail

Santiago mine adit and ore cart tracks

building of a tunnel allowing the Argentine Central to travel under the Continental Divide was attempted but abandoned during construction due to lack of funds.

The town of Waldorf was relatively small, with a peak population of 300. The town had a large mill, a boardinghouse, a small store, a machine shop, and a power house. A post office opened in 1906. Located at 11,666 feet, it registered as the highest post office in the nation. The Argentine Central went bankrupt in 1912. After the rail line's brief revival as the Argentine and Grays Peak Railway, the tracks were removed in 1920 and the roadbed turned into an automobile road. Over the life of the mines, about $4 million in silver and gold was produced.

The ghost town of Santiago was located just above Waldorf. William Rogers first discovered ore at the Santiago Mine in 1898. The name of the mine likely comes from the town of Santiago, Cuba, as

around the time of the mine's discovery the United States was engaged in the Spanish-American War and had just taken Santiago.

Like a number of other mines in Clear Creek County, the Santiago Mine was worked seasonally. The years of peak production for the Santiago occurred around the turn of the nineteenth century. A railroad spur off the Argentine Central Railroad was built in 1909–10 to help transport ore. A tramway built between Santiago and Waldorf in 1913 made transportation between the two towns easier. Little is known about when the town was abandoned.

The nearby Argentine Pass, previously named Sanderson Pass and Snake River Pass, once marked the divide between Spanish and French territory in North America. During the gold rush, the pass connected Georgetown to the rich mining districts above Peru Creek and the Snake River basin. Although Argentine Pass was

An old hoist at Waldorf town site

Santiago ghost town

close to the Peru Mining District, it was not named after the neighboring South American country Argentina. Rather, the name was derived from the Latin word "argentine," meaning "silver."

In 1869, Commodore Stephen Decatur and the Georgetown and Snake River Wagon Road Company built a toll road over the pass, the highest pass road over the Continental Divide during its years of operation. The road was not a commercial success because travelers increasingly found alternate routes over the divide in order to avoid the steep slopes of the frighteningly narrow road. The famous survey party led by Ferdinand V. Hayden crossed Argentine Pass in 1873. Photographer William H. Jackson, accompanying Hayden's party, took many photographs of the area. Argentine Pass is no longer accessible to motor vehicles, as numerous rock slides over the years have made the route impassable.

Description

Waldorf and Santigo Ghost Town Trail branches off of Central #2: Guanella Pass Trail and immediately climbs several switchbacks. Embedded rock makes the drive slow going. For much of its length, the road is narrow enough to require using a pullout or backing up for a short distance if you meet an oncoming vehicle.

Aggressively gaining elevation, the trail climbs more than 1,000 feet in about a mile. Below timberline, views are limited as it mostly follows a corridor through the trees. The stands of aspen trees here have brilliant yellow leaves in fall.

Most of the section of trail that runs above Leavenworth Creek is a shelf road, climbing higher and higher up the side of the valley until it reaches the town site of Waldorf. Above tree line, views of the surrounding peaks and alpine meadows, which bloom with wildflowers in spring, are expansive. There are also several good campsites along the section of trail up to Waldorf.

The most notable thing about the site of Waldorf is the abundance of tailings piles. Other than that, there are a few buildings left as well as a Quonset hut. A couple of tracks make their way around the few remaining structures and continue up the steep side of McClellan Mountain to additional mining remains and past a cluster of bristlecone pines. Branching off the track to McClellan Mountain is the spur to Santiago ghost town.

Set among the rugged and exposed mountain peaks, the remains of the old mining camp of Santiago are interesting to explore. Many well-preserved buildings and much mining equipment are left at Santiago. The buildings, including a large mill and a small cabin that served as living quarters, are clustered around the prominent mine adit. Sections of track for the ore carts

Old living quarters at Santiago

Extensive mill remains at Santiago

Mill foundations at Waldorf

that transported earth from inside the mine to the mill still remain.

Past Waldorf, the trail starts to climb again along FR 248.1V. This part of the trail is much looser and rockier than before but still well within the capabilities of a stock high-clearance 4WD. These last couple miles make for slow travel; however, the views back down the Leavenworth Creek Valley as well as the views of Argentine Peak and Mount Wilcox just keep getting better. Once on the pass, you can see the old vehicle route (now a hiking trail) that descends the other side toward Central #4: Peru

Creek Trail. Many peaks are visible, but Mount Edwards, Grays Peak, and Ruby Mountain are the most prominent.

Current Road Information

Arapaho & Roosevelt National Forests
Clear Creek Ranger District
101 Chicago Creek Road
Idaho Springs, CO 80452
(303) 567-3000

Map References

USFS   Arapaho & Roosevelt National Forests

Mill remains at Santiago

Maptech CD:
    Denver/Steamboat Springs/North
    Central
Benchmark's *Colorado Road & Recreation
    Atlas*, p. 74
Colorado Atlas & Gazetteer, p. 39
The Roads of Colorado, p. 79
Trails Illustrated, #104

Route Directions

▼0.0   From Georgetown, take Central #2:
          Guanella Pass Trail 2.5 miles; make a
          right on a sharp curve. Zero trip meter
          and head south on dirt road (FR
          248.1), following signs for Waldorf.
          GPS: N39°40.99′ W105°42.13′

▼0.2   SO   Track on left.
▼0.4   SO/BR   Cross over Leavenworth Creek; then
          two tracks on right lead to campsites;
          bear right on right-hand switchback;
          track on left is narrow and overgrown
          and climbs hill.
▼0.6   SO   Track on right leads to campsite.
▼0.9   TR   Turn sharp right; track FR 248.1B

continues ahead, leading to mine
remains and many campsites.
GPS: N39°40.99′ W105°42.53′

▼1.1   TL   FR 248.1Q (dead end) straight ahead;
          turn left on left-hand switchback.
▼2.3   SO   Cross through wash; then track on
          left.
▼2.7   SO   Narrow crossing over wash.
▼3.4   BR   Fork in road. Zero trip meter.
          GPS: N39°39.99′ W105°44.38′

▼0.0   Proceed southwest up the hill.
▼0.2   SO   Cross over creek.
▼0.7   SO   Track on sharp right; then cross
          through wash.
          GPS: N39°39.46′ W105°44.62′

▼1.2   SO   FR 248.1A on left; then right.
▼1.8   SO   Track on left to campsite.
▼1.9   SO   Cross through wash.
▼5.9   SO   Enter Waldorf town site; track on
          sharp right is 248.1; mill and mine
          remains on left; Quonset hut on right
          up hill. Zero trip meter.
          GPS: N39°38.27′ W105°45.87′

View to the west from Argentine Pass and what remains of the old vehicle trail

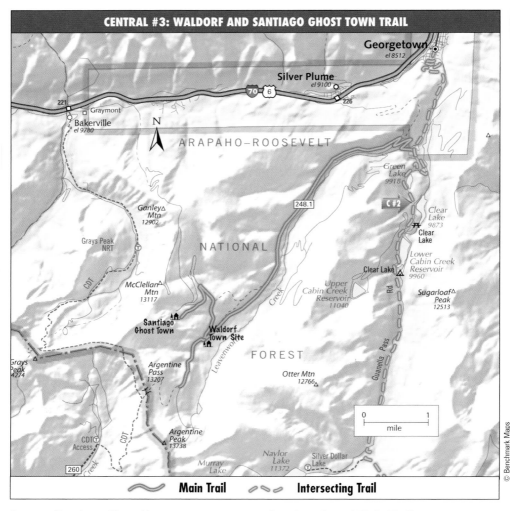

~~~ **Main Trail**   ⌒⌒⌒ **Intersecting Trail**

© Benchmark Maps

Spur to Santiago Ghost Town

▼0.0   Proceed northeast on FR 248.1.

▼0.6 **SO** Track on left; then track on right.

▼0.7 **SO** Track on left and right (FR 248.1N).

▼1.0 **UTL** Track straight on goes up to McClellan Mountain; track on sharp left proceeds to Santiago ghost town.
GPS: N39°39.05' W105°45.98'

▼1.4 **BL** Intersection with FR 248.1N to the left and right.

▼1.6 **SO** Gate.

▼1.7 **SO** Track on left; then grave on left and foundations on right.

▼1.8   Spur ends at Santiago Mine and ghost town.
GPS: N39°38.59' W105°46.30'

Continuation of Main Trail

▼0.0   Continue to the west; then pass two tracks on right through Waldorf.

▼0.1 **SO** Continue on FR 248.1V.

▼0.3 **SO** Cross through wash; then track on left goes to mine.

▼0.5 **BL** Track on right; then cross through wash; then bear left when trail forks.

▼0.6 **SO** Track on right rejoins.

▼0.8 **SO** Trail forks then immediately rejoins.

▼0.9 **BR** FR 248.1U continues ahead. Bear right following FR 248.1V.
GPS: N39°37.62' W105°46.25'

▼2.5   Trail ends at Argentine Pass.
GPS: N39°37.53' W105°46.90'

A cluster of bristlecone pines beside the trail

Leavenworth Creek near the beginning of the trail

Peru Creek Trail

STARTING POINT Intersection of CR 5 (Montezuma Road) and FR 260

FINISHING POINT Gate at Shoe Basin Mine ore bin

TOTAL MILEAGE 4.7 miles (one-way)

UNPAVED MILEAGE 4.7 miles

DRIVING TIME 1 hour (one-way)

ROUTE ELEVATION 10,007 to 11,149 feet

USUALLY OPEN Late May to October

DIFFICULTY RATING 2

SCENIC RATING 10

Special Attractions

- The substantial Pennsylvania Mine and Mill.
- Abundant mining remains along the entire the length of the trail.
- Popular ATV, dirt bike, and mountain bike trail.
- Rugged, above-timberline scenery of Peru Creek Valley.
- Spring wildflowers and large beaver dams in Peru Creek.
- Numerous hiking trailheads.
- Good backcountry campsites and picnic spots.
- Snowmobile trail in winter.

Peru Creek runs alongside the trail

Boilers and shaft at the Pennsylvania Mine

History

In 1865, newspaperman D. C. Collier and future Colorado senator H. M. Teller were among the first men to arrive in the valley just south of the site where silver ore was reportedly first discovered in Colorado Territory. It was Collier who suggested that the town be named for the Aztec emperor Montezuma. The town grew quickly and by 1868 rivaled Breckenridge as one of Summit County's largest towns.

Transportation proved problematic for Montezuma as it was for many other mining towns. However, the population escalated with the development of multiple wagon routes in the district. By 1880, more than 800 people lived in Montezuma, and the town boasted a schoolhouse, post office, three hotels, a steam sawmill, a smelting furnace, and concentration works. A larger schoolhouse even had to be built in 1884 to accommodate the growing number of students.

Montezuma was well known as a social and hospitable town, famous for its poker playing. It was said the game never stopped, as there was always someone willing to take the place of anyone who dropped out. Like many other mining towns, Montezuma had a red-light district. One "soiled dove" in particular, Dixie, was recognized throughout the town, as she would go to local baseball games to support the home team. She also fed all of the town's stray animals, buying cans of milk and beef by the caseload.

A fire ravaged the town in 1915, and the population continued to dwindle until it numbered about a dozen in 1956. In the 1950s, the Roberts Tunnel project, built to carry water from Lake Dillon to Denver via an underground tunnel, brought about a small revival, as construction workers moved into town. Another fire, however, destroyed half the homes in town in 1958. Today there are a few remaining residents

Pennsylvania Mill tipple

Inside the Pennsylvania Mill

A beaver lodge, dam, and pond in Peru Creek

Ruins at the Pennsylvania Mill

in Montezuma, although the town is much diminished from its mining heyday.

Farther up Peru Creek is the ghost town of Argentine. First established in 1868 as Decatur, the town took off upon J. W. Hall's 1879 discovery of silver at the Pennsylvania Mine, one of the best producers in the area. Production declined at the Pennsylvania in the 1890s, and the silver crash of 1893 forced most of the silver mines in the area to close. However, the Pennsylvania managed to remain in operation throughout the silver crash, and in 1893 the town was revived with the new name of Rathbone. From 1893 to 1898, the Pennsylvania not only survived but prospered, producing over $3 million in earnings during this period. An avalanche in the winter of 1898 destroyed most of the town.

New silver discoveries in 1902 drew prospectors to the region, and the town experienced a final rebirth as Argentine. The Decatur Mining Syndicate sold the Pennsylvania Mine to the Ohio Mines Company in 1902. The Rothschild Company later purchased the mine, which continued to function into the 1940s.

Description

This backcountry adventure begins less than a mile north of Montezuma in a parking area at the intersection of CR 5 and FR 260. Starting off as an easygoing drive through pine forest, the wide, gravel road (which is well maintained for its entire length) gradually gains elevation. The trail crosses Peru Creek and proceeds past several hiking trailheads and many good backcountry campsites. For the first several miles, views are limited because the road follows Peru Creek through the trees. Also along this

Ore cart trestle at Pennsylvania Mine

Old abandoned cabin in Peru Creek Valley

Tramhouse perched on the hill above the Pennsylvania Mill

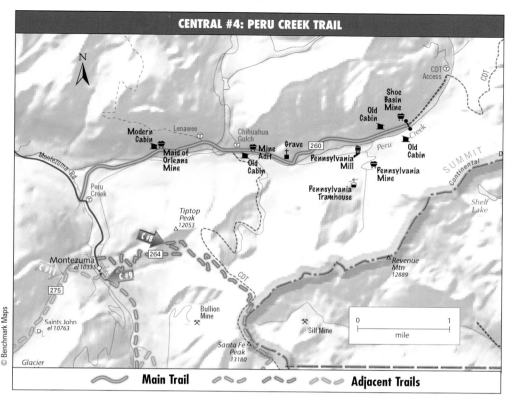

Main Trail 〰️ 〰️ 〰️ **Adjacent Trails**

© Benchmark Maps

section, several forest roads branch off the main trail, and old cabins and other abandonded mining equipment remain among the trees.

In around 3.5 miles, the trail reaches timberline and the trees thin out, revealing expansive views of Peru Creek Valley. Rugged peaks enclose the valley's alpine meadows. The Pennsylvania Mine and Mill ruins appear on the south side of the valley. The wooden mill building is collapsing around the old ore processing equipment that remains inside. An old tramhouse is also perched on the hillside above the mill, and there are several more interesting buildings to explore on the maze of tracks just off the main trail in Cinnamon Gulch. The remains of the mine are well worth the diversion to explore.

Beyond the Pennsylvania Mine complex, the trail continues alongside Peru Creek through alpine meadows, which are blanketed with wildflowers in spring. There are several more old cabins and some more mining equipment scattered throughout

the valley. Numerous beaver ponds and dams are another point of interest in Peru Creek. The patient observer is likely to spot a beaver in the clear creek waters.

About a mile beyond Cinnamon Gulch, the trail ends at a gate and an ore bin from the nearby Shoe Basin Mine. Hikers can proceed beyond the gate to the Argentine Pass Trailhead, a strenuous 2-mile climb to Argentine Pass and the Continental Divide.

Current Road Information
White River National Forest
Dillon Ranger District
680 Blue River Parkway
Silverthorne, CO 80498
(970) 468-5400

Map References
USFS   White River National Forest
Maptech CD:
> Denver/Steamboat Springs/North Central

Benchmark's *Colorado Road & Recreation Atlas,* p. 73

Colorado Atlas & Gazetteer, p. 38
The Roads of Colorado, p. 79
Trails Illustrated, #104

Route Directions

▼0.0　　　Trail begins at intersection of
Montezuma Road (CR 5) and FR 260.
Zero trip meter and proceed northeast
on FR 260 through seasonal gate.
GPS: N39°35.53' W105°52.25'

▼1.0　　**BL**　Track on right.
GPS: N39°35.92' W105°51.46'

▼1.1　　**SO**　Cross over Peru Creek.
▼1.4　　**SO**　Cabin with mine loader on left and
sheds on right.
▼1.6　　**SO**　Lenawee Hiking Trailhead on left.
▼1.9　　**SO**　Cross over creek.
▼2.1　　**SO**　Track on right is FR 265, signed
Warden Gulch and Morgan Creek to
the right and Argentine Pass Trailhead
straight ahead.
▼2.2　　**SO**　FR 263 on right; then track on left

signed to Chihuahua Gulch Road and
Chihuahua Lake Trailhead.
GPS: N39°36.03' W105°50.29'

▼2.3　　**SO**　Old cabin on right; then old mine adit
on left.
▼2.4　　**SO**　Grave on left.
▼2.8　　**SO**　Picnic area on left.
▼3.3　　**SO**　Cabin remains on right.
▼3.7　　**SO**　Road on right ends in 0.2 miles at
Pennsylvania Mine and Mill ruins in
Cinnamon Gulch. Zero trip meter.
GPS: N39°36.16' W105°48.79'

▼0.0　　　Proceed east on FR 260.
▼0.4　　**SO**　Old cabin on left.
GPS: N39°36.25' W105°48.34'

▼0.8　　**SO**　Parking lot on left.
▼0.9　　**SO**　Cabin on right.
▼1.0　　　Trail ends near Shoe Basin Mine ore
bin at gate.
GPS: N39°36.59' W105°47.92'

View of the west side of Argentine Pass from the trail

Handcart Gulch Trail

STARTING POINT Intersection of US 285 and CR 60 (FR 120) at the town site of Webster

FINISHING POINT Webster Pass

TOTAL MILEAGE 9.6 miles

UNPAVED MILEAGE 9.6 miles

DRIVING TIME 1.75 hours

ROUTE ELEVATION 9,200 to 12,096 feet

USUALLY OPEN Mid-August to late September

DIFFICULTY RATING 6

SCENIC RATING 9

Special Attractions

- Varied four-wheel driving challenges, including an extremely narrow shelf road.
- Spectacular views, particularly of Red Cone Peak.
- Access to an extensive network of 4WD trails.

History

The area is named for two prospectors who in 1860 brought their handcart loaded with supplies up the valley and made the area's

Lower section of the trail

first gold discovery while panning the creek.

Towns that developed in the vicinity included Webster, Hall Valley, and Handcart Gulch. Webster was a staging point for pas-

The narrow shelf section of Handcart Gulch Trail descending from Webster Pass before switchbacking into the valley

sengers and freight headed across Webster Pass. For a time in the 1870s it was the end of the line for the Denver, South Park & Pacific Railroad. It was known as a wild town where gunplay was common; traffic was heavy to the boot hill cemetery north of town. As the railroad was extended and better pass routes were opened, Webster went into decline. Its post office closed in 1909.

The town of Hall Valley, also known as Hall's Gulch, Hallville, and Hall City, was centered on the fortunes of the Whale Mine. At the town's peak, around 1876–77, the population reached about 500. Hall Valley was renowned as a very rowdy place where the saloons were open all day and all night. When two of the mine foremen who had earned the wrath of the miners for their bullying management were in town, the miners lynched them both!

It is not clear if Col. J. W. Hall was the owner or the manager of the Whale Mine, but it is clear that both he and the English

company that subsequently operated it were incompetent, and as the fortunes of the mine declined, so did the town.

The town of Handcart Gulch, located a short distance farther up the valley, was also short-lived, and its prosperity mirrored that of Hall Valley.

Description

The route starts at the town site of Webster (nothing remains of the town) at the intersection of US 285 and CR 60 (FR 120), 3.2 miles west of Grant.

Initially, this is the same route that leads to Webster Pass by way of Red Cone Peak. The well-maintained 2WD road travels along Hall Valley beside the headwaters of the North Fork of the South Platte River though pine and aspen groves.

After the intersection with Central #6: Red Cone Peak Trail 5 miles along the route, the road soon becomes rough and rocky. Large rocks in the road make selecting the correct line important. There is a

Rocky, difficult section of the trail

The intersection of Handcart Gulch Trail and Red Cone Peak Trail

North Fork of the South Platte River near the beginning of the trail

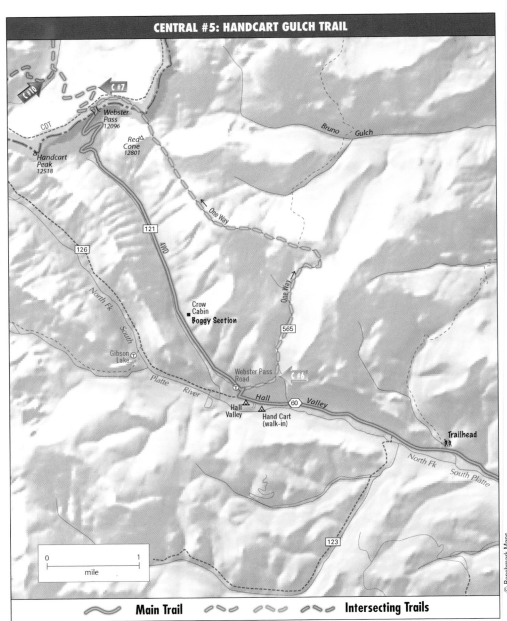

~~~ Main Trail   **◦◦◦ ◦◦◦ ◦◦◦ Intersecting Trails**

boggy spot that has been repaired by the Colorado Association of 4 Wheel Drive Clubs just in front of a cabin 1.7 miles after the turnoff to Red Cone. Be aware that logs used to repair this muddy section may have become dislodged, uncovering sharp stakes. Remain on the trail through this section to prevent further damage to the ground around the trail or worst of all, trail closure.

The road continues through two manageable creek crossings and then commences its final assault on the pass. The ascent begins with a number of switchbacks and culminates in a long, very narrow, off-camber rough shelf cut into the steep talus mountainside. This stretch of road is frequently obstructed by rocks that you must clear in order to pass; it is only just wide

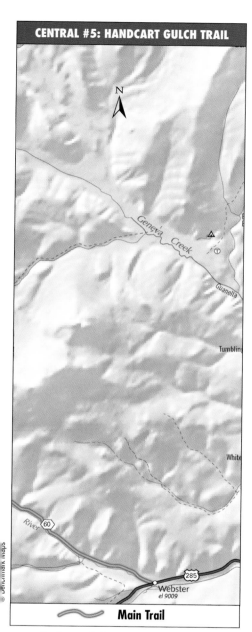

CENTRAL #5: HANDCART GULCH TRAIL

N

Geneva Creek

Guanella

Tumblin

White

River 60

Webster
el 9009

Main Trail

© Benchmark Maps

Current Road Information
Pike National Forest
South Platte Ranger District
19316 Goddard Ranch Court
Morrison, CO 80465
(303) 275-5610

Map References
USFS   Pike National Forest
Maptech CD:
>Colorado Springs/Ski Areas/Central;
>Denver/Steamboat Springs/North
>Central

Benchmark's *Colorado Road & Recreation
>Atlas,* p. 73
Colorado Atlas & Gazetteer, pp. 38, 48
The Roads of Colorado, p. 79
Trails Illustrated, #104 (incomplete)

Route Directions

▼0.0   From intersection of US 285 and CR 60 (FR 120) at the site of Webster, zero trip meter. Proceed west on unpaved road marked with sign to Red Cone Road and Handcart Gulch.

5.0▲   End at intersection with US 285 at the site of Webster.

        GPS: N 39°27.46' W 105°43.27'

▼0.9   SO   Enter Pike National Forest.
4.1▲   SO   Leave Pike National Forest.

▼1.7   SO   Track on left with campsite. Cattle guard.
3.3▲   SO   Cattle guard. Track on right with campsite.

▼2.9   SO   Burning Bear hiking trail on right. Town site of Hall Valley.
2.1▲   SO   Burning Bear hiking trail on left. Town site of Hall Valley.

        GPS: N 39°28.46' W 105°45.70'

▼3.1   SO   Road on left to Beaver Creek (FR 123).
1.9▲   SO   Road on right to Beaver Creek (FR 123).

▼4.6   SO   USFS Handcart Campground and FR 120A on left.
0.3▲   SO   USFS Handcart Campground and FR

enough for a full-sized vehicle to squeeze through. The last hundred feet are usually blocked by a snowdrift until late into summer.

The view from the pass is wonderful: To the east is the one-way (downhill only) road off Red Cone Peak, southeast is the west face of Red Cone, north is the Snake River Valley, and southwest is the shelf road you have just ascended.

120A on right.

▼4.9   SO   Hall Valley Campground and Gibson
                    Lake Trailhead (FR 120B) to the left.
                    Town site of Handcart Gulch.

0.1▲   SO   Hall Valley Campground and Gibson
                    Lake Trailhead (FR 120B) to the right.
                    Town site of Handcart Gulch.
                    GPS: N 39°28.98' W 105°48.20'

▼5.0   TL   T-intersection. Turn left onto road to
                    Handcart Gulch (FR 121). Track on
                    right is Central #6: Red Cone Peak
                    Trail, which also leads to Webster
                    Pass. Zero trip meter.

0.0▲   Proceed along Handcart Gulch Trail
                    (FR 120).
                    GPS: N 39°29.02' W 105°48.27'

▼0.0   Proceed along Handcart Gulch Trail.

4.6▲   BR   Intersection. Left goes to Central #6:
                    Red Cone Peak Trail and loops back to
                    Webster Pass. Right leads to US 285.
                    Zero trip meter.

▼0.1   SO   Track on right.
4.5▲   BR   Track on left.

▼0.4   BL   Intersection. FR 5652 on right.
4.1▲   BR   Intersection. FR 5652 on left.

▼0.5   SO   Track on right to walking trail.
4.0▲   SO   Track on left to walking trail.

▼1.7   SO   Building on right. Potentially very
                    boggy and rutted section of the track.

2.9▲   SO   Building on left. Potentially very
                    boggy and rutted section of the track.

▼2.8   SO   Cross through creek.
1.8▲   SO   Cross through creek.

▼3.1   SO   Cross through creek.
1.5▲   SO   Cross through creek.
                    GPS: N 39°31.31' W 105°49.89'

▼4.2-4.6 SO   Travel along a very narrow shelf.
0.0-0.4▲ SO   Travel along a very narrow shelf.

▼4.6   End at Webster Pass.
0.0▲   From the summit of Webster Pass,
                    zero trip meter and proceed south on
                    Handcart Gulch Trail (FR 120) along a
                    narrow shelf.
                    GPS: N 39°31.86' W 105°49.92'

Narrow shelf road near Webster Pass

Red Cone Peak Trail

STARTING POINT Intersection of US 285 and Park CR 60 (FR 120), at the town site of Webster

FINISHING POINT Webster Pass

TOTAL MILEAGE 11.2 miles (one-way)

UNPAVED MILEAGE 11.2 miles

DRIVING TIME 2 hours (one-way)

ROUTE ELEVATION 9,200 to 12,600 feet

USUALLY OPEN Early July to late September

DIFFICULTY RATING 7

SCENIC RATING 10

Special Attractions

- Spectacular alpine views.
- The adventure of tackling a very challenging 4WD trail.
- Access to an extensive network of 4WD trails.

Description

The main part of this trail starts 5 miles from US 285. Navigating this trail is easy, as there are no other side roads.

The start of Red Cone Peak Trail is quite rocky. The road travels through pine and aspen forest that becomes just pine as the road ascends. The clearance between the trees is just wide enough for a full-sized vehicle. The road crosses a creek bed that is often heavily eroded. Along the way, you will also encounter a number of switchbacks and rocks. A couple of uphill sections (although short) are quite challenging because of large rocks and a loose, eroded surface.

After emerging from timberline, the road travels along a lengthy, open tundra ridge before making its final, sharp ascent to a narrow perch above the steep, dangerous descent to Webster Pass. This is a good place to stop and admire one of the most

Steep section of Red Cone Peak Trail

breathtaking views in Colorado while gathering yourself for the last section, now in clear view.

The distance from the summit of Red Cone Peak to Webster Pass is about three-quarters of a mile and is broken into three short, steep sections, with the first being the hardest.

From Webster Pass, you get to look back on the slope you have just negotiated and across to the vivid red surface of Red Cone Peak.

Special Note on the Difficulty of This Road

This trail is one of the most difficult included in this book. We have limited the scope of this book primarily to trails with difficulty ratings up to a maximum of 5. So why include one rated 7? First, the views are fabulous. Second, it provides a route for those four-wheelers who want to test their skills on a truly demanding road. However, be warned. Some experienced four-wheel drivers consider this the most dangerous 4WD trail in the state.

Heading down the steep section of the Red Cone Peak Trail

The trail climbs Red Cone Peak before descending to Webster Pass and Radical Hill Trail in the distance on the left

The route offers a range of challenges. Clearance is very tight between the trees in the early part of the trail. There are also a number of very tight switchbacks, severely eroded sections, and quite large (and not al-ways embedded) rocks. However, these obstacles by themselves would warrant a difficulty rating of only 5.

By far the most challenging and potentially dangerous obstacle is the very steep

Looking across Hall Valley to Red Cone Peak Trail as it descends to Webster Pass (marked)

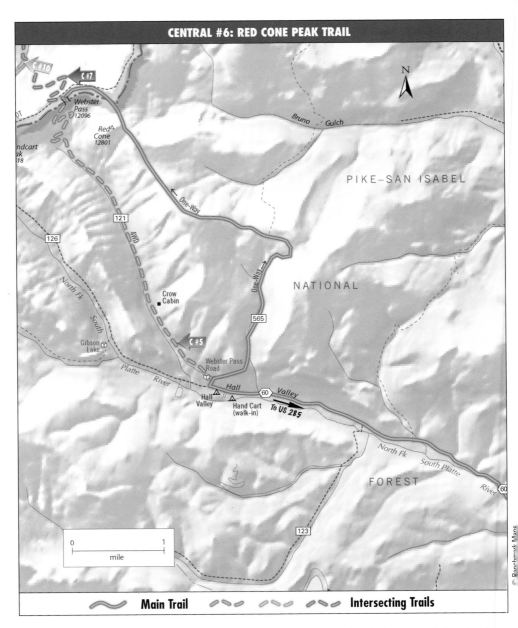

~~~ Main Trail   ⌒⌒⌒ ⌒⌒⌒ ⌒⌒⌒ **Intersecting Trails**

downhill section of loose talus at the end of the trail. It is because of this section that the U.S. Forest Service has banned travel on this road from the Webster Pass direction, making the road one-way only. If you do not handle your vehicle properly when descending the talus slope, the rear of the vehicle is likely to swing around, causing it to roll. The floor of Handcart Gulch is about 1,500 feet below—and that is where you will stop!

However, there is a safe way to make the descent: Select first gear in low range and go down slowly. You must exercise particular care if you use the brakes because if the wheels lock up, the rear of the vehicle will swing around. If the back of the vehicle starts to come around, the only way to

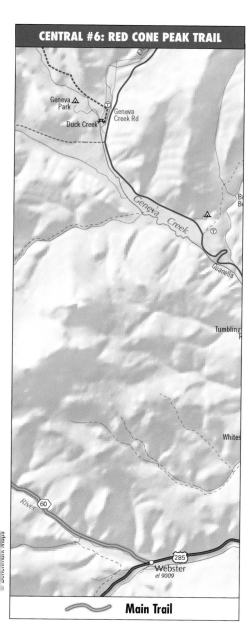

Main Trail

straighten it is to accelerate. In the heat of a crisis, however, many drivers will find the need to accelerate the opposite of their instincts. If you need to employ this technique, be careful not to overdo it. This steeply descending section of road is bumpy because of broad corrugations caused by vehicles sliding on the talus; if you have to accelerate, be prepared to bounce all over the place.

Current Road Information
Pike & San Isabel National Forests
South Platte Ranger District
19316 Goddard Ranch Court
Morrison, CO 80465
(303) 275-5610

Map References
USFS   Pike National Forest
Maptech CD:
    Colorado Springs/Ski Areas/Central;
    Denver/Steamboat Springs/North
    Central
Benchmark's *Colorado Road & Recreation
    Atlas,* pp. 73, 74
Colorado Atlas & Gazetteer, pp. 39, 48, 49
The Roads of Colorado, p. 79
Trails Illustrated, #104 (incomplete)

Route Directions

▼0.0   From intersection of US 285 and CR 60 (FR 120) at the site of Webster, zero trip meter. Proceed northwest on unpaved road marked with sign to Red Cone Road and Handcart Gulch.
        GPS: N 39°27.46' W 105°43.27'

▼0.9   SO Enter Pike National Forest.
▼1.7   SO Track on left with campsite. Cattle guard.
▼2.9   SO Burning Bear walking trail on right.
▼3.1   SO Road on left to Beaver Creek (FR 123).
▼4.6   SO USFS Handcart Campground.
▼4.9   SO Hall Valley Campground and Gibson Lake Trailhead (FR 120B) to the left.
        GPS: N 39°28.98' W 105°48.20'

▼5.0   TR T-intersection. Road on left is Central #5: Handcart Gulch Trail (FR 121), which also leads to Webster Pass. Zero trip meter.
        GPS: N 39°29.02' W 105°48.27'

▼0.0   Proceed along Red Cone Peak Trail (FR 565.)
▼0.1   TR Sign for Webster Pass.
▼1.0   SO Cross through creek.
▼3.6   BL Fork in road.
▼5.5   SO First steep descent.
▼6.2   End at Webster Pass crossing.
        GPS: N 39°31.90' W 105°49.92'

Webster Pass Trail

STARTING POINT Webster Pass, at the intersection of FR 285, Central #5: Handcart Gulch Trail (FR 121) and Central #6: Red Cone Peak Trail

FINISHING POINT Intersection with Central #11: Saints John and Glacier Mountain Trail (FR 275)

TOTAL MILEAGE 5.1 miles

UNPAVED MILEAGE 5.1 miles

DRIVING TIME 45 minutes

ROUTE ELEVATION 10,300 to 12,096 feet

USUALLY OPEN Early July to late September

DIFFICULTY RATING 3

SCENIC RATING 9

Special Attractions

- Views from the summit.
- Access to an extensive network of 4WD trails.
- Attractive Snake River Valley.

History

Native Americans used Webster Pass for many years before the arrival of the white man. Prospectors first traveled the pass in the 1860s, and in 1878 a partnership of the Webster brothers and the Montezuma Silver Mining Company built a wagon road over the crossing. The route was the main freight route to the Snake River Mining District. The itinerant Father Dyer traveled across the route regularly to deliver the mail and conduct his far-flung ministry. In the early 1890s, David Moffat, the president of the Denver & Rio Grande Railroad, surveyed the crossing at Webster Pass as a possible rail route. The road fell into disuse and was reopened in 1971 through the efforts of 4WD clubs.

Description

This route takes you from Webster Pass, where it intersects the roads over Red Cone Peak and through Handcart Gulch, down the Snake River Valley and into the township of Montezuma. From the pass, there is a magnificent view of the Handcart Gulch area to the southeast and the Snake River Valley to the northwest. The road up Red Cone Peak is one-way and cannot be entered from Webster Pass. A snowdrift usu-

Fording the Snake River

ally blocks the alternative road into Handcart Gulch until late in summer.

The route remains above timberline as it switchbacks down from Webster Pass on a reasonably wide road that has a sound surface. Passing other vehicles is easy at the switchbacks. As you reach the valley floor, you will cross the headwaters of the Snake River and pass the road toward Radical Hill, which departs to the left.

This route is simple to navigate.

Current Road Information

White River National Forest
Dillon Ranger District
680 Blue River Parkway
Silverthorne, CO 80498
(970) 468-5400

Map References

USFS   White River National Forest
Maptech CD:
    Denver/Steamboat Springs/North
    Central
Benchmark's *Colorado Road & Recreation
    Atlas*, p. 73
Colorado Atlas & Gazetteer, p. 38
The Roads of Colorado, p. 79
Trails Illustrated, #104

Route Directions

▼0.0   From the summit of Webster Pass, zero trip meter and proceed down FR 285.

1.5▲   End at intersection with Central #6: Red Cone Peak Trail straight ahead (a one-way road with no entry from this point) and Central #5: Handcart Gulch Trail to the right.
    GPS: N 39°31.90′ W 105°49.92′

▼1.5 SO Intersection with Central #10: Radical Hill Trail on left. Zero trip meter.

0.0▲   Proceed southeast on FR 285.
    GPS: N 39°32.29′ W 105°50.50′

▼0.0   Proceed north on FR 285.

2.6▲ BL Intersection with Central #10: Radical Hill Trail on right. Zero trip meter.

▼1.2 SO/TL Cross through Snake River; then intersection.

1.4▲ TR Intersection; then cross through Snake River.
    GPS: N 39°33.31′ W 105°50.65′

▼1.4 SO Track on right; then cross through creek.

1.2▲ SO Cross through creek; then track on left.

▼1.9 SO Seasonal closure gate.

0.7▲ SO Seasonal closure gate.

Mountain goats grazing near Webster Pass

Webster Pass viewed from Radical Hill Trail

One of the tight switchbacks near the end of the trail at Webster Pass

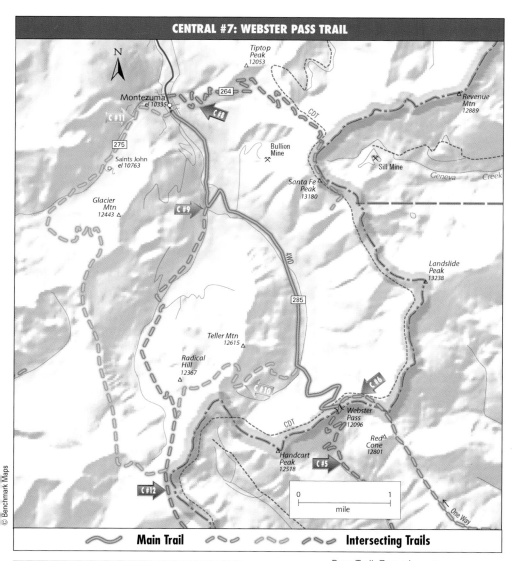

~~ **Main Trail** ~~~ ~~~ ~~~ **Intersecting Trails**

▼2.2   **SO**   Private Bullion Mine Road on right.

0.4▲   **SO**   Private Bullion Mine Road on left.

▼2.6   **TR**   Intersection of Webster Pass Trail and Central #9: Deer Creek Trail (CR 5/FR 5). Zero trip meter.

0.0▲   Proceed along Webster Pass Trail (FR 285).

GPS: N 39°34.10' W 105°51.57'

▼0.0   Proceed north along CR 5.

1.0▲   **TL**   Intersection of Central #9: Deer Creek Trail (CR 5/FR 5) and Webster Pass Trail. Zero trip meter.

▼0.3   **SO**   Ruins of mine and log buildings.

0.7▲   **SO**   Ruins of mine and log buildings.

▼1.0   End at the intersection with Central #11: Saints John and Glacier Mountain Trail (FR 275).

0.0▲   From the intersection of Central #11: Saints John and Glacier Mountain Trail (FR 275), zero trip meter and proceed south on CR 5 (FR 5).

GPS: N 39°34.80' W 105°52.05'

Santa Fe Peak Trail

STARTING POINT Montezuma

FINISHING POINT Santa Fe Peak near the Silver Wave Mine, at the end of a dead-end road (FR 264)

TOTAL MILEAGE 5.2 miles (one-way)

UNPAVED MILEAGE 5.2 miles

DRIVING TIME 1.5 hours (one-way)

ROUTE ELEVATION 10,300 to 12,800 feet

USUALLY OPEN Early June to early October

DIFFICULTY RATING 5

SCENIC RATING 9

Special Attractions

- Spectacular, panoramic alpine views.
- Shelf road with some very challenging sections.
- Many other 4WD trails in the vicinity.

Description

This route commences at the first intersection on the left as you drive into Montezuma from Keystone (or, coming from the fire station, the last intersection on the right). The unpaved route heads uphill

View to the north from Webster Pass

through the homes within the town limits. At this point, there are a number of side roads, but stay on the main road and proceed up a series of mild switchbacks. As the road ascends from timberline, it begins a tighter series of switchbacks.

Once you are out of town, navigation becomes fairly straightforward. The road levels out as it travels along an open ridge that provides some wonderful views. It then

Webster Pass Trail follows the Snake River through the valley

A view of Santa Fe Peak Trail crossing a ridgeline

commences another series of short switchbacks before leveling off at an open, rocky meadow that offers spectacular 360-degree views.

As you leave this meadow, the road becomes significantly more difficult—especially if you are in a full-sized vehicle. It narrows, becomes rougher, and has a looser

Looking across toward Radical Hill from the trail

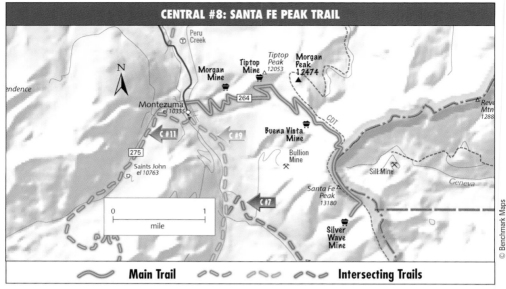

Main Trail ⌇⌇⌇ ⌇⌇⌇ **Intersecting Trails**

surface. As you proceed, the road starts to descend gently around a rocky, narrow shelf with a steep drop-off along the west side of Santa Fe Peak. We recommend that from this point you park your vehicle in an out-of-the-way spot and walk down to the Silver Wave Mine, as there is no place to turn around at the mine. You may park along a ridge just under half a mile from the mine or at the last switchback, about 150 yards before the mine. The ridge provides a great view of Geneva Creek Valley to the east, the

Snake River Valley to the southwest, and Red Cone Peak and Webster Pass to the south.

Current Road Information
White River National Forest
Dillon Ranger District
680 Blue River Parkway
Silverthorne, CO 80498
(970) 468-5400

Map References
USFS   White River National Forest

A narrow, rough section of the trail

Maptech CD:
Denver/Steamboat Springs/North
Central
Benchmark's *Colorado Road & Recreation
Atlas*, p. 73
Colorado Atlas & Gazetteer, p. 38
The Roads of Colorado, p. 79
Trails Illustrated, #104

Route Directions

▼0.0   From the Montezuma Snake River Fire Station, zero trip meter and proceed north on CR 5 (FR 5).
      GPS: N 39°34.85' W 105°52.03'

▼0.1   **TR** Intersection with Santa Fe Peak Road (FR 264).

▼0.2   **SO** Enter National Forest.
      GPS: N 39°34.96' W 105°51.92'

▼0.9   **SO** Track on left—closed.

▼1.3   **SO** Mine ruins on right (private property).

▼1.4   **SO** Track to cabin (private property) on right; then mine ruins on right.

▼1.7   **SO** Track to mine on right (private property).

▼1.9   **SO** Mine on right.

▼2.6   **SO** Track on right. Stay on FR 264.

▼2.7   **SO** Timberline.

▼3.0   **SO** Quail Mine on right.
      GPS: N 39°34.83' W 105°50.72'

▼3.3   **SO** View down onto Montezuma and Snake River Valley.

▼3.8   **SO** Intersection. Track on right goes to Buena Vista Mine. Remain on FR 264.
      GPS: N 39°34.67' W 105°50.33'

▼4.1   **SO** Enter large plateau with spectacular 360-degree views.

▼4.6   **SO** Turn-around and parking opportunity prior to shelf road.

▼4.8   **SO** Ridge. Full-sized vehicles should stop at this point. Last good spot for turning around.
      GPS: N 39°34.09' W 105°50.08'

▼5.1   **BR** Last switchback.

▼5.2   End at Silver Wave Mine.
      GPS: N 39°34.02' W 105°50.11'

Deer Creek Trail

STARTING POINT Intersection with Central #11: Saints John and Glacier Mountain Trail (FR 275)

FINISHING POINT Three-way intersection with Central #12: Middle Fork of the Swan Trail and Central #11: Saints John and Glacier Mountain Trail

TOTAL MILEAGE 5.0 miles

UNPAVED MILEAGE 5.0 miles

DRIVING TIME 45 minutes

ROUTE ELEVATION 10,300 to 12,400 feet

USUALLY OPEN Mid-June to late September

DIFFICULTY RATING 4

SCENIC RATING 8

Special Attractions

- Provides access to an extensive network of 4WD trails.
- A relatively easy road that provides a good introduction to roads in the area.

History

Montezuma, a silver camp named after the last Aztec emperor of Mexico, was founded in the 1860s. Henry Teller, who went on to serve as a U.S. senator for 29 years, was possibly one of the first to locate silver in the area. The camp grew slowly, mainly be-

Sign at the end of the trail

Deer Creek

cause silver rather than gold was found and because of its inaccessibility. Ore shipments had to be made via the newly opened but difficult route across Argentine Pass, which led to high transportation costs.

When the Loveland and Webster Passes were built in the late 1870s and silver mining was booming, Montezuma began to flourish. A regular stage traveled across both passes. Soon Montezuma was the focal point for the many mining camps in the district, offering supplies, a school, and entertainment such as dance halls, saloons, and poker games—which are said to have gone on 24 hours a day. Montezuma reached its peak population of about 800 residents around 1880, and the following year the city was incorporated. In 1882, Montezuma's new trustees set about cleaning up the town, establishing fines for drunkenness and outlawing gambling and prostitution.

Montezuma suffered greatly from the silver crash of 1893, although it never did become a ghost town. In 1958, a fire start-ed at the Summit House hotel and blazed through town, completely destroying the hotel, the town hall, houses, garages, and other buildings. Almost half of the 75 residents were rendered homeless—a week before Christmas. In 1972, it lost its post office. Today, the town is a mixture of old and new buildings. The one-room schoolhouse, which operated from 1884 to 1958, still stands on a slope east of Main Street.

Franklin was the site of the headquarters of the Montezuma Silver Mining Company. It was deliberately located an appropriate distance from the jarring activity of the company's mines and was intended to become an elite community of the company's management. The first building was a large two-story house built for the mine superintendent. It was the showpiece of the town and was used to entertain visiting dignitaries. Today the foundations of the house are all that remain. At some point, a sawmill was also built at the site. Little else was ever built and the community was short-lived.

A lower section of Deer Creek Trail

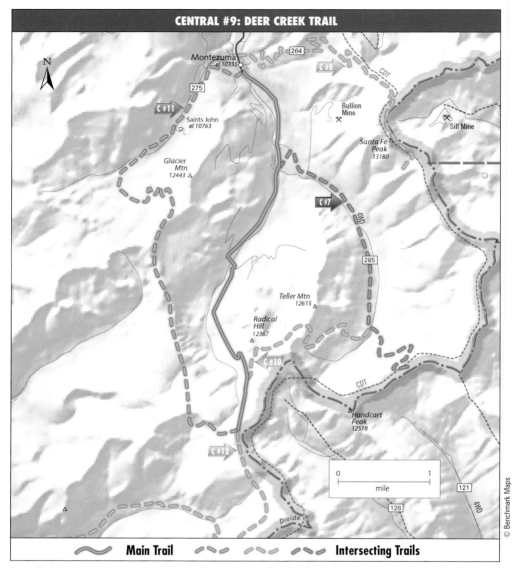

Main Trail ～～ ∂∿∂ ∂∿∂ ∂∿∂ **Intersecting Trails**

Description

Deer Creek Trail serves as the backbone for an extensive network of 4WD roads branching in all directions. Many of the roads are poorly marked, and navigation can be difficult. We strongly recommend that you use a copy of the Trails Illustrated #104 map for the area. It is not entirely accurate but is more detailed than most of the alternative maps.

Other than navigation, this route presents no major difficulties. The road is bumpy and includes some easy switch-backs, but the surface is sound.

Franklin is located just north of the intersection with Central #7: Webster Pass Trail. It is private property.

Current Road Information

White River National Forest
Dillon Ranger District
680 Blue River Parkway
Silverthorne, CO 80498
(970) 468-5400

Map References

USFS   White River National Forest

Maptech CD:
    Denver/Steamboat Springs/North
    Central
Benchmark's *Colorado Road & Recreation
    Atlas*, p. 73
Colorado Atlas & Gazetteer, p. 38
The Roads of Colorado, p. 79
Trails Illustrated, #104

Route Directions

▼0.0   From the intersection with Central
            #11: Saints John and Glacier
            Mountain Trail (FR 275), zero trip
            meter and proceed south on CR 5 (FR
            5).
1.0▲   End at the intersection with Central
            #11: Saints John and Glacier
            Mountain Trail (FR 275).
            GPS: N 39°34.80' W 105°52.05'

▼0.7   SO   Ruins of mine and log buildings.
0.3▲   SO   Ruins of mine and log buildings.

▼1.0   SO   Track on left is Central #7: Webster
              Pass Trail. Town site of Franklin. Zero
              trip meter.
0.0▲   Continue along CR 5/FR 5.
              GPS: N 39°34.08' W 105°51.57'

▼0.0   Continue on CR 5/FR 5.
4.0▲   SO   Track on right is Central #7: Webster
              Pass Trail. Town site of Franklin. Zero
              trip meter.

▼0.3   SO   Parking area. Cross over creek.
3.7▲   SO   Cross over creek. Parking area.

▼0.6   SO   Gated track on right.
3.4▲   SO   Gated track on left.

▼0.9   SO   Track on right dead-ends at mines.
3.1▲   SO   Track on left dead-ends at mines.

▼1.0   SO   Arapaho National Forest information
              board. Seasonal closure gate.
3.0▲   SO   Seasonal closure gate. Arapaho
              National Forest information board.

▼1.5   SO   Track to the right goes to mines.
2.4▲   SO   Track to the left goes to mines.

▼1.6   SO   Cross over Deer Creek. Track on left.
2.4▲   SO   Track on right. Cross over Deer Creek.

▼1.7   SO   Track on left goes to numerous
              mines.
2.3▲   SO   Track on right goes to numerous
              mines.

The trail climbing above timberline

▼2.0	SO	Short track to the right.
2.0▲	SO	Short track to the left.

▼2.2	BL	Track on the right.
1.8▲	BR	Track on the left.

▼3.4	BR	Track on left is first turnoff to Central #10: Radical Hill Trail (FR 286).
0.6▲	BL	Track on right is second turnoff to Radical Hill.

▼3.5	SO	Track on left is second turnoff to Radical Hill.
0.5▲	SO	Track on right is first turnoff to Central #10: Radical Hill Trail (FR 286).

▼4.0		End at 3-way intersection signpost that points to the Middle Fork of the Swan to the south and to Glacier Mountain, the North Fork of the Swan, and Saints John to the west.
0.0▲		Begin at 3-way intersection signpost that points to the Middle Fork of the Swan to the south and to Glacier Mountain, the North Fork of the Swan, and Saints John to the west. Zero trip meter and proceed north. **GPS: N 39°31.24' W 105°52.09'**

View from the end of Deer Creek Trail

Looking into the beautiful Deer Creek Valley

Radical Hill Trail

STARTING POINT Intersection of Central #9: Deer Creek Trail and FR 286

FINISHING POINT Central #7: Webster Pass Trail (FR 285)

TOTAL MILEAGE 2.5 miles

UNPAVED MILEAGE 2.5 miles

DRIVING TIME 45 minutes

ROUTE ELEVATION 11,400 to 12,600 feet

USUALLY OPEN Mid-June to late September

DIFFICULTY RATING 6

SCENIC RATING 10

Special Attractions

- Very challenging 4WD trail.
- Interconnects with a network of other 4WD trails.
- Wonderful alpine scenery.

Description

This is a short, challenging road with a steep, loose, and very narrow shelf section. If you start at Central #9: Deer Creek Trail, the difficult section is downhill. This route is the easier way of tackling it.

From Central #9: Deer Creek Trail, the route commences a gentle ascent through a broad expanse of alpine tundra across the top of Radical Hill and over to Teller Mountain. After only about the first mile of the route, from the top of Teller Mountain, there is a particularly good view down into the Snake River Valley.

As you proceed from this point, the road turns, descends sharply, and switchbacks onto a very narrow shelf cut into the face of the mountain. The road is significantly eroded in spots as well as being off-camber and having a loose surface. As it curves around the mountain, it levels off and becomes wide enough to accommodate two vehicles when passing is necessary.

The balance of this short trail is a rough, rocky ride, but the worst is definitely over.

Current Road Information

White River National Forest
Dillon Ranger District
680 Blue River Parkway
Silverthorne, CO 80498
(970) 468-5400

Map References

USFS White River National Forest
Maptech CD:
    Denver/Steamboat Springs/North Central

A view across Teller Mountain

Another view of the narrow, dangerous shelf road at the end of the trail

The trail where it switchbacks down into the Swan River Valley

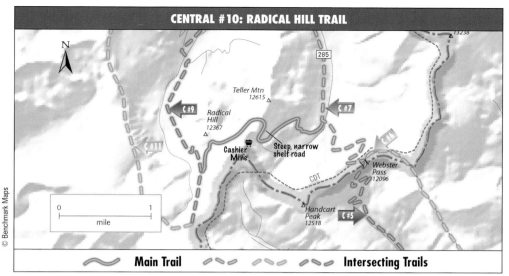

~~~ **Main Trail** ∽∽∽ ∽∽∽ ∽∽∽ **Intersecting Trails**

Benchmark's *Colorado Road & Recreation Atlas*, p. 73
Colorado Atlas & Gazetteer, p. 38
The Roads of Colorado, p. 79
Trails Illustrated, #104

Trail (FR 286), zero trip meter and proceed along FR 286.
GPS: N 39°32.29' W 105°50.46'

Route Directions

▼0.0   From intersection of Central #9: Deer Creek Trail (FR 5) and FR 286, zero trip meter and turn onto FR 286.
2.5▲   End at intersection with Central #9: Deer Creek Trail (FR 5).
        GPS: N 39°31.66' W 105°51.91'

▼0.1   **SO** Track on right is alternative track to Deer Creek Trail.
2.4▲   **BL** Track on left is alternative track to Deer Creek Trail.

▼0.9   **SO** Scenic overlook and start of steep, narrow descent.
1.6▲   **SO** Scenic overlook.

▼1.4   **SO** Track on right to cabin.
1.1▲   **SO** Track on left to cabin.
        GPS: N 39°32.05' W 105°51.18'

▼2.5   **BL** Track on right; then end at intersection with Central #7: Webster Pass Trail.
0.0▲   At intersection of Central #7: Webster Pass Trail and Radical Hill

A rocky section close to the intersection with Webster Pass Trail

Saints John and Glacier Mountain Trail

STARTING POINT Intersection of CR 5 and FR 275

FINISHING POINT Three-way intersection with Central #9: Deer Creek Trail and with Central #12: Middle Fork of the Swan Trail

TOTAL MILEAGE 7.2 miles

UNPAVED MILEAGE 7.2 miles

DRIVING TIME 1.5 hours

ROUTE ELEVATION 10,300 to 12,200 feet

USUALLY OPEN Mid-July to late September

DIFFICULTY RATING 4

SCENIC RATING 8

Special Attractions

- Moderately challenging 4WD trail that offers a mix of historic sites, varied trail conditions, and excellent scenery.
- Access to a network of 4WD trails.

History

Saints John was originally named Coleyville, after John Coley, who located the first ore in 1863. Legend has it that hunters in the area in 1861 ran out of bullets and resorted to using pieces of rock in their guns. Two years later, they were in Nevada and noticed a great similarity between the rich ore they saw there and the rocks that they had used as ammunition. They contacted Coley, who set up camp in the area and subsequently located silver ore.

A prospector named Bob Epsey is also celebrated for an unusual strike. Suffering from a hangover one day, Epsey lay down to sleep it off under a shady tree. When he awoke, he steadied himself by grasping a rock as he stood. When the rock broke off in Epsey's hand, he discovered in it a big chunk of solid ore.

The town was renamed Saints John by Freemasons who gave it the biblical name after John the Baptist and John the Evangelist. Saints John became a company town when it was taken over by the Boston Silver Mining Association, an East Coast company, in 1872. At great expense, the company erected a sophisticated milling and smelter work, complete with bricks imported from Europe. A few years later it was taken over by the Boston Mining Company. For such a remote mining town, Saints John had a large library of 350 volumes (complete with regularly stocked newspapers from Boston and Europe), a boardinghouse, a dining

Saints John in the early 1870s

hall, a company store, an assay office, various cabins, and a beautiful superintendent's house with elegant furnishings from Europe and the eastern United States. However, the mining companies did not allow a saloon, so the miners regularly traveled down the mountain to Montezuma, where they indulged to their hearts' content in brothels, saloons, and poker dens.

Poor access, harsh winters, and waning silver finds caused the decline of Saints John. Argentine and Webster Passes were impassable because of snow in the winter and at other times from rock slides. The post office was closed by 1881, and the town was deserted by the 1890s.

The Wild Irishman Mine was discovered by a New York City policeman named Michael Dulhaney, who came to Colorado and struck it rich in the late 1870s. It operated throughout the 1880s but remained just a camp and was never formally incorporated as a town. The camp had no church or school. Several cabins were situated around the mine so that the miners could be close to their work. The Wild Irishman camp is typical of a number of camps where men and their families worked during the mining boom. The ruins of the mine and the miners' cabins are still evident in a beautiful timberline meadow.

Description

This route offers a variety of attractions: the historic mining town of Saints John, old mines, creek crossings, and stunning alpine views.

As the roads in the area are frequently unmarked, we recommend that you take a copy of the Trails Illustrated map #104. It is not completely accurate but is more detailed than most of the alternatives and will prove helpful.

The road is rough in sections but sound. Some sections are steep but should prove well within the capability of a 4WD vehicle.

The road starts in Montezuma and ascends some switchbacks to the Saints John town site. It passes by the Wild Irishman

Mine before switchbacking a steep slope onto the exposed Glacier Mountain. It then winds along the narrow ridge past the General Teller Mine and ends at the three-way intersection with Central #9: Deer Creek Trail and Central #12: Middle Fork of the Swan Trail.

Current Road Information

White River National Forest
Dillon Ranger District
680 Blue River Parkway
Silverthorne, CO 80498
(970) 468-5400

Map References

USFS   White River National Forest
Maptech CD:
    Denver/Steamboat Springs/North Central
Benchmark's *Colorado Road & Recreation Atlas,* p. 73
Colorado Atlas & Gazetteer, p. 38
The Roads of Colorado, p. 79
Trails Illustrated, #104 (minor inaccuracies)

Route Directions

▼0.0		At the intersection of CR 5 and FR 275 in Montezuma, zero trip meter and proceed onto FR 275 toward Saints John.
7.2▲		End at intersection of CR 5 and FR 275 in Montezuma.
		GPS: N 39°34.80′ W 105°52.05′

▼0.2	SO	Track on left goes to the Equity Mine with old buildings in 0.2 miles.
7.0▲	SO	Track on right goes to the Equity Mine with old buildings.

▼0.5	SO	Enter Arapaho National Forest.
6.7▲	SO	Leave Arapaho National Forest.

▼0.6	SO	Track on right crosses Saints John Creek and leads to Grizzly Gulch.
6.6▲	SO	Track on left crosses Saints John Creek and leads to Grizzly Gulch.

▼1.3	SO	Town site of Saints John.
5.9▲	SO	Town site of Saints John.
		GPS: N 39°34.33′ W 105°52.85′

▼1.4   **TR**   Follow Jeep trail sign. Cross Saints John Creek. Track on left.

5.8▲   **TL**   Track on right. Cross Saints John Creek.

▼1.8   **SO**   Cross Saints John Creek. Arapaho National Forest information board. Seasonal closure gate.

5.4▲   **SO**   Seasonal closure gate. Cross Saints John Creek.

        GPS: N 39°34.00′ W 105°53.23′

▼2.3   **TL**   T-Intersection. Right goes to camping possibilities. Cross creek.

4.9▲   **TR**   Cross creek. Track on left goes to camping possibilities.

▼2.5   **SO**   Creek crossing.

4.7▲   **SO**   Creek crossing.

▼2.8   **SO**   Wild Irishman Mine is approximately 100 yards off the road on left.

4.4▲   **SO**   Wild Irishman Mine is approximately 100 yards off the road on right.

▼2.9   **SO**   Wild Irishman Mine tailings.

4.3▲   **SO**   Wild Irishman Mine tailings.

▼3.0   **TR**   Trail on left goes to Wild Irishman Mine.

4.2▲   **TL**   Trail on right goes to Wild Irishman Mine.

▼3.5   **SO**   Short trail on left.

3.7▲   **SO**   Short trail on right.

▼3.7   **SO**   Trail on left.

3.5▲   **SO**   Trail on right.

▼3.8   **SO**   General Teller Mine remains on left exposed on mountain ridge.

3.4▲   **SO**   General Teller Mine remains on right exposed on mountain ridge.

The Wild Irishman Mine and site of the 1880s town

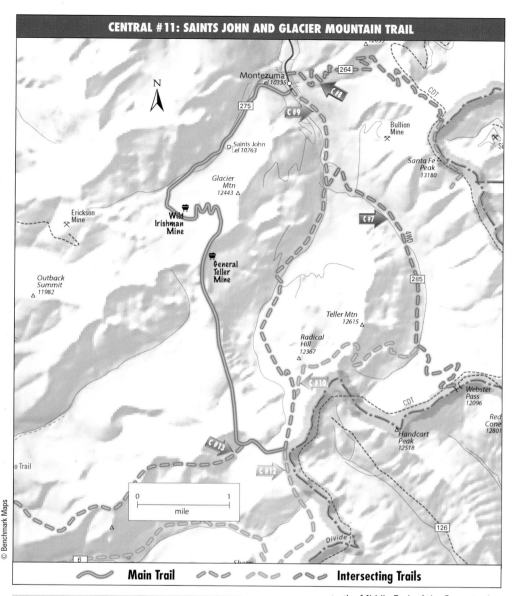

Main Trail — Intersecting Trails

▼4.5   **SO**   Track on left dead-ends at old mine.

2.7▲   **SO**   Track on right dead-ends at old mine.

▼6.5   **TL**   T-intersection. Track on right is Central #13: North Fork of the Swan and Wise Mountain Trail.

0.7▲   **TR**   Intersection. Straight ahead leads to Central #13: North Fork of the Swan and Wise Mountain Trail.
      GPS: N 39°31.39′ W 105°52.89′

▼7.2   End at T-intersection. Signpost points

to the Middle Fork of the Swan to the south and to Glacier Mountain, the North Fork of the Swan, and Saints John to the west.

0.0▲   Begin at 3-way intersection signpost that points to the Middle Fork of the Swan to the south and to Glacier Mountain, the North Fork of the Swan, and Saints John to the west. Zero trip meter and proceed west.
      GPS: N 39°31.24′ W 105°52.09′

© Benchmark Maps

Middle Fork of the Swan Trail

STARTING POINT Three-way intersection with Central #9: Deer Creek Trail and with Central #11: Saints John and Glacier Mountain Trail

FINISHING POINT Intersection of Colorado 9 and Tiger Road in Breckenridge

TOTAL MILEAGE 12.2 miles

UNPAVED MILEAGE 9.6 miles

DRIVING TIME 1 hour

ROUTE ELEVATION 9,250 to 12,200 feet

USUALLY OPEN Mid-June to early October

DIFFICULTY RATING 5

SCENIC RATING 8

Special Attractions

- Interesting, though unsightly, remains of extensive placer mining by dredge boats.
- Beautiful, wooded valley along the upper reaches of the Middle Fork of the Swan River.
- Challenging uphill section.
- Access to a network of 4WD trails.

History

Towns along this route were Swandyke, Tiger, Swan City, Delaware Flats, and Braddocks.

Swandyke boomed briefly in the late 1890s, considerably later than most other Colorado mining camps. The gold camp was divided into two sections called Swandyke and Upper Swandyke, about a mile apart. Stagecoach service connected the camp to Breckenridge and over Webster Pass to Jefferson; and from there, railroad service ran regularly to Denver. Swandyke's population peaked at about 500 in 1899, when the post office was set up. Few of the miners remained through the winter. During the camp's first winter, in 1898–99, extremely heavy snowfalls led to a number of snow slides, which destroyed most of the buildings in the new town. One avalanche carried Swandyke's mill down one side of the mountain and across a deep gulch, leaving the wreckage on the opposite mountainside. Swandyke was a ghost town by 1902, although the post office was not officially closed until 1910.

Tiger, another mining camp, was established following discovery of the Tiger Lode in 1864. Soon additional discoveries were made in the area. Shortly after the turn of the century, the Royal Tiger Mining Company was formed and bought up most of the mines. It established the company town of Tiger and provided well for the miners. They had free electricity, steam heat, and a

Tiger township, circa 1940

Remains of Tiger Dredge #1 boat near the Breckenridge end of the trail

school for the children; the company even held regular dances and free movie shows. The mine closed in 1940 and Tiger quickly became a ghost town. Because the town was much younger than most ghost towns, the buildings remained in good condition, and in the 1960s the town was reoccupied as a hippy commune. However, authorities responded by burning it to the ground in 1973.

About a half mile past the site of Tiger, Swan City sprang to life in May 1880, and within three months it had a post office, a general store, a saloon, and a hotel, but within ten years the gold mines were no longer profitable and the town was deserted. Although mining in the area was revitalized with the arrival of dredge boats, Swan City was obliterated—buried beneath tons of rubble left by the dredges.

Delaware Flats was established in 1860 during the initial gold rush to the area. This

View over Hall Valley from the overlook

An old cabin near the trail

was eight years prior to the Kit Carson Treaty, when the district was ceded by the Ute. Within a year, the town had a post office and several hundred prospectors. In 1875, the name of the town was changed to Preston. The post office closed in 1880, and twenty years later the dredge boats completely buried the site. Today, a golf course is on the western end of the reclaimed town site.

Braddocks, at the intersection of Tiger Road and Colorado 9, was founded by Dave Braddocks who operated the local stage line and livery stable. In 1884, the Denver, South Park & Pacific Railroad built a station at the location.

Description

This route commences at the three-way intersection at the end of Central #9: Deer Creek Trail and travels along an alpine ridge toward the headwaters of the Middle Fork

One of the many panoramic views afforded by this trail

of the Swan River.

At the 0.8-mile point, there is a sign to Hall Valley. This road does not go through to Hall Valley but goes to an overlook of the valley. It is a worthwhile side trip that not only provides a wonderful view down into the valley but also offers a spectacular panoramic view across the top of Handcart Gulch to Red Cone Peak and the trail descending from it (Central #7) to Webster Pass. The shelf road from Webster Pass that leads down into Handcart Gulch (Central #5) is also clearly visible from this vantage point.

Shortly after, the road travels along the side of the mountain before beginning the steep descent down to the valley floor. The surface during the descent is quite loose in sections and can be considerably looser if wet. Traveling uphill under such conditions in a stock vehicle can be nearly impossible. It is for this short section of road that the route warrants its difficulty rating; otherwise a rating of 4 would be more appropriate. The road continues along the extreme-ly attractive Middle Fork of the Swan River before intersecting with Central #14: Georgia Pass Trail.

From this point, the road is easily accessible to 2WD vehicles as it threads a path through an almost continual line of huge tailings dumps from the dredge mining in the early 1900s. At the 3.6-mile point from the intersection with Georgia Pass Trail, in a pond among tailings, lie the remains of the mining boat Tiger Dredge #1.

The route ends at the intersection of Colorado 9 and Tiger Road (at the Highlands at Breckenridge Public Golf Course). This intersection was the site of the towns of Delaware Flats and Braddocks, named for the Denver, South Park & Pacific Railroad station that was located there.

Current Road Information

White River National Forest
Dillon Ranger District
680 Blue River Parkway
Silverthorne, CO 80498
(970) 468-5400

Loose, steep, and rocky section of the trail

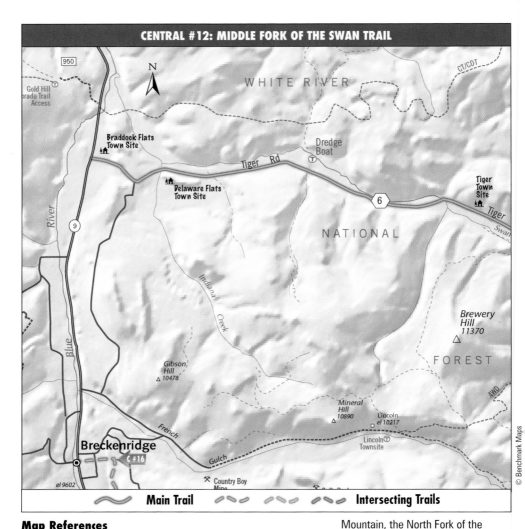

CENTRAL #12: MIDDLE FORK OF THE SWAN TRAIL

~~~ **Main Trail** 〰〰〰 〰〰〰 〰〰〰 **Intersecting Trails**

© Benchmark Maps

Map References

USFS   White River National Forest
Maptech CD: Colorado Springs/Ski
  Areas/Central;
  Denver/Steamboat Springs/North
  Central
Benchmark's *Colorado Road & Recreation
  Atlas*, p. 73
Colorado Atlas & Gazetteer, p. 38
The Roads of Colorado, pp. 78, 79
Trails Illustrated, #104 (minor
  inaccuracies), #109

Route Directions

▼0.0   Begin at 3-way intersection signpost
         that points to the Middle Fork of the
         Swan to the south and to Glacier

Mountain, the North Fork of the
Swan, and Saints John to the west.
Zero trip meter and proceed south.

6.1▲   End at 3-way intersection signpost
         that points to the Middle Fork of the
         Swan to the south and to Glacier
         Mountain, the North Fork of the
         Swan, and Saints John to the west..
         GPS: N 39°31.24' W 105°52.09'

▼0.7 **TR** T-intersection. Straight ahead to Hall
             Valley overlook (this side road ends at
             a scenic overlook in 0.8 miles).
             Proceed toward Middle Fork of the
             Swan on FR 220.

5.4▲ **TL** T-intersection. Hall Valley scenic
             overlook is to the right. Follow sign to

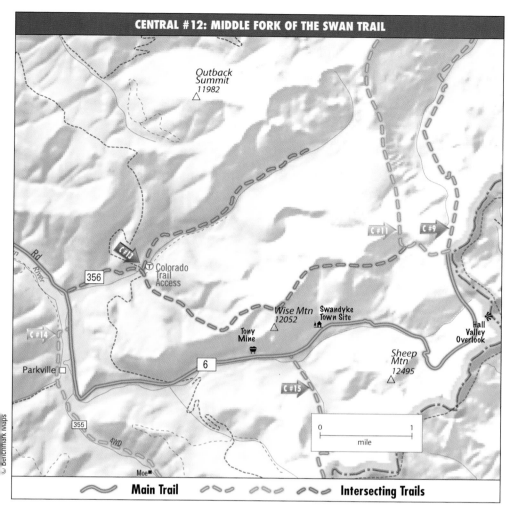

~~~ **Main Trail** ⌒⌒ ⌒⌒ ⌒⌒ **Intersecting Trails**

Montezuma. Then pass a small track on right.

GPS: N 39°30.83′ W 105°51.74′

▼1.5   **SO**   Track on left.
4.7▲   **SO**   Track on right.

▼2.2   **SO**   Cross through creek.
3.7▲   **SO**   Cross through creek.

▼2.4   **SO**   Track on right is Trail #62.
3.5▲   **SO**   Track on left is Trail #62.

▼2.8   **SO**   Deserted log cabin on right. Site of Swandyke.
3.3▲   **SO**   Deserted log cabin on left. Site of Swandyke.

GPS: N 39°30.49′ W 105°53.50′

▼3.0   **SO**   Cross through creek; then track on right.
3.1▲   **SO**   Track on left; then cross through creek.

▼3.2   **SO**   Cabin ruins on right.
2.9▲   **SO**   Cabin ruins on left.

▼3.3   **BL**   Track on right.
2.8▲   **SO**   Track on left.

▼3.4   **SO**   Private track to the Tony Mine on right.
2.7▲   **SO**   Private track to the Tony Mine on left.

GPS: N 39°30.14′ W 105°54.71′

▼3.5   **SO**   Track on left.

The benign-looking uphill section that can become impassable in wet conditions

2.6▲	SO	Track on right.

▼3.7	SO	Track on left.
2.4▲	BR	Fork.

▼5.3	SO	Seasonal gate and exit White River National Forest.
0.8▲	SO	Seasonal gate and enter White River National Forest.

▼6.1	SO	Road on left goes to Central #14: Georgia Pass Trail. Zero trip meter.
0.0▲		Continue straight on.
		GPS: N 39°30.39′ W 105°56.71′

▼0.0		Continue straight ahead on CR 6 (Tiger Road) toward Breckenridge.
6.1▲	SO	Road on right is Central #14: Georgia Pass Trail. Signed to Middle Fork

straight ahead and South Fork (Georgia Pass) to the right. Zero trip meter.

▼0.4	BL	Intersection with Central #13: North Fork of the Swan and Wise Mountain Trail on right.
5.7▲	BR	Intersection with Central #13: North Fork of the Swan and Wise Mountain Trail on left.

▼1.4	SO	Road on left. Tiger town site on right.
4.7▲	SO	Road on right. Tiger town site on left.
		GPS: N 39°31.37′ W 105°57.69′

▼3.5	SO	Pavement begins; then parking area for viewing historic dredge boat on right.
2.6▲	SO	Parking area for viewing historic dredge boat on left; then pavement ends.

▼6.1		End at intersection with Colorado 9. Breckenridge is to the left.
0.0▲		At intersection of Colorado 9 and CR 6 (Tiger Road), 3.2 miles north of Breckenridge Visitor Center, zero trip meter and proceed east along Tiger Road. This intersection is marked with a sign for the Breckenridge Public Golf Course.
		GPS: N 39°31.95′ W 106°02.58′

The trail follows alongside the Middle Fork of the Swan River

North Fork of the Swan and Wise Mountain Trail

STARTING POINT Intersection of Central #12: Middle Fork of the Swan Trail and FR 354

FINISHING POINT Intersection of Central #11: Saints John and Glacier Mountain Trail and FR 356

TOTAL MILEAGE 9.6 miles

UNPAVED MILEAGE 9.6 miles

DRIVING TIME 1.5 hours

ROUTE ELEVATION 10,000 to 12,400 feet

USUALLY OPEN Early July to early October

DIFFICULTY RATING 6 (5 traveling the reverse direction)

SCENIC RATING 9

Special Attractions

- Spectacular, expansive views.
- Town site of Rexford and views of mine and cabin ruins.
- Challenging, short, steep section along the trail.
- Access to a network of 4WD roads.

History

In 1880, Daniel Patrick discovered the Rochester lode. Two mines, the Rochester King and the Rochester Queen, were developed the following year by the Rexford Mining Corporation. To enable development of the mines in this remote location, the company also built the town of Rexford on land it owned. A mill was built near the mines to process the ore before shipment to a smelter in Denver. Within two years, declining production and high costs closed the mine, and the town was deserted.

Rexford had a post office from 1882 until the following year as well as a general store, a saloon, a boardinghouse for the miners, and several cabins. At its peak, the town had twice-weekly mail service from Montezuma. Several buildings are still evident at Rexford but all have, at least partially, collapsed. About three-quarters of a mile before Rexford, two buildings that were used by loggers when they were working the area are still standing. They were built after the demise of Rexford.

Description

The road commences at the intersection with Central #12: Middle Fork of the Swan Trail. Initially, the road is graded but becomes rough after a mile of so. Nonetheless, it remains easy for the first 2.2 miles; good backcountry camping sites exist along this section. However, after the turnoff for Rexford, water crossings, short sections that can be muddy, and progresively steeper sections make 4WD necessary.

The remains of Rexford in 1961

Sign to Wise Mountain with old miner's cabin in the background

After returning from the side road to Rexford, the main trail climbs above timberline and goes past a mine before intersecting a trail to a small cabin perched atop Wise Mountain, which, although very exposed to the elements, is still used. Turning to the left, the trail crosses the treeless ridgeline for about half a mile before encountering the most difficult section of the route: a very steep, loose section that transitions between two ridgelines. Until this point, the trail would have only been rated a 5 for difficulty, but this section increases the rating to a 6. (Going downhill, the rating remains a 5.)

From Wise Mountain, there are sweeping views in all directions. In particular, spectacular views are afforded down into the Middle Fork of the Swan River Valley and north toward Saints John.

The road ends at the intersection with Central #11: Saints John and Glacier Mountain Trail. From this point, you can select from a number of routes leading to Montezuma or Breckenridge.

Current Road Information

White River National Forest
Dillon Ranger District
680 Blue River Parkway
Silverthorne, CO 80498
(970) 468-5400

Map References

USFS   White River National Forest
Maptech CD:
        Denver/Steamboat Springs/North
        Central
Colorado Atlas & Gazetteer, p. 38
The Roads of Colorado, p. 79
Trails Illustrated, #104

Route Directions

▼0.0   From Central #12: Middle Fork of the
          Swan Trail (CR 6/Tiger Road), zero trip
          meter and proceed along FR 354,
          following sign to North Fork.
2.2▲   End at intersection with Tiger Road,
          which is also Central #12: Middle
          Fork of the Swan Trail. Right goes
          toward Breckenridge, and left
          continues the Middle Fork Trail and
          also goes toward Georgia Pass.
          GPS: N 39°30.80′ W 105°56.79′

▼0.5   SO Track on left.
1.7▲   SO Track on right.

▼0.6   SO Seasonal gate.
1.6▲   SO Seasonal gate.

▼0.9   SO Gated track on right.
1.2▲   SO Gated track on left.

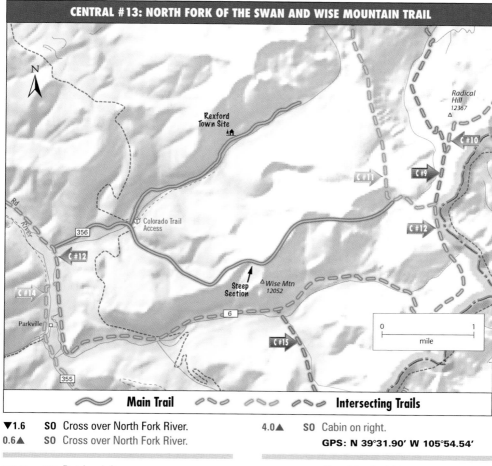

~~~ **Main Trail** 〜〜 〜〜 〜〜 **Intersecting Trails**

▼1.6   **SO**   Cross over North Fork River.
0.6▲   **SO**   Cross over North Fork River.

▼1.7   **SO**   Road on left.
0.4▲   **SO**   Road on right.
      GPS: N 39°31.43′ W 105°55.23′

▼2.2   **BL**   Fork in road. Remains of two cabins from a logging camp. Zero trip meter.
0.0▲   Continue along track toward the Middle Fork of the Swan River.
      GPS: N 39°31.65′ W 105°54.75′

▼0.0   Proceed along side road toward Rexford. (This road dead-ends, so you will have to return to this spot.)
4.4▲   **SO**   After returning to the intersection beside the two logging cabins, proceed straight on. Track on the left toward Wise Mountain. Zero trip meter.

▼0.4   **SO**   Cabin on left.

4.0▲   **SO**   Cabin on right.
      GPS: N 39°31.90′ W 105°54.54′

▼0.7   **SO**   Site of Rexford. Numerous cabin ruins on left and right.
3.7▲   **SO**   Rexford town site.
      GPS: N 39°32.04′ W 105°54.25′

▼1.8   **SO**   Cabin ruins on right.
2.6▲   **SO**   Cabin ruins on left.
      GPS: N 39°32.48′ W 105°53.35′

▼1.9   **BR**   Track on left. Cross through creek.
2.5▲   **BL**   Cross through creek. Track on right.

▼2.0   **BL**   Fork in the road.
2.4▲   **BR**   Fork in the road.
      GPS: N 39°32.49′ W 105°53.18′

▼2.2   **UT**   End of track at mine.
2.2▲   **UT**   End of track at mine.
      GPS: N 39°32.40′ W 105°53.18′

▼2.4 BR Fork in the road.
2.0▲ BL Fork in the road.

▼2.5 BL Cross through creek. Track on right.
1.9▲ BR Track on left. Cross through creek.

▼2.6 SO Cabin ruins on left.
1.8▲ SO Cabin ruins on right.
GPS: N 39°32.48′ W 105°53.35′

▼3.7 SO Rexford town site.
0.7▲ SO Site of Rexford. Numerous cabin ruins on left and right.

▼4.0 SO Cabin on right.
0.4▲ SO Cabin on left.

▼4.4 TL Upon returning to the intersection beside the two old logging cabins, zero trip meter and turn left.
0.0▲ Turn right and proceed along the side road to Rexford. (This road dead-ends, so you will have to return to this spot.)
GPS: N 39°31.65′ W 105°54.75′

▼0.0 Cross through the North Fork of the Swan and proceed toward Wise Mountain.
1.3▲ TR Cross through the North Fork of the Swan. Intersection and the remains of two logging cabins. Zero trip meter.

▼0.1 SO Cross through creek.
1.2▲ SO Cross through creek.

▼0.3 SO Cabin on right.
1.1▲ SO Cabin on left.

▼1.3 SO Mine on left.
0.1▲ SO Mine on right.
GPS: N 39°30.87′ W 105°54.17′

▼1.4 TL Intersection. Mine on Wise Mountain and cabin are 0.1 miles to the right. Deer Creek is to the left. Zero trip meter.
0.0▲ Proceed toward North Fork.
GPS: N 39°30.80′ W 105°54.13′

▼0.0 Proceed toward Deer Creek.

1.6▲ TR Intersection. Mine on Wise Mountain and cabin are 0.1 miles straight ahead. North Fork is to the right. Zero trip meter.

▼1.6 SO End at intersection with Central #11: Saints John and Glacier Mountain Trail on left.
0.0▲ From Central #11: Saints John and Glacier Mountain Trail, zero trip meter and proceed south on FR 356 toward North Fork and Wise Mountain.
GPS: N 39°31.39′ W 105°52.89′

Creek crossing

Georgia Pass Trail

STARTING POINT Central #12: Middle Fork of the Swan Trail and FR 355

FINISHING POINT Intersection of US 285 and CR 35 in Jefferson

TOTAL MILEAGE 16.2 miles

UNPAVED MILEAGE 14.7 miles

DRIVING TIME 1.5 hours

ROUTE ELEVATION 9,500 to 11,585 feet

USUALLY OPEN Mid-June to late September

DIFFICULTY RATING 4

SCENIC RATING 7

Special Attractions

- Historic route and mining sites.
- Parkville Cemetery.
- Can be combined with Central #7: Webster Pass Trail to form a loop.

History

Before the establishment of the Colorado Territory in 1861, Georgia Pass traversed the boundary of the Utah and Kansas Territories.

Crossing over the Continental Divide, the pass was traveled heavily by both the Ute, and after their migration south from Montana and Wyoming in the early 1800s, the Arapaho. The Arapaho were the more hostile of the two tribes. Many early prospectors and settlers avoided the pass when they were in the vicinity. John Frémont visited the area in 1844, but he chose to detour to Hoosier Pass to steer clear of the Arapaho.

Despite the threat of attack by the Arapaho, many early prospectors braved the route. It was heavily used in the 1859 gold rush to the Blue River diggings, which included the mining camps of Breckenridge, Lincoln City, and Frisco on the Blue River; Tiger and Parkville on the Swan River; and Montezuma, Saints John, and Argentine in the Snake River area.

Breckenridge produced Colorado's largest gold nugget, the 14-pound "Tom's Baby," which disappeared a few years after it was discovered and was presumed stolen to be broken down or melted. But in 1971, officials of the Denver Museum of Natural History found it in a box that was thought to contain dinosaur bones. The nugget is now on exhibit at the museum.

The first recorded wagon crossing over Georgia Pass was in November 1861; later that year, approval for a toll road was granted. A stagecoach service operated across the pass between Swandyke and Jefferson.

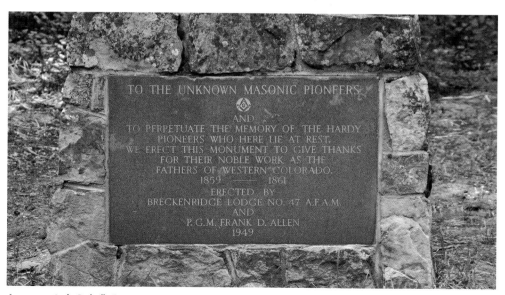

A monument in the Parkville Cemetery

Description

The route commences at the intersection with Central #12: Middle Fork of the Swan Trail. Initially, the road is easily accessible to 2WD vehicles but gradually becomes more difficult.

Soon after the start, the route passes the town site of Parkville, the main mining camp in Summit County during the gold rush of the 1860s. All that remains of the once bustling town of 10,000 is the cemetery, which can be reached via a short walking track.

After Parkville, the road forks. This route follows the left fork; the right fork turns toward Georgia Gulch and leads to Breckenridge via Georgia Gulch, American Gulch, French's Gulch, and the town site of Lincoln City.

From here to the summit, stay on the main road rather than follow any of the intersecting roads—most are dead ends. The summit is an open, grassy saddle with good views of Mount Guyot to the west.

The south side of the pass down to Jefferson is narrow initially but much easier

ATVs on Georgia Pass Trail

than the north side. From Jefferson, it is 16 miles southwest to Fairplay, 23 miles east to Bailey, and 8.4 miles northeast to the turnoff for Central #5: Handcart Gulch Trail.

Current Road Information

White River National Forest
Dillon Ranger District
680 Blue River Parkway
Silverthorne, CO 80498
(970) 468-5400

Pike & San Isabel National Forests
South Park Ranger District
320 US 285
Fairplay, CO 80440
(719) 836-2031

Map References

USFS   White River National Forest; Pike
    National Forest
Maptech CD:
    Colorado Springs/Ski Areas/Central;
    Denver/Steamboat Springs/North
    Central
Benchmark's *Colorado Road & Recreation
    Atlas,* p. 73

Colorado Atlas & Gazetteer, p. 48
The Roads of Colorado, p. 79
Trails Illustrated, #104, #105, #109

Route Directions

▼0.0   Begin at intersection of CR 6/Tiger Road (Central #12: Middle Fork of the Swan Trail) and FR 355. Zero trip meter and proceed toward Georgia Pass on FR 355.

4.5▲   End at intersection of CR 6 (Tiger Road). This is Central #12: Middle Fork of the Swan Trail.

           GPS: N 39°30.37′ W 105°56.73′

▼0.6   SO Cross through creek bed. Town site of Parkville on right.

3.9▲   SO Cross through creek bed. Town site of Parkville on left.

▼0.8   SO Walking track on left. Parkville Cemetery and Masonic marker are about 150 yards down the trail.

3.7▲   SO Walking track on right. Parkville Cemetery and Masonic marker are about 150 yards down the trail.

Old log cabin beside the trail

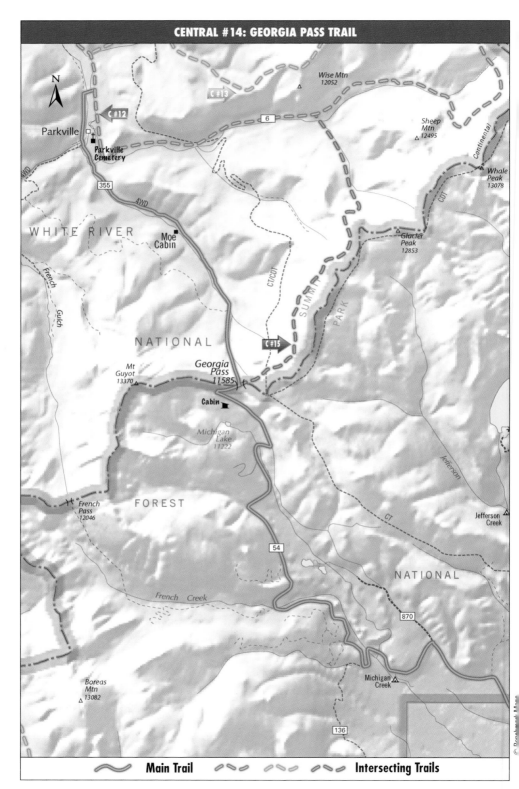

Main Trail ~~~ **Intersecting Trails**

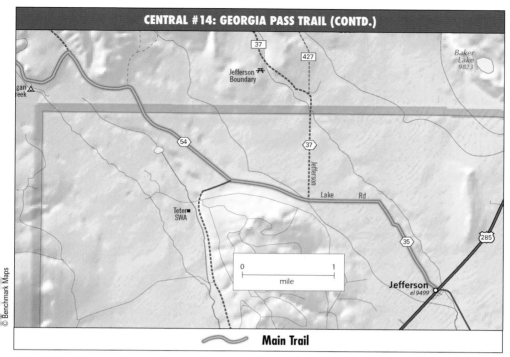

© Benchmark Maps

〰️ **Main Trail**

▼0.9   **BL**   Fork in the road. Track on right goes to Georgia Gulch. Cross bridge; then track on left.

3.6▲   **BR**   Track on right; then cross bridge to intersection. Track on the left goes to Georgia Gulch.
      GPS: N 39°27.70′ W 105°56.82′

▼1.6   **SO**   Log cabin ruins on left.
2.9▲   **SO**   Log cabin ruins on right.

▼2.3   **SO**   White cabin (private property) on right.
2.2▲   **SO**   White cabin (private property) on left.

▼2.8   **BL**   Follow FR 355. Track on right crosses through creek.
1.7▲   **BR**   Track on left crosses through creek.
      GPS: N 39°28.73′ W 105°55.33′

▼2.9   **BL**   Cross through creek.
1.6▲   **BR**   Cross through creek.

▼3.0   **BR**   Fork in road. Take right fork and cross through creek.
1.5▲   **BL**   Cross through creek. Track on right.

▼3.1   **BR**   Fork in road. Track on left.
1.4▲   **SO**   Track on right.

▼3.2   **BR**   Track on left.
1.3▲   **BL**   Track on right.

▼3.4   **SO**   Seasonal closure gate.

Georgia Pass summit

1.1▲	SO	Seasonal closure gate.
		GPS: N 39°28.31′ W 105°55.08′

▼3.6	TL	Intersection.
0.9▲	TR	Intersection.
		GPS: N 39°28.15′ W 105°55.18′

▼3.7	SO	Cross over creek.
0.8▲	SO	Cross over creek.

▼4.4	SO	Intersection. Proceed up hill.
0.1▲	SO	Intersection.

▼4.5	SO	Summit of Georgia Pass. Central #15: Glacier Peak Trail is to the left. Zero trip meter at the summit marker.
0.0▲		Continue along Georgia Pass Road.
		GPS: N 39°27.50′ W 105°54.98′

▼0.0		Continue toward Jefferson and Michigan Creek USFS Campground on FR 54.
12.2▲	SO	Summit of Georgia Pass. Central #15: Glacier Peak Trail is to the left. Zero trip meter at the summit marker.

▼0.3	SO	Track on right is FR 541.
11.9▲	BR	Track on left is FR 541.

▼0.4	SO	Track on right is FR 545.
11.8▲	SO	Track on left is FR 545.

▼0.7	SO	Cabin on right.
11.5▲	SO	Cabin on left.

▼2.5	SO	Cross over creek.
9.7▲	SO	Cross over creek.

Loose, rocky descent from Georgia Pass

▼3.9　**SO**　Track on left to camping spots; then cross over creek.

8.3▲　**SO**　Cross over creek; then track on right to campsites.

▼5.6　**SO**　FR 136 on right.

6.6▲　**SO**　FR 136 on left.

▼6.3　**SO**　USFS Michigan Creek Campground on right.

5.9▲　**SO**　USFS Michigan Creek Campground on left.

　　　　GPS: N 39°24.68′ W 105°53.01′

▼6.9　**TR**　Intersection.

5.3▲　**TL**　Intersection.

▼7.2　**SO**　Leave Pike National Forest.

5.0▲　**SO**　Enter Pike National Forest.

▼9.3　**BL**　Intersection.

2.9▲　**BR**　Intersection.

▼10.2　**SO**　Pavement begins; then road on left to Jefferson Lake.

2.0▲　**SO**　Road on right to Jefferson Lake; then pavement ends.

▼11.7　　　Trail ends at the intersection of US 285 and CR 35 in Jefferson.

0.0▲　　　At intersection of US 285 and CR 35 in Jefferson, zero trip meter and proceed along CR 35 toward Georgia Pass. This intersection is marked with a National Forest sign to Jefferson Lake Road and Michigan Creek Road.

　　　　GPS: N 39°22.67′ W 105°48.01′

Michigan Creek flowing over the road

Glacier Peak Trail

STARTING POINT Summit of Central #14: Georgia Pass Trail
FINISHING POINT S.O.B. Hill
TOTAL MILEAGE 4.2 miles (one-way)
UNPAVED MILEAGE 4.2 miles
DRIVING TIME 1 hour (one-way)
ROUTE ELEVATION 11,000 to 11,585 feet
USUALLY OPEN Mid-July to mid-September
DIFFICULTY RATING 5
SCENIC RATING 8

Special Attractions

- Short side road from Georgia Pass.
- Great scenery, particularly the view of Mount Guyot.

Description

This trail is an interesting side road from Georgia Pass. At the summit of the pass there are a number of trails, and it can be difficult to distinguish one from another. The Glacier Peak Trail departs to the northeast, heading directly away from the face of the information board at the summit.

A pickup truck (circled) that has crashed down the mountain

Initially, it is rough but not difficult. A little more than half a mile from the summit two 4WD roads intersect to the right. The road to the right is easy and offers a mile or so of scenic alpine meadow to explore. The center, shorter road climbs the hill and provides a very good view of the area. It is more difficult than the other side road.

View from near the beginning of the trail

Overlooking the Colorado Trail to the south

A hiker on the Colorado Trail takes in the sweeping panorama to the north

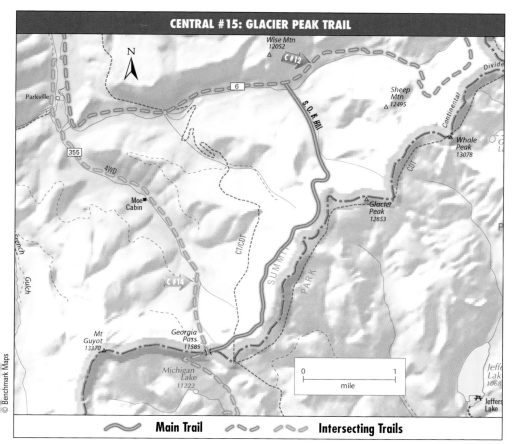

Main Trail ‿‿‿ ‿‿‿ **Intersecting Trails**

The main route continues to the left. As you continue along this rough, off-camber, narrow shelf road, there is a great view across to Mount Guyot. The ski runs of Breckenridge and Dillon Reservoir can also be sighted in the distance. Although rough, the surface of the road is mostly embedded rock and is generally sound.

As you continue, the road descends back below timberline. At one point, as you travel along a narrow shelf road, you can look across the valley and glimpse (between the trees on the left-hand side of the road) a turquoise pickup that has crashed down the slope and landed near the bottom of the valley.

Toward the end of the route, after you pass some alpine meadows, there is a creek crossing with a short, steep descent and an even steeper ascent. This is the most difficult section. At this point we end the direc-

tions because the road deteriorates dramatically as it descends the aptly named S.O.B. Hill, which has a difficulty rating of 8. This is an extremely challenging, steep slope interspersed with many large boulders. To proceed further would certainly risk damage to any larger stock vehicle.

If you proceed despite the risk, you will come out close to an intersection with Central #12: Middle Fork of the Swan Trail. Once down S.O.B. Hill, the road crosses through the Middle Fork of the Swan River and then, almost immediately, intersects the trail between the Tony Mine and Swandyke town site.

Current Road Information

White River National Forest
Dillon Ranger District
680 Blue River Parkway
Silverthorne, CO 80498
(970) 468-5400

Map References

USFS   White River National Forest

Maptech CD:
> Colorado Springs/Ski Areas/Central;
> Denver/Steamboat Springs/North
> Central

Benchmark's *Colorado Road & Recreation
Atlas*, p. 73

The Roads of Colorado, p. 79

Trails Illustrated, #109

Route Directions

▼0.0   From the summit marker on Central
#14: Georgia Pass Trail, zero trip
meter and proceed toward sign for
Glacier Ridge and Colorado Trail on FR
268.
GPS: N39°27.50′ W105°54.98′

▼0.4   **SO** Colorado Trail hiking trail crosses
track.

▼0.7   **BL** Intersection with FR 268.1 and 268.2.

▼2.4   **SO** Short track on right to a scenic view
down into Missouri Gulch. Zero trip
meter.
GPS: N39°29.14′ W105°53.81′

▼0.0   Continue along track.

▼1.1   **SO** On mountainside to the left, you can
see a turquoise-colored car that has

View of Glacier Peak Trail from Georgia Pass

crashed down the slope.

▼1.2   **SO** Cross through creek.

▼1.4   **SO** Several cabin ruins on left.

▼1.6   **SO** Cross through creek and cabin ruins
on left; then cross through another
creek.

▼1.7   **SO** Cross through creek and climb steep
embankment.

▼1.8   **SO** End here unless you want to venture
down S.O.B. Hill. The road continues
to the right but is not passable at the
level of this book.
GPS: N39°29.75′ W105°53.68′

Glacier Peak Trail at timberline

Boreas Pass Trail

STARTING POINT Breckenridge Welcome Center

FINISHING POINT Como at the intersection of US 285 and CR/FR 33

TOTAL MILEAGE 31.9 miles

UNPAVED MILEAGE 27.0 miles

DRIVING TIME 1.25 hours

ROUTE ELEVATION 9,600 to 11,481 feet

USUALLY OPEN Late May to mid-October

DIFFICULTY RATING 1

SCENIC RATING 8

Special Attractions

- Travel the route of a famous old narrow gauge railway, which in its time was the highest in the United States.
- Narrow railway cuttings, fine views, and the sites of many old mining camps.
- In fall, excellent views of the changing aspens.

History

This pass was called by many names—Ute, Hamilton, Tarryall, and Breckenridge—before receiving its present name in the late 1880s. Boreas, the Greek god of the north wind, is an appropriate namesake for this gusty mountain route.

The Ute crossed the pass going south to spend their winters in warmer regions. In 1839, Thomas Farnham, a Vermont lawyer, traveled the pass on his trek across Colorado. In the late 1850s, prospectors poured over the pass from South Park to reach the gold discoveries in the Blue River District. At this time, the crossing was nothing more than a burro trail, but miners braved the winter snow to walk the pass on snowshoes.

In the 1860s, the road was upgraded, and a daily stage traveled across Boreas Pass. In 1884, the Denver, South Park & Pacific Railroad laid narrow gauge tracks over the pass. For a time, the line was the highest in the United States and required over a dozen snowsheds. Steep grades of more than 4 percent made the route difficult for trains pulling heavy loads. The grades were such a problem that when P. T. Barnum's circus came to Breckenridge, it had to unload the elephants to help pull the train the last 3 miles to the summit. The railroad continued to operate until 1937.

Tailings piles in Tarryall Creek

Overlook from along Boreas Pass Trail

In 1952, the U.S. Army Corps of Engineers converted the old railroad grade for automobile use but bypassed the most dangerous portion near Windy Point.

Description

This scenic and extremely popular route is suitable for passenger vehicles, although it is unpaved and frequently scarred by numerous potholes.

The route starts in Breckenridge and joins Boreas Pass Road a short distance south of town. Windy Point, identifiable by a large rock outcropping, lies about a half mile from the turnoff onto Boreas Pass Road. The route continues past the restored Bakers Tank.

The summit of Boreas Pass was the site of a Denver, South Park & Pacific Railroad station. The station house, which has been restored as an interpretative center, is only one of the buildings that was located at the site. There was also a two-room telegraph house and a storehouse, as well as a wye in the tracks to allow the trains to turn around. Today, several cabins and a train car are located at the summit, and information boards tell the history of the site.

At Como, the stone roundhouse still

Visitors center at Boreas Pass

stands, but the wooden portion of the roundhouse and the 43-room Pacific Hotel were destroyed by fire. The roundhouse is being restored.

Current Road Information
White River National Forest
Dillon Ranger District
680 Blue River Parkway
Silverthorne, CO 80498
(970) 468-5400

Pike & San Isabel National Forests
South Park Ranger District
320 US 285
Fairplay, CO 80440
(719) 836-2031

Map References
USFS   White River National Forest; Pike
    National Forest
Maptech CD:
    Colorado Springs/Ski Areas/Central
Benchmark's *Colorado Road & Recreation*
    Atlas, p. 73
Colorado Atlas & Gazetteer, p. 48
The Roads of Colorado, pp. 78, 79, 95
Trails Illustrated, #109

Route Directions

▼0.0   Outside Breckenridge Welcome Center at 203 South Main Street, zero trip meter and proceed south.

10.6▲   End at Breckenridge Welcome Center at 203 South Main Street.
    GPS: N 39°28.82' W 106°02.76'

▼0.5   **TL**   Onto Boreas Pass Road (CR 33/FR 33).

10.1▲ **TR**   T-intersection with Colorado 9.

▼4.0   **SO**   Pavement ends.

6.6▲   **SO**   Road becomes paved.

▼4.1   **SO**   Cross through gate.

6.5▲   **SO**   Cross through gate.

▼5.6   **SO**   Walking track on left.

5.0▲   **SO**   Walking track on right.

▼7.1   **SO**   Bakers Tank on left with walking track behind it.

3.5▲   **SO**   Bakers Tank on right with walking track behind it.

▼7.7   **SO**   Track on left.

2.9▲   **SO**   Track on right.

▼8.0   **SO**   Track on left.

2.6▲   **SO**   Track on right.

▼9.0   **SO**   Site of Farnham Station, post office, and store on left. On right is a walking track to Dyersville site, about 0.5 miles from road.

1.6▲   **SO**   Site of Farnham Station, post office, and store on right. On left is a walking track to Dyersville site, about 0.5 miles from road.
    GPS: N 39°25.50' W 105°58.88'

▼10.6   **SO**   Exit Pike National Forest and cross through seasonal closure gate; then summit of Boreas Pass and historic buildings. Zero trip meter.

0.0▲   Proceed northwest on Boreas Pass Road; then cross through seasonal closure gate and enter Pike National Forest.
    GPS: N 39°24.64' W 105°58.07'

▼0.0   Proceed southeast on Boreas Pass Road.

21.3▲   **SO**   Summit of Boreas Pass and historic buildings. Zero trip meter.

▼13.2   **SO**   Cross over Selkirk Gulch Creek.

8.1▲   **SO**   Cross over Selkirk Gulch Creek.

▼14.4   **SO**   Track on right goes to Upper Tarryall Road and access to Selkirk Campground.

6.9▲   **BR**   Track on left goes to Upper Tarryall Road and access to Selkirk Campground.

▼15.2   **SO**   Cross over Halfway Gulch Creek.

6.1▲   **SO**   Cross over Halfway Gulch Creek.

▼17.5   **SO**   Seasonal gate.

3.8▲   **SO**   Seasonal gate.

▼17.7   **TL**   Intersection of CR 50 and CR33.

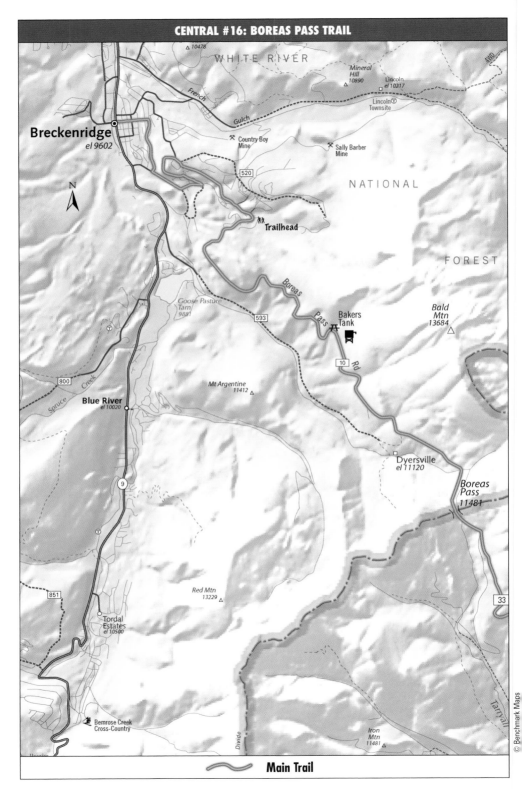

WHITE RIVER

△ 10478

French

Gulch

Mineral
Hill
10890 △

Lincoln
el 10217

Lincoln ⊕
Townsite

Breckenridge
el 9602

⚒ Country Boy
Mine

⚒ Sally Barber
Mine

N A T I O N A L

520

N

Trailhead

Boreas

F O R E S T

*Goose Pasture
Tarn
9881*

593

Pass

Bakers
Tank

Bald
Mtn
13684
△

Rd

10

800

Spruce

Creek

Blue River
el 10020

*Mt Argentine
11412* △

9

Dyersville
el 11120

**Boreas
Pass
11481**

851

*Red Mtn
13229* △

33

Tordal
Estates
el 10500

⛷ Bemrose Creek
Cross-Country

Divide

*Iron
Mtn
11481* △

Tarryall

© Benchmark Maps

🌊🌊 **Main Trail**

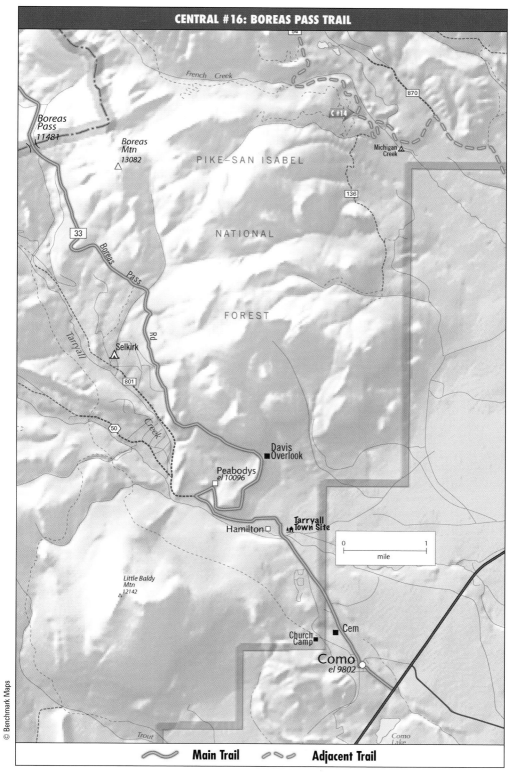

Main Trail   Adjacent Trail

A cutting in the rock made for the railroad

Bakers Tank

3.6▲	TR	Intersection of CR 50 and CR 33.
▼18.4	SO	Site of Tarryall City mining camp.
2.9▲	SO	Site of Tarryall City mining camp.
▼18.8	SO	Cross Tarryall Creek. Mining ruins on right.
2.5▲	SO	Mining ruins on left. Cross Tarryall Creek.
▼20.0	SO	Site of Hamilton mining camp.
2.3▲	SO	Site of Hamilton mining camp.
▼20.4	SO	Road becomes paved.
0.9▲	SO	Pavement ends.
▼20.5	SO	Town of Como.

0.8▲	SO	Leaving Como.
▼20.7	TL	Intersection.
0.6▲	TR	Intersection.
▼20.8	SO	Old stone roundhouse on left.
0.5▲	SO	Old stone roundhouse on right.
▼21.3		Cattle guard. End at intersection with US 285.
0.0▲		At intersection of Boreas Pass Road (CR 33/FR 33) and US 285 in Como, zero trip meter and proceed along CR 33 toward Boreas Pass.
		GPS: N 39°18.64' W 105°53.15'

Denver, South Park & Pacific roundhouse in Como at the beginning of Boreas Pass Trail

Shrine Pass Trail

STARTING POINT Redcliff
FINISHING POINT Interstate 70, at exit 190 near Vail Pass
TOTAL MILEAGE 10.8 miles
UNPAVED MILEAGE 10.7 miles
DRIVING TIME 45 minutes
ROUTE ELEVATION 8,800 to 11,089 feet
USUALLY OPEN Mid-June to late September
DIFFICULTY RATING 2
SCENIC RATING 8

Special Attractions

- Spectacular views of the Mount of the Holy Cross.
- Fall viewing of the aspens.
- Summer wildflowers.

History

Shrine Pass is so named because it overlooks and provides a wonderful view of the Mount of the Holy Cross, a famous 14,000-foot peak. The route was an Indian trail. It rose to prominence in the 1920s when Orion W. Daggett, a Redcliff newspaper publisher, proposed a shrine be built there. His amazing plans included not only viewing facilities but also an airport and a golf course. In 1931, he opened the road

Mount Holy Cross overlook

that he intended to use for this project, attracting a crowd of hundreds to the event. The project was never undertaken, but proponents continued to raise it periodically for some years. Before 1940, the pass road

Hikers at Shrine Ridge Trailhead

Log cabin remains along the trail

served as the main route between Denver and Grand Junction.

The Mount of the Holy Cross was declared a national monument by President Herbert Hoover, but it lost its status in 1950 due to the deterioration of the right arm of the cross.

Description

The route leaves Redcliff and travels initially beside Turkey Creek through the narrow, wooded valley. As the route gains altitude, there are a number of viewing spots along the way that provide distant but spectacular views of the Mount of the Holy Cross to the southwest. Closer to the broad, open pass are alpine meadows that are famous for their vivid wildflower displays in summer. The huge stands of aspens also attract many sightseers in fall. In winter, the area is very popular for cross-country skiing.

The road is easy and accessible to 2WD vehicles the entire distance.

Even the most straightforward trail requires care especially when passing

Main Trail   Intersecting Trail

Current Road Information

White River National Forest
Holy Cross Ranger District
24747 US 24
Minturn, CO 81645
(970) 827-5715

Map References

USFS   White River National Forest
Maptech CD:
     Colorado Springs/Ski Areas/Central
Benchmark's *Colorado Road & Recreation
Atlas*, pp. 72, 73
Colorado Atlas & Gazetteer, p. 37
The Roads of Colorado, p. 78
Trails Illustrated, #108

Route Directions

▼0.0   At intersection of US 24 and FR 709
          in Redcliff, zero trip meter and
          proceed east, following sign to Shrine
          Pass (FR 709).
2.4▲   End at intersection with US 24 in
          Redcliff.
          GPS: N 39°30.78′ W 106°22.03′

▼0.1   SO Cross bridge; then pavement ends.
2.3▲   SO Pavement begins; then cross bridge.

▼1.9   SO Seasonal gate. FR 745 on left.
0.5▲   SO FR 745 on right. Seasonal gate.

▼2.4   SO Track on right over bridge is Central
              #18: Ptarmigan Pass and McAllister
              Gulch Loop. Zero trip meter.
0.0▲   Continue along FR 709 toward
              Redcliff.
          GPS: N 39°31.39′ W 106°19.49′

▼0.0   Continue along FR 709 toward Shrine
              Pass.
8.4▲   SO Track on left over bridge is Central
              #18: Ptarmigan Pass and McAllister
              Gulch Loop. Zero trip meter.

▼1.6   SO FR 758 on right. Cabins.
6.8▲   SO Cabins. FR 758 on left.

▼1.7   SO Cross over Turkey Creek.
6.7▲   SO Cross over Turkey Creek.

▼3.2   SO Cross over creek.
5.2▲   SO Cross over creek.

▼3.4   SO Track on right.
5.0▲   SO Track on left.

▼4.0   **TL**   FR 713 on right.

4.4▲   **TR**   FR 713 on left.

      GPS: N 39°33.41′ W 106°16.07′

▼4.7   **BR**   Lime Creek Road (FR 728) on left.

3.7▲   **BL**   Lime Creek Road (FR 728) on right.

▼4.9   **SO**   Sign for Mount Holy Cross overlook. Public restrooms, parking lot, and walking track on right.

3.5▲   **SO**   Sign for Mount Holy Cross overlook. Public restrooms, parking lot, and walking track on left.

▼5.3   **SO**   Track on right.

3.1▲   **SO**   Track on left.

▼6.2   **SO**   Summit of Shrine Pass. Hiking trail and public restrooms on right.

2.2▲   **SO**   Hiking trail and public restrooms on right. Summit of Shrine Pass.

      GPS: N 39°32.72′ W 106°14.45′

▼8.4   Seasonal gate; then stop sign and pavement begins. Trail ends at I-70.

0.0▲   The intersection for Shrine Pass is on I-70 at exit 190, approximately 1 mile east of Vail Pass summit. Zero trip meter where the side road ends.

      GPS: N 39°31.74′ W 106°13.06′

Aspen stands along the trail

Ptarmigan Pass and McAllister Gulch Loop

STARTING POINT Intersection of Central #17: Shrine Pass Trail (FR 709) and FR 747

FINISHING POINT Intersection of Central #17: Shrine Pass Trail (FR 709) and FR 747

TOTAL MILEAGE 21.4 miles

UNPAVED MILEAGE 21.4 miles

DRIVING TIME 3 hours

ROUTE ELEVATION 9,200 to 11,765 feet

USUALLY OPEN Mid-June to late September

DIFFICULTY RATING 4

SCENIC RATING 9

Special Attractions

- Panoramic views of the Mount of the Holy Cross, a 14,000-foot peak.
- Numerous creek crossings.
- Historic site of the Camp Hale Army Base.
- Interesting loop route that is only moderately difficult.

History

During World War II, this area was used as a training ground for the 10th Mountain Division of the U.S. Army, based at the now decommissioned Camp Hale Army Base. The base was the only facility that offered training in mountain and winter warfare. The division fought with distinction, and after the war a number of the veterans from the 10th Mountain Division were instrumental in establishing Colorado's ski industry.

Description

This route is a side road off of Central #17: Shrine Pass Trail. Initially, it travels through a very scenic, narrow canyon with barely enough room at its base for the road and Wearyman Creek. The road crosses through the shallow creek a number of times before reaching FR 708 in less than a mile.

FR 708 immediately starts to climb steeply and continues through the dense forest with numerous switchbacks, where passing oncoming vehicles is possible. The

Camp Hale Army Base in the 1940s

road rises above timberline into a broad alpine meadow and continues to the top of Hornsilver Mountain, from which point there is a spectacular 360-degree view; to the southwest is the Holy Cross Wilderness Area and the Mount of the Holy Cross, a famous 14,000-foot peak. This mountain was declared a national monument by President Herbert Hoover, but it lost its status in 1950 due to the deterioration of the right arm of the cross.

The route continues across a fairly level ridge to Resolution Mountain. At around the 6-mile point, the road commences a steep descent for about half a mile. As you turn onto FR 702 (Resolution Road), a right turn takes you to the old Camp Hale Army Base and US 24. The route continues to the left toward Ptarmigan Pass. The road to the pass is wide and well maintained.

The descent from the pass via FR 747 (Wearyman Road) heads back below tim-berline and is rough, narrow, and often boggy. There is also another short section of shelf road. You will have to cross the creek several times before returning to the inter-section with Shrine Pass Road.

We highly recommend the Trails Illus-trated maps listed below to assist with nav-igation of this route.

Current Road Information

White River National Forest
Holy Cross Ranger District
24747 US 24
Minturn, CO 81645
(970) 827-5715

Map References

USFS   White River National Forest
Maptech CD:
    Colorado Springs/Ski Areas/Central
Benchmark's *Colorado Road & Recreation Atlas,* p. 73
Colorado Atlas & Gazetteer, pp. 37, 47
The Roads of Colorado, p. 78
Trails Illustrated, #108, #109

Route Directions

▼**0.0**   From intersection of Central #17: Shrine Pass Trail (FR 709) and FR 747, zero trip meter at Wearyman Creek bridge and proceed toward Ptarmigan Pass and McAllister Gulch.

0.7▲   Cross bridge and end at Central #17: Shrine Pass Trail (FR 709).

        GPS: N 39°31.39′ W 106°19.49′

▼**0.2** **SO** Cross through creek; then 100 yards farther, cross through creek again.

0.5▲ **SO** Cross through creek; then 100 yards farther, cross through creek again.

▼**0.3** **SO** Cross through creek.
0.4▲ **SO** Cross through creek.

▼**0.4** **SO** Cross through creek.
0.3▲ **SO** Cross through creek.

▼**0.7** **TR** Cross through creek. Intersection with McAllister Gulch Road (FR 708). Zero trip meter.

0.0▲   Proceed along FR 747.

        GPS: N 39°31.20′ W 106°18.87′

A section of trail typical of this route

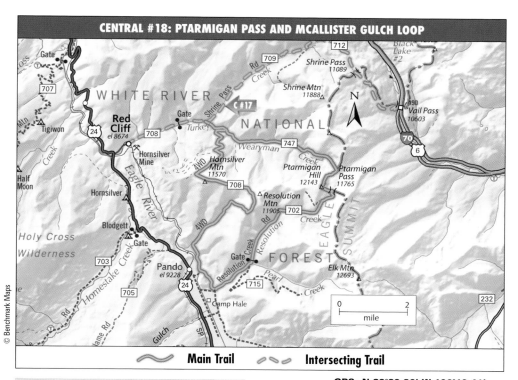

Main Trail ~~~ **Intersecting Trail** ∞∞∞

GPS: N 39°29.86' W 106°19.41'

▼0.0   Proceed along FR 708.

10.0▲   **TL**   Intersection with Wearyman Road (FR 747) Cross through creek. Zero trip meter.

▼4.3   **BR**   Intersection.

5.7▲   **BL**   Intersection.

GPS: N 39°29.27' W 106°17.82'

▼1.1   **BR**   Fork in road.

8.9▲   **BL**   Fork in road.

▼2.1   **BL**   Track on right.

7.9▲   **BR**   Track on left.

▼2.2   **BL**   Track on right.

7.8▲   **BR**   Track on left.

▼2.9   **BL**   Intersection. Spot on right with broad, panoramic views of Eagle River Valley to the southwest and northwest.

7.9▲   **BR**   Intersection. Spot on left with broad, panoramic views of Eagle River Valley to the southwest and northwest.

GPS: N 39°29.98' W 106°19.88'

▼3.6   **SO**   Meadow at top of Hornsilver Mountain with 360-degree views.

6.4▲   **SO**   Meadow at top of Hornsilver Mountain with 360-degree views.

Rocky section of the trail

▼8.4   SO   Private cabin on right. National Forest boundary.

1.6▲   SO   National Forest boundary. Private cabin on left.

▼8.8   TL   Intersection. Track on right dead-ends.

1.2▲   TR   Intersection. Sign to McAllister Gulch. Dead end is straight ahead.
     GPS: N 39°27.76′ W 106°19.76′

▼9.2   TL   Intersection. Follow Ptarmigan Pass sign to the left.

0.8▲   TR   Intersection.

▼10.0   TL   Intersection with Resolution Road (FR 702). Road on right connects with US 24 in 1.1 miles and site of old Camp Hale U.S. Army Base. Zero trip meter.

0.0▲   Continue along FR 708.
     GPS: N 39°26.90′ W 106°19.12′

▼0.0   Continue along FR 702.

5.3▲   TR   Onto FR 708. Zero trip meter.

▼0.2   SO   Seasonal gate.

5.1▲   SO   Seasonal gate.

▼1.3   SO   Track on right dead-ends. Remain on Resolution Road (FR 702).

4.0▲   SO   Track on left dead-ends.

▼4.8   TR   Intersection with FR 751.

0.5▲   TL   Intersection with Resolution Road (FR 702).

▼5.3   SO   Summit of Ptarmigan Pass. Road becomes FR 747. Zero trip meter.

0.0▲   Continue along FR 702.
     GPS: N 39°29.59′ W 106°15.14′

▼0.0   Continue along FR 747.

5.4▲   SO   Summit of Ptarmigan Pass. Road becomes FR 702. Zero trip meter.

▼1.4   SO   Cross through creek.

4.0▲   SO   Cross through creek.

▼2.1   SO   Cross through creek.

3.3▲   SO   Cross through creek.

▼3.1   SO   Cross through creek.

2.3▲   SO   Cross through creek.

▼4.6   SO   Cross through creek.

0.8▲   SO   Cross through creek.

▼4.7   SO   Intersection with FR 708 to McAllister Gulch on left. Cross through creek.

0.7▲   SO   Cross through creek. Intersection with FR 708 to McAllister Gulch on right.
     GPS: N 39°31.20′ W 106°18.87′

▼5.0   SO   Cross through creek.

0.4▲   SO   Cross through creek.

▼5.1   SO   Cross through creek.

0.3▲   SO   Cross through creek.

▼5.2   SO   Cross through creek.

0.2▲   SO   Cross through creek.

▼5.3   SO   Cross through creek.

0.1▲   SO   Cross through creek.

▼5.4   Cross bridge and end at Shrine Pass Trail (FR 709).

0.0   From intersection of Central #17: Shrine Pass Trail (FR 709) and FR 747, zero trip meter at Wearyman Creek bridge and proceed toward Ptarmigan Pass and McAllister Gulch.
     GPS: N 39°31.39′ W 106°19.49′

The trail crossing the beautiful alpine meadow on Hornsilver Mountain

Weston Pass Trail

STARTING POINT Intersection of US 24 and CR 7, 5.1 miles south of Leadville Airport

FINISHING POINT Intersection of Park CR 5 and US 285

TOTAL MILEAGE 25.7 miles

UNPAVED MILEAGE 23.4 miles

DRIVING TIME 1.5 hours

ROUTE ELEVATION 9,400 to 11,921 feet

USUALLY OPEN Late June to late September

DIFFICULTY RATING 2

SCENIC RATING 7

Special Attractions

- Attractive scenery along an easy 4WD trail.
- Access to a network of 4WD trails.

History

Like so many passes in the Colorado Rockies, Weston Pass was a Ute trail before being developed as a wagon road. In 1860, during the first gold boom in the Leadville area, the new wagon road was known as the Ute Trail. The stagecoach way station on the eastern side of the pass grew into the town of Weston. Father Dyer made early use of the pass and in 1861 was caught in a blizzard and nearly perished.

Four freight and passenger service companies sprang up to meet the enormous demand. One, the Wall & Witter Stage Company, maintained 400 horses, 11 freight wagons, and 7 stagecoaches to service its operations. In 1873, the Hayden survey party found a good wagon road over Weston Pass at a time when there was barely a burro trail over Mosquito Pass.

The Denver, South Park & Pacific Railroad reached Weston in 1879, adding new impetus to the town's growth. In that year, the Wall & Witter Stage Company collected $1.5 million in fares; on just one day in September, 225 teams were counted as they crossed the pass, pulling either wagons or stagecoaches. As proof that traveling the pass road was thirsty work, Park County issued no fewer than eight new liquor licenses in 1879 to establishments between the town and the top of the pass.

A section of trail typical of this route

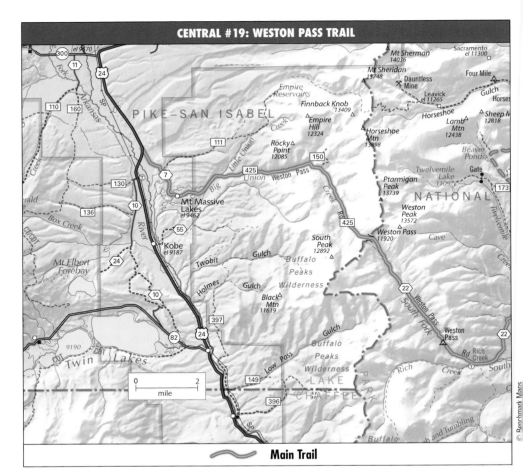

Main Trail

© Benchmark Maps

However, in 1881, the railroad made it into Leadville, sending Weston Pass into rapid decline.

In the 1950s, the pass road was renovated and has been well maintained ever since as a recreational road.

Description

The route commences at the intersection of US 24 and CR 7, 5.1 miles south of the Leadville Airport entrance on the left as you leave Leadville.

Navigation along the Weston Pass route is a simple matter, and the road is suitable for cars—except for a couple of miles on the west side of the summit, where high clearance is preferable.

The road travels beside Union Creek on the west side and along the South Fork of the South Platte River on the east side. Both offer numerous, good backcountry camping sites. Additionally, on the west side there is a U.S. Forest Service campground.

Current Road Information

Pike & San Isabel National Forests
Leadville Ranger District
810 Front Street
Leadville, CO 80461
(719) 486-0749

Map References

USFS   Pike National Forest; San Isabel
        National Forest
Maptech CD:
        Colorado Springs/Ski Areas/Central
Benchmark's *Colorado Road & Recreation
        Atlas,* p. 87
Colorado Atlas & Gazetteer, pp. 47, 48
The Roads of Colorado, p. 94
Trails Illustrated, #110

CENTRAL #19: WESTON PASS TRAIL

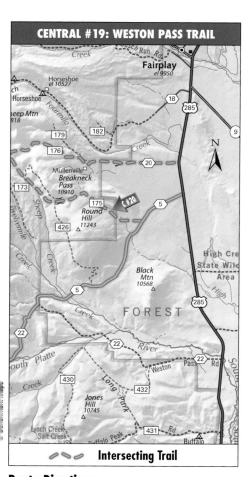

Intersecting Trail

Route Directions

▼0.0   At intersection of US 24 and CR 7, zero trip meter and proceed southeast along CR 7 (FR 425) toward Weston Pass. There is a sign for Massive Lakes.

10.5▲   End at intersection with US 24.
      GPS: N 39°10.58' W 106°19.27'

▼3.0   SO Cattle guard.
7.5▲   SO Cattle guard.

▼7.1   SO Cross over creek.
3.4▲   SO Cross over creek.

▼7.5   SO Track on left.
3.0▲   SO Track on right.

▼8.4   SO Track on left.
2.1▲   SO Track on right.

▼8.7   SO Cabin ruins on right.
1.8▲   SO Cabin ruins on left.

▼8.8   SO Track on left.
1.7▲   SO Track on right.

▼9.3   SO Cabin ruins below shelf road.
1.2▲   SO Cabin ruins below shelf road.

▼10.4   SO Track on right.
0.1▲   SO Track on left.

▼10.5   SO Summit of Weston Pass. Zero trip meter.
0.0▲   Continue along FR 425.
      GPS: N 39°07.88' W 106°10.88'

▼0.0   Continue along FR 425.
8.4▲   SO Summit of Weston Pass. Zero trip meter.

▼0.1   SO Cabin ruins on the left and right. Track on left to small lake.
8.3▲   SO Track on right to small lake. Cabin ruins on the left and right.

▼0.2   SO Site of the Ruby Mine.
8.2▲   SO Site of the Ruby Mine.

▼0.8   SO Track on left.
7.6▲   SO Track on right.

▼1.7   SO Track on left.
6.7▲   SO Track on right.

▼1.9   SO Site of Park Place roadside restaurant on left.
6.5▲   SO Site of Park Place roadside restaurant on right.

▼4.5   SO Road on right to USFS Weston Pass Campground.
3.9▲   SO Road on left to USFS Weston Pass Campground.
      GPS: N 39°04.63' W 106°07.99'

▼5.6   SO Rich Creek Trailhead on right and cattle guard. Leave the National Forest.
2.8▲   SO Enter the National Forest. Cattle

guard; then Rich Creek Trailhead on left.

▼6.8   **BL**   Road on right goes to a private ranch.
1.6▲   **CR**   Road on left goes to a private ranch.

▼7.5   **SO**   Cattle guard.
0.9▲   **SO**   Cattle guard.

▼7.9   **SO**   Road on left.
0.5▲   **SO**   Road on right.

▼8.4   **TL**   FR 425 ends at fork in the road. Left fork goes to US 285 via CR 5. Right fork goes to US 285 via CR 22. Both alternatives reach the highway in 7 miles. Zero trip meter.
0.0▲   Proceed along FR 425.
    GPS: N 39°05.85′ W 106°05.28′

▼0.0   Proceed along CR 5.
6.8▲   **BR**   Onto FR 425. Zero trip meter.

▼1.6   **SO**   Cattle guard.
5.2▲   **SO**   Cattle guard.

▼1.9   **BR**   Road on left.
4.9▲   **BL**   Road on right.

▼2.2   **SO**   Cattle guard.
4.6▲   **SO**   Cattle guard.

▼3.6   **SO**   Cattle guard.
3.2▲   **SO**   Cattle guard.

▼5.2   **SO**   Central #20: Breakneck Pass and Browns Pass Trail on left. Cattle guard.
1.6▲   **SO**   Cattle guard. Central #20: Breakneck Pass and Brown Pass Trail on right.
    GPS: N 39°08.39′ W 106°01.42′

▼6.8   Cattle guard; then end at intersection with US 285.
0.0▲   At intersection of US 285 and Park CR 5, zero trip meter and proceed west on Weston Pass Road, CR 5. Cross cattle grid and follow sign to Weston Pass.
    GPS: N 39°09.20′ W 105°59.93′

A view of one of the stands of aspens along the Weston Pass route

Breakneck Pass and Browns Pass Trail

STARTING POINT Intersection of US 285 and Park CR 5

FINISHING POINT Intersection of CR 20 and US 285

TOTAL MILEAGE 13.9 miles

UNPAVED MILEAGE 11.8 miles

DRIVING TIME 1.5 hours

ROUTE ELEVATION 9,600 to 11,372 feet

USUALLY OPEN Early June to early October

DIFFICULTY RATING 3

SCENIC RATING 7

Special Attractions

- Access to a network of 4WD trails.
- Fairly easy 4WD trail that travels under the canopy of the dense forest.
- Aspen viewing in the fall.

History

Little is known about the history of these two pass roads, but it is likely that they were built, or at least improved, in the early 1900s to open access to the mines in the Sheep Park area.

Description

The route commences at the intersection of US 285 and Central #19: Weston Pass Trail (CR 5) about 4.5 miles south of Fairplay and travels through attractive ranchland for 1.6 miles before turning onto Breakneck Pass Road (FR 175).

Proceeding from the intersection, the road is fairly steep and rocky in sections. It might also be boggy if it has rained recently. The clearance between the trees is tight in spots, especially for full-sized vehicles. Nonetheless, although the road becomes rough and narrow, it is not difficult.

The unmarked Breakneck Pass is at the intersection with FR 426, at which point the main road proceeds straight on, the road on the left is closed, and FR 426 (to the right) takes you on an alternative loop past ruins of a mine and a cabin. FR 426 is a more interesting route than FR 175 from this point and rejoins the main road at the start of Sheep Park. The route directions for FR 426 are provided below.

As you travel through Sheep Park, Browns Pass Road (FR 176) turns off to the right. The track climbs uphill steeply for about three-tenths of a mile and can be quite difficult if it is wet (under which circumstances the road's difficulty rating would be higher than 3). After this initial ascent, the road levels out and is easy except for some tight clearance between the trees. Browns Pass is marked with a rough sign.

This little-used route lacks the drama of many 4WD roads in Colorado but offers a variety of scenery from the tranquil meadows of Sheep Park to dense forests with thick stands of aspen that cover the road in gold during fall. Some higher sections of the route also provide good views of the Mosquito Range to the west.

Current Road Information

Pike & San Isabel National Forests
South Park Ranger District
320 US 285
Fairplay, CO 80440
(719) 836-2031

A stand of aspens envelops the road near Breakneck Pass

Map References

USFS   Pike National Forest

Maptech CD:

    Colorado Springs/Ski Areas/Central

Benchmark's *Colorado Road & Recreation Atlas*, p. 87

Colorado Atlas & Gazetteer, p. 48

The Roads of Colorado, p. 94

Trails Illustrated, #110

Route Directions

▼0.0   At intersection of US 285 and Park CR 5, zero trip meter and proceed west on Weston Pass Road, CR 5. Cross cattle grid and follow sign to Weston Pass.

5.0▲   End at intersection with US 285.

        GPS: N 39°09.20' W 105°59.93'

▼1.6 **TR** Cross cattle guard. Turn onto Breakneck Pass Road (FR 175).

3.4▲ **TL** Turn onto CR 5. Cross cattle guard.

        GPS: N 39°08.39' W 106°01.42'

▼3.2 **SO** Cattle guard. Enter Pike National Forest.

1.8▲ **SO** Leave Pike National Forest. Cattle guard.

▼3.5 **SO** Track on left to camping.

1.5▲ **SO** Track on right to camping.

▼5.0 **TR** Intersection with Round Hill Road (FR 426) on right. To the left, FR 426 is closed a little farther on. Zero trip meter.

0.0▲   Continue along FR 175.

        GPS: N 39°08.91' W 106°04.65'

▼0.0   Proceed along FR 426.

2.8▲ **TL** Intersection with Breakneck Pass Road (FR 175). Zero trip meter.

▼1.4 **BL** Track on right. Cabin ruins and mine.

1.4▲ **BR** Track on left. Cabin ruins and mine.

▼1.6 **SO** Cabin ruins on right.

1.2▲ **SO** Cabin ruins on left.

▼2.0 **TR** Intersection to rejoin FR 175.

0.8▲ **TL** Intersection with FR 426, a faint trail to the left near the end of Sheep Park.

The remains of a miners' cabin near Breakneck Pass

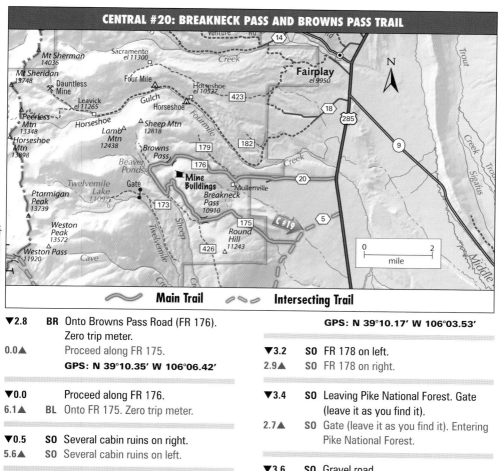

~~~ **Main Trail** ◦◦◦◦ **Intersecting Trail**

▼2.8 **BR** Onto Browns Pass Road (FR 176). Zero trip meter.

0.0▲ Proceed along FR 175.
  GPS: N 39°10.35′ W 106°06.42′

▼0.0 Proceed along FR 176.

6.1▲ **BL** Onto FR 175. Zero trip meter.

▼0.5 **SO** Several cabin ruins on right.

5.6▲ **SO** Several cabin ruins on left.

▼0.6 **SO** Summit of Browns Pass. FR 1761 track on the left.

5.5▲ **SO** Summit of Browns Pass. FR 1761 track on the right.
  GPS: N 39°10.47′ W 106°05.77′

▼1.1 **SO** Cabin ruins on right.

5.0▲ **SO** Cabin ruins on left.

▼1.4 **BR** Track on left.

4.7▲ **BL** Track on right.

▼2.8 **SO** Cross through creek.

3.3▲ **SO** Cross through creek.

▼2.9 **BR** Track on left (FR 179). Remain on FR 176.

3.2▲ **BL** Track on right (FR 179). Remain on FR 176.

GPS: N 39°10.17′ W 106°03.53′

▼3.2 **SO** FR 178 on left.

2.9▲ **SO** FR 178 on right.

▼3.4 **SO** Leaving Pike National Forest. Gate (leave it as you find it).

2.7▲ **SO** Gate (leave it as you find it). Entering Pike National Forest.

▼3.6 **SO** Gravel road.

2.5▲ **SO** Gravel road.

▼4.0 **TL** Intersection with CR 20.

2.1▲ **TR** Turn from CR 20 onto FR 176. Signs read: "Browns Pass, Fourmile Road, National Forest Access."
  GPS: N 39°09.99′ W 106°02.45′

▼4.5 **SO** Cattle guard.

1.6▲ **SO** Cattle guard.

▼6.1 Cattle guard. End at intersection with US 285.

0.0▲ At intersection of CR 20 and US 285 (there is a sign for National Forest access and Browns Pass), zero trip meter and proceed along CR 20.
  GPS: N 39°10.14′ W 106°00.06′

Mosquito Pass Trail

STARTING POINT Colorado 9 and Mosquito
   Pass Road (CR 12) at Alma Junction
FINISHING POINT Leadville
TOTAL MILEAGE 16.7 miles
UNPAVED MILEAGE 15.2 miles
DRIVING TIME 2 hours
ROUTE ELEVATION 10,200 to 13,186 feet
USUALLY OPEN Early August to mid-
   September
DIFFICULTY RATING 6
SCENIC RATING 10

Special Attractions
- The highest pass road in America.
- Great historic significance.
- Wonderful alpine views.

History
According to legend, this pass got its name
in 1861 at a meeting of local residents who
gathered to try to choose one of the many
names proposed at their previous, incon-
clusive meeting. When they opened the
minutes from that meeting, they found that

Father Dyer memorial at the summit of Mosquito Pass

a mosquito had been squashed in the middle of their list of proposed names. The new
name was approved by acclamation!

The Indians used the pass, but the first
white men recorded to have crossed it were
Thomas Farnham and his party in their ex-
ploratory journey across Colorado in 1839.
In 1861, the Mosquito gold mining camp
was established to the east of the pass.

From 1864, the pass was used by the
itinerant Methodist preacher Father Dyer,
who carried the mail across the pass for pay
of $18 per week. In winter, he traveled on
snowshoes at night when the surface of the
snow was harder. A small memorial to him
stands at the summit of the pass.

Horace A. W. Tabor crossed the pass
with Augusta, his wife, on horseback in
1870 but noted that a road barely existed.
In 1873, Hayden's survey team crossed the
pass and noted only a well-used burro trail.

Western Union built a telegraph line
over the pass in 1878. Later that year, Horace Tabor and other investors formed the
Mosquito Pass Wagon Road Company to
construct a toll road over the pass. This
wagon road was completed the following
year, when freight wagons and stagecoaches
were among the 150 vehicles crossing the
pass each day. The pass became known as
the "highway of frozen death" because of
the many travelers who froze to death while
walking across the pass road in winter to
avoid paying the stagecoach fare.

In 1880, both the Denver, South Park &
Pacific Railroad and the Denver & Rio
Grande Railroad commenced service to
Leadville, ringing the death knell for the
pass road. The road fell into disuse and was
closed from 1910 until 1949, when local
residents restored it to hold the first Get
Your Ass Over the Pass burro race. The race
is now a well-established event, held every
July.

The town of Alma Junction is located at
the intersection of Mosquito Pass Road and
the road between Alma and Fairplay. It was
also called London Junction and Alma Station, and although it was never incorporated, 150 people lived there in 1884. At its
peak, the population reached 300. The

Old miners' cabins near the beginning of Mosquito Pass Trail

town served as a stop for travelers to and from Leadville and Fairplay as well as a home to those who worked in the nearby London Mines. The McLaughlin stagecoach line ran between Alma and Fairplay, providing transfers at London Junction for travelers heading west across the pass.

In 1882, a spur of the London, South Park & Leadville Railroad was completed—a 6-mile segment leading from London Junction, through Park City, to the London Mountain mining area. Used for hauling ore from the London Mines, the spur was abandoned two years later when the mines closed down.

The London Mines were established in the 1870s, and small settlements grew up in the area to house the miners. A concentration works was constructed at London Junction in 1883 to process ore. The South

Mosquito Creek has washed out a section of the trail

American Mill with tram remains perched on the hill above

London Mine, which opened in 1874, lies on the eastern slope of Mosquito Pass. It was the terminus of the London, South Park & Leadville spur up Mosquito Gulch. The North London Mine was high on London Mountain (12,280 feet). The mine had its own boardinghouses and an aerial tram, with wooden tram towers that are still visible among the trees. The tram was constructed to span the 3,300-foot distance between the North London Mine and its mill because a conventional chute was not sufficient. Ruins of cabins and the bunkhouse can be seen at the site.

A scenic alpine lake near the trail

Remains of the North London Mill

The North London and South London Mines merge via a tunnel beneath them that goes through the mountain. In total, more than 100 miles of tunnels burrow through London Mountain in all directions and have yielded millions of dollars' worth of ore.

Description

The route commences at Alma Junction, the intersection of Colorado 9 and Mosquito Pass Road (CR 12), which was the junction of the railway spur to the London Mill and the main line.

The easy 2WD road continues past the

Switchbacks where the trail begins to climb steeply

Narrow, rocky, and eroded section of shelf road on Mosquito Pass Trail

A hoist at the North London Mill site

town of Park City, an old stagecoach stop, and then past the Orphan Boy Mine, which operated well into the twentieth century, at the 3.3-mile point. At the 4.4-mile point, the route continues past the intersection of FR 696 on the left, which travels around the south of London Mountain and reconnects with the pass road but is usually closed to through traffic. A couple of miles farther, FR 12 turns left, crosses Mosquito Creek, and commences the ascent toward the pass, providing scenic views of the valley.

The side road to Cooney Lake has several creek crossings and passes through the water at the bottom tip of the lake. The wa-

The view to the west over Leadville from Mosquito Pass

ter at these crossings can be more than 18 inches deep, and the road can be very rutted and boggy in places. It is an interesting 4WD road but considerably more challenging than the main pass road.

At the summit, the view is spectacular: South Park spreads out to the east, and to the west is Leadville, Turquoise Lake, and the massive Sawatch Range with its 15 fourteeners, including the three highest peaks in the Rockies.

The road descending toward Leadville, although it begins steeply, is generally easier than the road on the east side. About 1.5 miles from the summit, a track to Birdseye Gulch intersects on the right. This road heads north toward Colorado 91 but has some extremely boggy sections at about the 1.5-mile point. To avoid damage to the terrain, do not attempt this trail without a winch (and a long winch extension strap to reach the sometimes distant winching points).

The main road from this point affords a straightforward drive into Leadville, past Horace Tabor's Matchless Mine.

Mosquito Creek runs beside the American Mill

Current Road Information

Pike & San Isabel National Forests
Leadville Ranger District
810 Front Street
Leadville, CO 80461
(719) 486-0749

Map References

USFS   Pike National Forest; San Isabel National Forest
Maptech CD:
     Colorado Springs/Ski Areas/Central
Benchmark's *Colorado Road & Recreation Atlas*, p. 87
Colorado Atlas & Gazetteer, pp. 47, 48
The Roads of Colorado, p. 94
Trails Illustrated, #109

Route Directions

▼0.0   Start at Alma Junction, which is the intersection of Colorado 9 and CR/FR 12, 1.3 miles south of Alma. Turn onto CR 12, zero trip meter, and proceed west along Mosquito Pass Road. Sign points toward Mosquito Gulch.
7.8▲   End at intersection with Colorado 9.
           GPS: N 39°16.23′ W 106°02.83′

▼0.2   SO   Site of cabins and other buildings that were part of Alma Junction. Grade of old railroad wye is visible between the river and the highway.
7.6▲   SO   Site of cabins and other buildings that were part of Alma Junction. Grade of old railroad wye is visible between the river and the highway.

▼2.4   SO   Road on right to Park City.
5.4▲   SO   Road on left to Park City.

▼2.5   SO   Site of Park City, a stage stop that grew into a town.
5.3▲   SO   Site of Park City, a stage stop that grew into a town.

▼3.4   SO   Orphan Boy Mine.
4.4▲   SO   Orphan Boy Mine.

▼4.5   BR   Intersection. Remain on FR 12. South London Mine ruins are to the left

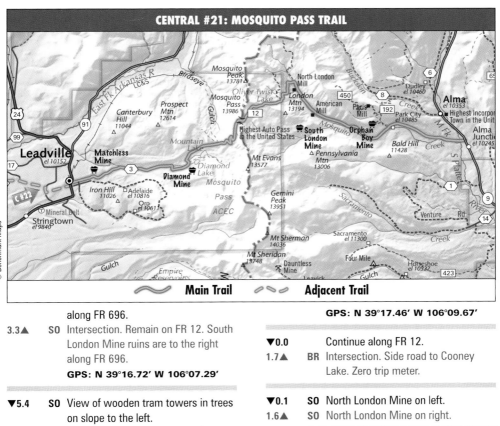

~~~ **Main Trail**   ⌒⌒⌒ **Adjacent Trail**

along FR 696.

3.3▲ **SO** Intersection. Remain on FR 12. South London Mine ruins are to the right along FR 696.

GPS: N 39°16.72' W 106°07.29'

▼5.4 **SO** View of wooden tram towers in trees on slope to the left.

2.4▲ **SO** View of wooden tram towers in trees on slope to the right.

▼6.2 **SO** Track on left to North London Mill and tailings dump.

1.6▲ **SO** Track on right to North London Mill and tailings dump.

▼6.7 **TL** Intersection. Turn left, remaining on FR 12. On the right is FR 856; then cross creek.

1.1▲ **TR** Cross creek; then intersection with FR 856 on left.

▼7.4 **SO** Track on right to Champaign Mine.

0.4▲ **SO** Track on left to Champaign Mine.

▼7.5 **SO** Cross through creek.

0.3▲ **SO** Cross through creek.

▼7.8 **TL** Intersection. Road on right goes to Cooney Lake. Zero trip meter.

0.0▲ Continue along FR 12.

GPS: N 39°17.46' W 106°09.67'

▼0.0 Continue along FR 12.

1.7▲ **BR** Intersection. Side road to Cooney Lake. Zero trip meter.

▼0.1 **SO** North London Mine on left.

1.6▲ **SO** North London Mine on right.

▼0.2 **SO** Track on right and mining machinery on left.

1.5▲ **SO** Mining machinery on right and track on left.

▼0.7 **SO** Track on left (FR 696) is gated farther on.

1.0▲ **SO** Track on right dead-ends.

▼1.7 **SO** Tracks on the left and right. Then summit of Mosquito Pass. Zero trip meter.

0.0▲ Proceed toward Leadville. Mosquito Pass Road changes to FR 12 on this side.

GPS: N 39°16.86' W 106°11.12'

▼0.0 Proceed toward Leadville. Mosquito Pass Road changes to FR 438 on this side.

7.2▲ **SO** Summit of Mosquito Pass. Tracks on the left and right. Zero trip meter.

▼**0.3**   **BL**   Bypass trail on right is one-way downhill and rejoins at 0.8 miles.
6.9▲   **SO**   Track from 6.4-mile point rejoins on left.

▼**0.4**   **SO**   Track on left.
6.8▲   **SO**   Track on right.

▼**0.8**   ·   **SO**   Track from 0.3-mile point rejoins on right.
6.4▲   **BR**   Track on left (no entry—one-way).

▼**1.4**   **SO**   Track to Birdseye Gulch on right. Stay on main road toward Leadville.
5.8▲   **SO**   Track on left to Birdseye Gulch. Stay on main road toward Mosquito Pass.
           GPS: N 39°16.15′ W 106°11.74′

▼**2.8**   **TL**   Road forks. Stay to the left.
4.4▲   **BR**   Road forks. Stay to the right.
           GPS: N 39°15.69′ W 106°13.15′

▼**3.0**   **SO**   Cross over creek. Then gate to Diamond Mine on left. Follow main road.
4.2▲   **SO**   Gate to Diamond Mine on right. Cross over creek.
           GPS: N 39°15.57′ W 106°13.06′

▼**3.2**   **TR**   Intersection.
4.0▲   **TL**   Intersection.

▼**3.3**   **SO**   Mine structure on right.
3.9▲   **SO**   Mine structure on left.

▼**3.6**   **SO**   Cross over creek.
3.6▲   **SO**˙ Cross over creek.

▼**3.8**   **SO**   Mine on right and left.
3.4▲   **SO**   Mine on right and left.

▼**4.6**   **SO**   Road on left.
2.6▲   **SO**   Road on right.

▼**5.4**   **SO**   Intersection. Road on right.
1.8▲   **SO**   Intersection. Road on left.

▼**5.6**   **SO**   Road on left.
1.6▲   **SO**   Road on right.

▼**6.0**   **SO**   Matchless Mine on right.
1.2▲   **SO**   Matchless Mine on left.

▼**6.9**   **SO**   Leadville, Colorado & Southern Railway station on right.
0.3▲   **SO**   Leadville, Colorado & Southern Railway station on left.

▼**7.2**   End at intersection of 7th Street and Harrison Avenue in Leadville.
0.0▲   At the intersection of Harrison Avenue and 7th Street in Leadville, zero trip meter and proceed east along 7th Street.
           GPS: N 39°14.99′ W 106°17.47′

Mosquito Pass is the highest pass road open to automobiles in the United States

Hagerman Pass Trail

STARTING POINT Leadville
FINISHING POINT Basalt
TOTAL MILEAGE 63.3 miles, plus 5.9-mile spur to Hagerman Tunnel
UNPAVED MILEAGE 22.5 miles, plus 5.9-mile spur to Hagerman Tunnel
DRIVING TIME 3 hours, plus 1 hour for spur
ROUTE ELEVATION 6,600 to 11,982 feet
USUALLY OPEN Mid-July to late September
DIFFICULTY RATING 3, 4 for spur
SCENIC RATING 9

Special Attractions

- Historic railroad route.
- Network of 4WD trails to explore.
- Excellent fall aspen viewing.
- Fishing, boating, and camping at Turquoise Lake.
- Good for ATVs, motorbikes, and mountain bikes.
- Snowmobiling and cross-country skiing in winter.

History

Hagerman Pass Road is the product of one of the great railroad stories of the 1880s, the golden period of railroad expansion in Colorado. The pass was named for James J. Hagerman, the president of the Colorado Midland Railroad. Previously it had been known as Cooke Pass, and before that the Hayden survey party had called it Frying Pan Pass in 1873.

In 1885, the Colorado Midland Railway began construction on a railway running from Aspen to Leadville. The railway was remarkable at that time because it was a standard gauge track rather than the prevalent narrow gauge. To enable trains to cross the Continental Divide, the company commenced construction of the Hagerman Tunnel in 1885, completing the project the following year. It was 2,164 feet long and located only 450 feet from the pass's summit at 11,528 feet, the highest standard gauge railroad in the United States at the time. To reach the tunnel, the tracks made three horseshoe turns at a grade of 1.5 percent. One of the turns was made with the help of an enormous 1,084-foot curved trestle bridge.

On the east side of the tunnel was Douglass City, a notorious mining camp that boasted six saloons and a brothel. The camp was home to the railroad construction workers as well as to miners.

The railroad opened in 1887 but faced financial difficulties right from the start. The operating costs were prohibitive. Six locomotives had to operate full-time to clear the rails in the winter, embankments

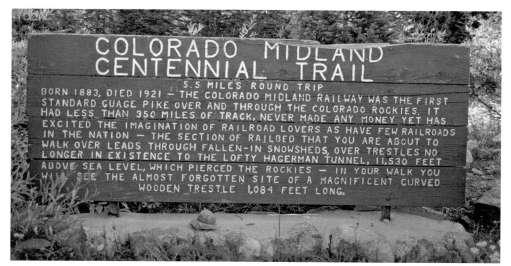

Sign at the trailhead to the site of Douglass City

East portal of Carlton Tunnel

collapsed from water damage, and the trestle bridge required constant upkeep. In 1893, the rail line was closed, and the train was rerouted to the new Busk-Ivanhoe Tunnel that had been constructed 600 feet lower. The new tunnel had proved much more difficult to build than anticipated because of liquid mud floods. When completed, it was nearly 2 miles long, 15 feet wide, and 21 feet high. Construction had taken three years, claimed 20 lives, and cost three times the budget of $1 million.

In 1897, after suffering continuous financial troubles since its formation, the Colorado Midland Railway was sold at a foreclosure. The new owners initially reverted to using the Hagerman Tunnel but went back to the Busk-Ivanhoe Tunnel in 1899. From 1922 until 1943, after the tracks had been torn up, the Busk-Ivanhoe Tunnel was known as the Carlton Tunnel and used as State Highway 104. As it was only wide enough for a single lane of motor vehicles, an alternating system of traffic

A small lake near the summit of Hagerman Pass

control was used. A water pipeline laid through the tunnel to transfer water from the Western Slope to the east is still in use today.

In the 1960s, a new tunnel was built to divert additional water to the Eastern Slope as part of the multimillion-dollar Frying-pan-Arkansas Project, which provides electricity to many Front Range cities. This lower 4-mile-long tunnel is known as the Charles H. Bousted Tunnel.

Description

The Hagerman Pass turnoff is 2.2 miles past the Turquoise Lake dam wall. The road is not difficult, but high clearance is recommended for the embedded rock and erosion. In the narrower sections, adequate pull-offs facilitate passing. Below timberline, the road travels through pine and aspen forest.

The east entrance to the Carlton (Busk-Ivanhoe) Tunnel is about 3.5 miles along Hagerman Pass Road. A mile farther on is a hiking trail that leads to the remains of Douglass City, the site of the trestle bridge, Hagerman Lake, and the east entrance of

The collapsed west end of Hagerman Tunnel

the Hagerman Tunnel. It is an easy walk along the old railway grade that takes about 2 hours and 30 minutes.

The road continues through the pine forest that opens before the summit to an impressive view. Also evident is the high-voltage line between Denver and Grand Junction; the Hagerman Pass Road was used in the construction of the line.

On the west side of the pass, a spur provides an opportunity to visit Ivanhoe Lake and the west side of the Carlton (Busk-Ivanhoe) Tunnel. By driving the entire 6 miles of the spur, you will reach the western entrance of the Hagerman Tunnel, which is now collapsed. The scenic drive over this abandoned section of the original railroad grade is well worth the extra time.

Beyond the spur, Hell Gate gauging station is ahead on the left, a scenic stop on the Colorado Midland Railroad. This section of the trail is a wide shelf road traveling high above Ivanhoe Creek. Driving through the large cuttings that were origi-

Traveling the embankments of the spur to Hagerman Tunnel it is easy to envisage the original steam train chugging along

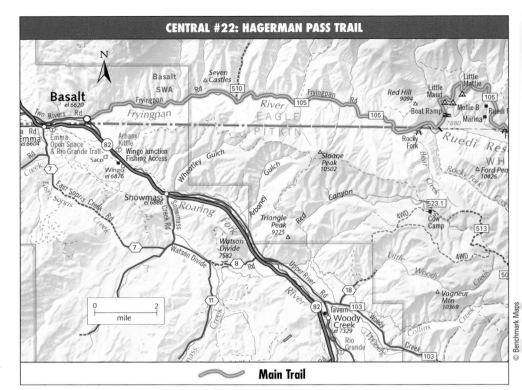

Main Trail

© Benchmark Maps

nally made for the railroad is evocative of the days when trains carried their loads over this route.

The road, which continues past the open expanse of Sellar Park, becomes an easy 2WD road before returning to pavement about 14 miles from the summit.

Current Road Information
San Isabel National Forest
Leadville Ranger District
810 Front Street
Leadville, CO 80461
(719) 486-0749

Summit of Hagerman Pass

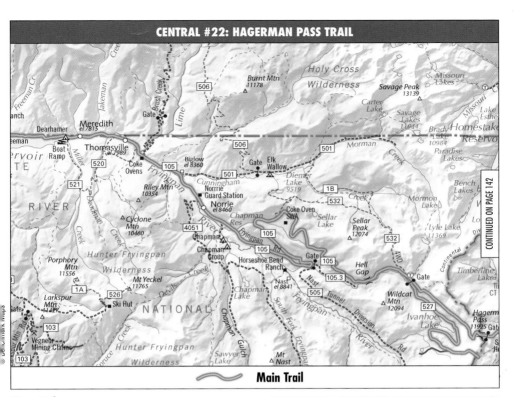

~~~~ **Main Trail**

Map References

USFS   San Isabel National Forest; White
    River National Forest
Maptech CD:
    Colorado Springs/Ski Areas/Central
Benchmark's *Colorado Road & Recreation
    Atlas,*
    pp. 71, 72, 86
Colorado Atlas & Gazetteer, pp. 46, 47
The Roads of Colorado, pp. 76, 77, 93, 94
Trails Illustrated, #109, #110, #126, #127

Route Directions

▼0.0		In Leadville, from the intersection of West 6th Street and Harrison Avenue, zero trip meter and proceed west from the traffic light toward Turquoise Lake.
7.8▲		End at intersection with Harrison Avenue in Leadville.
		GPS: N 39°14.93′ W 106°17.49′

| ▼0.8 | TR | T-intersection. Follow signs to Turquoise Lake. |
| 7.0▲ | TL | Stop sign at intersection. |

| ▼3.1 | SO | Cross railway line. |
| 4.7▲ | SO | Cross railway line. |

| ▼3.5 | BR | Fork in road. |
| 4.3▲ | BL | Road on right. |

| ▼4.3 | SO | Road on right. |
| 3.5▲ | SO | Road on left. |

| ▼4.4 | SO | Dam wall—Turquoise Lake. |
| 3.4▲ | SO | Dam wall—Turquoise Lake. |

| ▼5.7 | SO | Road on right. |
| 2.1▲ | SO | Road on left. |

▼7.8	BL	Onto Hagerman Pass Road (FR 105) and pavement ends. Zero trip meter.
0.0▲		Proceed along Turquoise Lake Road.
		GPS: N 39°16.12′ W 106°25.00′

| ▼0.0 | | Proceed along unpaved FR 105. |
| 7.9▲ | TR | Onto paved Turquoise Lake Road. Zero trip meter. |

| ▼1.8 | SO | Track on left is Sugarloaf Mountain |

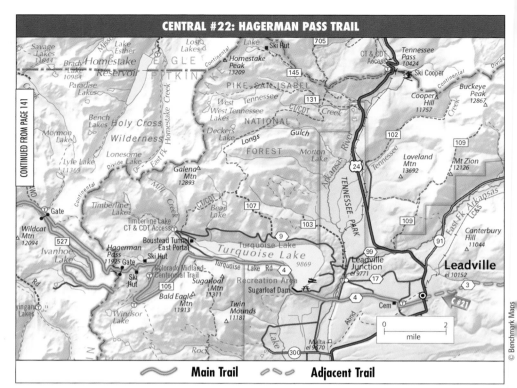

CENTRAL #22: HAGERMAN PASS TRAIL

~~~ **Main Trail**   ⌒⌒⌒ **Adjacent Trail**

Road (FR 105.1A).

6.1▲ **SO** Track on right is Sugarloaf Mountain
Road (FR 105.1A).

▼3.6 **SO** Cross over Busk Creek.
4.3▲ **SO** Cross over Busk Creek.

▼3.7 **BR** East entrance (sealed) of the Carlton
(Busk-Ivanhoe) Tunnel on left.

4.2▲ **BL** East entrance (sealed) of the Carlton
(Busk-Ivanhoe) Tunnel on right.

Crooked Creek Reservoir

View of Ivanhoe Lake with the old railroad embankment crossing the lake toward the Carlton Tunel western entrance

▼4.7　SO　Colorado Midland Centennial Trail marker on left. Walking trail to trestle, tunnel, and Hagerman Lake via TR 1491.

3.2▲　SO　Colorado Midland Centennial Trail marker on right. Walking trail to trestle, tunnel, and Hagerman Lake via TR 1491.

GPS: N 39°15.56' W 106°27.51'

▼6.7　SO　Track on right to Skinner Hut.

1.2▲　SO　Track on left to Skinner Hut.

▼7.4　SO　Seasonal closure gate.

The western end of the Carlton Tunnel is now collapsed

Coke ovens beside the trail

0.5▲	SO	Seasonal closure gate.

▼7.9	SO	Hagerman Pass summit. Zero trip meter.
0.0▲		Continue along FR 105.
		GPS: N 39°15.80′ W 106°28.83′

▼0.0		Continue along FR 105.
3.7▲	SO	Hagerman Pass summit. Zero trip meter.

▼3.8	SO	Seasonal gate; then hiking trailhead on right.
0.1▲	SO	Hiking trailhead on left; then seasonal gate.

▼3.9	SO	Intersection with FR 532 on the right and FR 527 (to Ivanhoe Lake) on the left. Zero trip meter.
0.0▲		Remain on 105 and follow sign to Hagerman Pass.
		GPS: N 39°17.53′ W 106°31.67′

Sections of Hagerman Pass Trail are shelf road traveling high above the Fryingpan River

Spur to Hagerman Tunnel

▼0.0   Proceed south on FR 527 signed to Ivanhoe Lake; then seasonal closure gate and cross over creek.

▼1.6   SO   Track on left.

▼1.7   SO   Dam wall and Ivanhoe Lake on right.

▼2.5   SO   Gated track on right.

▼3.0   SO   Cross through creek.

▼3.1   SO   Cross through creek.

▼5.2   SO   Track on right goes to Lily Lake.

        GPS: N 39°15.35′ W 106°30.68′

▼5.7   SO   Cross through creek.

▼5.9   SO   Spur ends at collapsed entry to Hagerman Tunnel. Return to main trail.

        GPS: N 39°15.33′ W 106°29.44′

Continuation of Main Trail

▼0.0   Remain on FR 105 and follow sign to Ruedi Reservoir.

10.7▲   SO   Intersection with FR 532 on the left and FR 527 (to Ivanhoe Lake) on the right. Zero trip meter.

▼1.2   SO   Track on right.

9.5▲   SO   Track on left.

▼2.0   SO   Hell Gate scenic overlook and gauging station in the valley on left among trees.

8.7▲   SO   Hell Gate scenic overlook and gauging station in the valley on right among trees.

▼7.4   SO   Sellar Park on left. Track on right goes to Sellar Lake and Diemer Lake and up to North Fork Road.

3.3▲   SO   Sellar Park on right. Track on left goes to Diemer Lake and up to North Fork Road.

        GPS: N 39°19.21′ W 106°36.63′

▼10.7   BR   Intersection with road on left. Proceed onto paved Fryingpan Road.

Hagerman Pass Trail travels along the old railroad grade through rock cuttings and aspen stands

		Zero trip meter.
0.0▲		Continue along main road.
		GPS: N 39°17.89' W 106°35.21'

▼0.0		Continue along main road.
33.0▲	BL	Intersection. Continue toward Hagerman Pass on unpaved FR 105. Zero trip meter.

▼0.1	SO	Road on left to Fryingpan Lakes Trailhead.
32.9▲	SO	Road on right to Fryingpan Lakes Trailhead.

▼3.5	SO	USFS Chapman Dam Campground.
29.5▲	SO	USFS Chapman Dam Campground.

▼3.8	SO	USFS Chapman Dam Campground.
29.2▲	SO	USFS Chapman Dam Campground.

▼7.0	SO	Road on right is FR 400, Brush Creek Road. It goes to Eagle.
26.0▲	SO	Road on left is FR 400, Brush Creek Road. It goes to Eagle.
		GPS: N 39°21.10' W 106°41.30'

▼8.2	SO	Thomasville.
24.8▲	SO	Thomasville.

▼9.6	SO	Meredith.
23.4▲	SO	Meredith.

▼10.0	SO	Ruedi Reservoir on left.
23.0▲	SO	Ruedi Reservoir on right.

▼30.7	SO	Basalt.
2.3▲	SO	Leaving Basalt.

▼30.9	TR	Intersection with Midland and Two Rivers Road (Business Route 82).
2.1▲	TL	Intersection with Fryingpan Road.

▼33.0		End at intersection with Colorado 82 in Basalt.
0.0▲		From traffic light at intersection of Colorado 82 and Business Route 82 (Two Rivers Road), zero trip meter and proceed along Business Route 82 toward Basalt.
		GPS: N 39°22.27' W 107°04.23'

Lincoln Creek Trail

STARTING POINT FR 106 off of Colorado 82
FINISHING POINT Collapsed mine portal
TOTAL MILEAGE 11.0 miles (one-way)
UNPAVED MILEAGE 11.0 miles
DRIVING TIME 2 hours (one-way)
ROUTE ELEVATION 9,639 to 11,897 feet
USUALLY OPEN Late May to September
DIFFICULTY RATING 4 to Ruby, 5 beyond
SCENIC RATING 10

Special Attractions

- Interesting remains in Ruby ghost town and the Lincoln Creek Mining District.
- Varied scenery along Lincoln Creek.
- Good camping opportunities.
- Access to hiking, mountain biking, fishing, picnicking, and swimming.
- Snowmobiling, cross-country skiing, and snowshoeing in winter.

History

In 1880, several miners from Independence, Colorado, discovered silver on the South Fork of the Roaring Fork River. Several mining camps were established, the

The rushing waters of Lincoln Creek

Aspen stands on the mountain slopes above Grizzly Reservoir

largest of which was called South Independence. That same year, the men decided to shorten the name of the South Fork of the Roaring Fork to Lincoln Creek, after the newly established Lincoln Creek Mining District.

At the turn of the nineteenth century, the Ruby Mining and Development Company began operating the silver mines in the valley. The town changed its name to Ruby, either after the company or because of the "ruby" silver ore found in the vicinity. The company brought some development to the town, building a large two-story boardinghouse and several other log structures.

Transportation was a significant problem for the town, as ore had to be moved by

Grizzly Reservoir

Interesting rock formations in Lincoln Creek

View of Lincoln Creek from the trail

pack train to Leadville. In 1906, a wagon road was built to reach Independence Pass Road so that ore could be hauled to Aspen. Ruby Mining and Development Company built a 50-ton concentrating plant to help reduce the amount of ore headed to Aspen.

Although tons of ore were transported to Aspen, mining activity largely stopped in 1912. Some prospectors continued on, leasing the mines until the 1950s. Many local geographical landmarks are named after Rudy's early prospectors, including Larson

Portal USFS Campground beside Grizzly Reservoir

The trail winds through the forest and enters Lincoln Creek Mining District

Peak (named after John Larson) and Anderson Lake (named after "Rattle Snake" Bill Anderson). Anderson is said to have kept the U.S. Forest Service out of the Anderson Lake area until the 1940s by force of his personality. Larson Peak stands at 12,900 feet and can be viewed to the west before reaching Ruby. Anderson Lake is located just west of Ruby and is accessible by a hiking trail.

Today a number of the mine properties are still owned by descendants of original settlers. A sign on one of the cabins reads that John A. Nichols founded his claim during June 1903. He worked the claim for the next 30 years in summer, walking from Twin Lakes to Lincoln Gulch. In 1921, John, his son, and grandson were the first to drive a car, a Model T Ford, into Lincoln Gulch. To travel from Twin Lakes over In-

Frenchman's cabin

Log cabin at Ruby ghost town

At first the road follows alongside Lincoln Creek through pine and aspen forest, and views are limited. This section of trail is generally well maintained with a few potholes and is as an easy although bumpy drive. Where the creek runs close to the road, keep an eye out for the remarkable rock formations that have been created over time by the rushing waters of Lincoln Creek. To get the best view, pull off the trail and park in an out-of-the-way location that does not block other travelers. It is a short walk to the bank of the creek and good view of the formations.

The Grizzly Reservoir and the Portal USFS Campground are located just beyond the halfway point. Rainbow trout are abundant in the reservoir, and the shady campground provides facilities, including picnic tables, vault toilets, fire grates, and trash disposal.

The difficulty rating increases to 4 beyond the Grizzly Reservoir. Since the trail beyond the reservoir is not frequently maintained, erosion has caused deeper potholes and corrugations around larger embedded rocks. The trees also begin to di-

dependence Pass took one day, and another day was required to drive 11 miles up Lincoln Gulch.

Description

Lincoln Creek Trail begins approximately 10 miles southeast of Aspen off of Colorado 82 at the intersection with FR 106. The trail follows FR 106, a vehicle corridor through the Collegiate Peaks Wilderness. Although the drive is bumpy and slow going for its entire length, the trail is one of our favorites and well worth spending the time to explore.

The first several miles of the trail are heavily used because the area is popular for outdoor recreation, including hiking, mountain biking, fishing, picnicking, and swimming. The forest service also maintains a number of popular dispersed campsites adjacent to the scenic Lincoln Creek. Camping is not allowed outside of the designated sites for the first 6 miles of the trail, and all the campsites are located within the initial 2.5 miles.

The end of the trail travels through fragile alpine tundra

minish at this point, revealing views of the Lincoln Creek Valley and the rugged peaks enclosing it. Although the taller trees start to recede, low oak scrub grows close to the trail. While not close enough to scratch the sides of your vehicle, the brush may complicate passing oncoming vehicles.

The trail climbs gradually through Lincoln Creek Mining District, revealing wider and more expansive views and crossing through a number of drainage streams and washes. You will come across an old abandoned miners' cabin, among other evidence of the mining era, and finally arrive at Ruby ghost town near the end of the trail. There are several old structures that have collapsed at Ruby, and information boards have been posted to explain some of the local history. There is also a modern cabin that appears to be frequently used at the town site.

Past Ruby the difficulty rating becomes a 5 for the additional complications of large rocks embedded in the road's surface. By picking a sensible line and careful wheel placement through the obstacles, you will not damage your stock high-clearance 4WD. This rating is also for the narrow, loose, and off-camber shelf road that leads

up the abandoned mine workings. The trail ends at the remnants of the Ruby Mine. The mine portals have collapsed, but the roads that branch off and climb the slopes of Red Mountain around the old mine workings are fun to explore.

Current Road Information

White River National Forest
Aspen Ranger District
806 West Hallam
Aspen, CO 81611
(970) 925-3445

Map References

USFS   White River National Forest
Maptech CD:
     Colorado Springs/Ski Areas/Central
Benchmark's *Colorado Road & Recreation
    Atlas,* p. 86
Colorado Atlas & Gazetteer, p. 47
The Roads of Colorado, p. 93
Trails Illustrated, #127 (incomplete)

Route Directions

▼0.0   Zero trip meter and proceed south on FR 106 from Colorado 182, 10 miles southeast of Aspen, through seasonal gate and over bridge over the Roaring Fork River.

View of Lincoln Creek Valley from the Ruby Mine

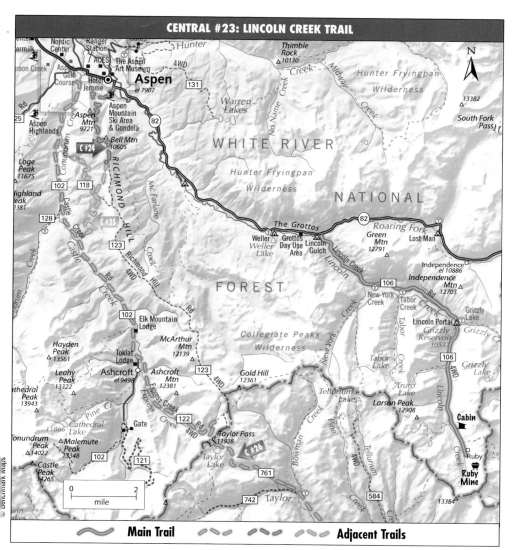

⌇⌇ Main Trail   ⌇⌇⌇   ⌇⌇⌇   ⌇⌇⌇ **Adjacent Trails**

GPS: N39°07.17' W106°41.31'

▼0.4	SO	Lincoln Gulch USFS Campground on right.
▼3.1	SO	New York Creek Trail on right.
		GPS: N39°05.69' W106°39.61'
▼4.1	SO	Tabor Creek Trail on right.
		GPS: N39°05.55' W106°38.66'
▼4.6	SO	Track on left.
▼6.0	SO	Maintenance Road, signposted Authorized Vehicles Only, on left and right; then Grizzly Reservoir on right.
▼6.1	BR	Proceed on FR 106 toward Ruby

ghost town, Grizzly hiking trail, and Portal Campground. Zero trip meter.

GPS: N39°04.77' W106°36.81'

▼0.0		Proceed uphill.
▼0.2	SO	Hiking Grizzly Lake Trailhead on left; then track on left.
▼0.25	SO	Cross over creek.
▼0.3	SO	Portal Campground on right; then seasonal closure gate.
		GPS: N39°04.55' W106°36.75'
▼0.9	SO	Cross through creek.
▼2.0	SO	Cross through creek.
▼2.8	SO	Cross through creek.

▼3.2 SO Frenchman's cabin on left.
GPS: N39°02.17′ W106°37.04′

▼3.3 SO Enter Lincoln Creek Mining District.
▼3.7 BL Road on right to Petroleum and
Anderson Lake hiking trail and old
cabin. Zero trip meter.
GPS: N39°01.86′ W106°36.92′

▼0.0 Proceed southeast on FR 106.
▼0.4 SO Old cabin on left.
▼0.5 SO Track on right to cabin remains (on
private property).
▼0.6 SO Old cabin on right.
GPS: N39°01.39′ W106°36.62′

▼0.7 SO Cross through creek.
▼0.8 SO Modern cabin on left; then town site
of Ruby.
GPS: N39°01.25′ W106°36.55′

▼1.0 TL Road on left. Proceed up narrow,
loose switchback.
▼1.2 Trail ends at collapsed mine portal.
GPS: N39°01.10′ W106°36.15′

Section of rocky, eroded trail enclosed by low shrubs

Collapsed adit and old ore cart tacks of the Ruby Mine

Aspen Mountain Trail

STARTING POINT Intersection of South Original Street and South Ute Avenue in Aspen

FINISHING POINT Sundeck complex and gondola lift station

TOTAL MILEAGE 4.7 miles

UNPAVED MILEAGE 4.6 miles

DRIVING TIME 1 hour

ROUTE ELEVATION 7,946 to 11,210 feet

USUALLY OPEN Mid-May to September

DIFFICULTY RATING 2

SCENIC RATING 10

Special Attractions

- Spectacular views from high on Aspen Mountain of the town of Aspen and the Roaring Fork Valley.
- Chance to explore the famous Aspen Mountain ski slopes in summer.
- Short, interesting trail that begins in downtown Aspen.
- Good trail for hiking, mountain biking, riding ATVs and motorbikes, and frisbee golf.

Intersection showing the entrance to the trail

History

Aspen Mountain Trail begins downtown and climbs Aspen Mountain, traversing its world-famous ski slopes. Although today the town is a destination for the rich and famous, it was originally established in 1879 as a remote mountain mining camp named Ute City. At the peak of its silver production in the late 1880s, Aspen was considered one of the richest centers of silver production in the world. Although the silver crash of 1893 dealt a hard blow to Aspen's silver production, the industry managed to

Chairlift above the switchbacks of Aspen Mountain Trail

A ski lift on Aspen Mountain sits motionless during summer

A fence made from old skis on one of the trail's switchbacks

survive. It was during World War I and the 1920s when the town's mining activity declined significantly. Although Aspen seemed as though it would fall into obscurity, the ski industry revived the town.

The 1928 Olympic gold medal winner in bobsledding, Billy Fiske, discussed popularizing the predominantly European sport of downhill skiing in 1936 with two friends, Thomas and Edward Flynn. The three formed a company and began developing ski facilities in Highland, near Aspen. The first ski run was cleared in 1937, and Aspen held its first official race in 1939. World War II derailed the group's plans when Fiske died fighting in the British Royal Air Force. The Flynns subsequently abandoned the project.

During the war, the U.S. Army's 10th Mountain Division trained as ski troopers at Colorado's Camp Hale, near Leadville, Colorado. After the war, Friedl Pfeifer, a

ATV on Aspen Mountain Trail

member of the 10th Mountain Division, returned to Aspen, determined to shape it into a top-notch ski resort. Pfeifer founded Aspen's first ski school and helped convince Chicago financier Walter Paepcke to invest in Aspen's first chairlift. The lift officially opened on January 12, 1947, with the distinction of being the longest chairlift in the world with the greatest vertical rise. The ski trails were named after the mining areas they crossed—Smugglers, Tourtellotte Park, Little Nell—as an acknowledgment of the town's roots.

Aspen ski resort continued to expand after Aspen Mountain opened in 1947. Three more mountains—Buttermilk (1958), Aspen Highlands (1958), and Snowmass (1968)—helped enhance Aspen's reputation as a premier resort. With further help from Paepcke, the town also developed as a cultural center, attracting tourists year-round.

Frisbee golf course on Aspen Mountain

Description

The entrance to Aspen Mountain Trail is not immediately evident, so be prepared when navigating to the starting point by using a GPS, reading the route directions carefully in advance, or having a passenger navigate. The trail begins at the intersection of South Original Street and South Ute Avenue in downtown Aspen. Proceed southwest through the intersection and take the narrow alleyway that swings around behind a cluster of condominiums. Proceed through the gate at the base of the moun-

View of Aspen from the trail

tain, and the trail immediately begins climbing the ski slopes. This trail, also known as Aspen Mountain Summer Road, is closed temporarily from time to time for maintenance to the ski runs.

The road climbs steeply, but it is an easy drive. Its surface is wide and well maintained with little or no loose or embedded rock depending upon how recently the road has been graded. The water bars across the road in places help prevent erosion, but their deep trenches make high clearance preferred (difficulty rating of 2). Although there are sections of shelf road that can be narrow, passing oncoming vehicles is not an issue because of the numerous pullouts.

Higher and higher the switchbacks ascend the ski hill beneath numerous lifts and the Silver Queen Gondola, revealing expansive views over Aspen and the Roaring Fork Valley. Stands of aspens on the slopes of Aspen Mountain make this a scenic and exciting fall color viewing drive. Popular for a multitude of outdoor recreation activities, including hiking, mountain biking, and riding ATVs and motorbikes, the road is heavily used when it is open for use in summer and fall. Near the trail's end, you will also pass through a frisbee golf course.

The trail concludes at the Sundeck and Silver Queen Gondola Station and the intersection with Central #25: Midnight Mine and Little Annie Trail. The experience of traversing the ski slopes of Aspen Mountain in summer along with the one-of-a-kind views are sure to make this trail a favorite.

Current Road Information

White River National Forest
Aspen Ranger District
806 West Hallam
Aspen, CO 81611
(970) 925-3445

Map References

USFS   White River National Forest

The Sundeck at the end of the trail

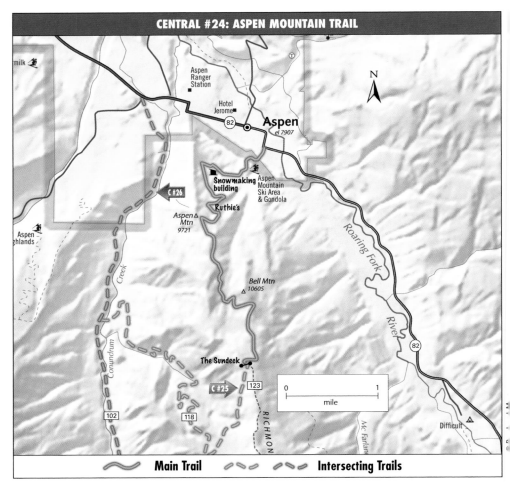

Main Trail   **Intersecting Trails**

Maptech CD:
    Colorado Springs/Ski Areas/Central
Benchmark's *Colorado Road & Recreation
    Atlas*, p. 86
Colorado Atlas & Gazetteer, p. 46
The Roads of Colorado, p. 93
Trails Illustrated, #127

Route Directions

▼**0.0**   From the intersection of South
            Original Street and South Ute Avenue
            in Aspen, zero trip meter and proceed
            southwest through the intersection
            and into the narrow alleyway
            between condominium blocks.
            Proceed up the hill behind buildings.

0.1▲   Trail ends at the intersection of South
            Original Street and South Ute Avenue

in Aspen.

GPS: N39°11.13′ W106°48.98′

▼**0.1**   **SO** Pavement ends. Seasonal gate at
                    gondola. Zero trip meter.

0.0▲   **SO** Proceed down the hill behind the
                    block of condominiums.

GPS: N39°11.11′ W106°49.06′

▼**0.0**   Proceed south on Aspen Mountain
                    Summer Road.

4.6▲   Seasonal gate at gondola; then
                    pavement begins. Zero trip meter.

▼**0.2**   **SO** Aspen Hiking Trail on left.

4.4▲   **SO** Aspen Hiking Trail on right.

▼**0.4**   **BL** Track on right; then proceed straight
                    on past road on left.

4.2▲	BL	Road on right; then proceed straight on past track on left.
▼0.8	SO	Aspen Mountain snowmaking building on left.
3.8▲	SO	Aspen Mountain snowmaking building on right.
		GPS: N39°11.05′ W106°49.59′
▼1.0	SO	Short track on left.
3.6▲	SO	Short track on right.
▼1.7	SO	Track on right to ski lift; then Ruthie's on left.
2.9▲	BR	Track on left to ski lift; then Ruthie's on right.
		GPS: N39°10.61′ W106°49.58′
▼1.8	SO	Ski lift on left.
2.8▲	SO	Ski lift on right.
▼2.3	SO	Gated track on right.
2.3▲	SO	Gated track on left.
▼3.0	SO	Old cabin ruins on right.
1.6▲	SO	Old cabin ruins on left.
▼3.3	TL	Track on right to Bonnie's restaurant.
1.3▲	TR	Track on left to Bonnie's restaurant.
▼3.4	SO	Track on left to ski lift.
1.2▲	SO	Track on right to ski lift.
▼4.5	SO	Track on left to snow equipment building.
0.1▲	SO	Track on right to snow equipment building.
▼4.6		Trail ends at Sundeck complex, gondola lift station, and intersection with Central #25: Midnight Mine and Little Annie Trail.
0.0▲		Trail begins at the intersection with Central #25: Midnight Mine and Little Annie Trail at the Sundeck complex and gondola lift station. Zero trip meter and proceed east on Aspen Mountain Summer Road.
		GPS: N39°09.11′ W106°49.15′

Midnight Mine and Little Annie Trail

STARTING POINT Summit of Aspen Mountain at the intersection of Central #24: Aspen Mountain Trail and FR 118

FINISHING POINT Intersection with Central #26: Taylor Pass Trail (Castle Creek Road or CR 15)

TOTAL MILEAGE 5.6 miles, plus 3.1-mile spur

UNPAVED MILEAGE 5.6 miles, plus 3.1-mile spur

DRIVING TIME 45 minutes

ROUTE ELEVATION 8,960 to 11,211 feet

USUALLY OPEN Mid-May to October

DIFFICULTY RATING 2 for main trail, 1 for spur

SCENIC RATING 8

Special Attractions

- Popular trail for hiking, mountain biking, and riding ATVs and dirt bikes.
- Good snowmobile trail in winter.
- Numerous stands of aspen with spectacular fall color.

A steep switchback with Aspen Highlands ski runs in the distance

History

Midnight Mine and Little Annie Trail passes through a historic mining district that proved less sustainable than the mines north of Aspen Mountain. The area first saw prospectors when a group moved south from Aspen after failing to find silver. They founded the nearby town of Highland, which was located just east of the junction of Castle Creek and Conundrum Creek about midway between the end of the main trail (Midnight Mine Road, FR 118) and the end of the Little Annie Spur on Castle Creek Road (CR 15).

Some good strikes in 1879 drew more prospectors to the town. From a peak of 500 residents, the population of Highland leveled off at about 300 by 1880. Little gold was discovered, although other metals, as well as minerals, were found including galena, silver, copper, lead, carbonates, and iron.

By 1881, Highland's boom years were over, although the town experienced periods of revival in 1889 and 1890. The Hope Mining, Milling, and Leasing Company attempted to reach the Little Annie Mine with an ambitious tunnel project in 1910. The company managed to bore for roughly 3 miles, but the ore found was of inferior quality. The project was halted in the early 1920s.

The first ski run in the Aspen area was opened in Highland through the efforts of Billy Fiske and brothers Thomas and Edward Flynn. Fiske died while flying for the British Royal Air Force during World War II, and the ski experiment was abandoned until Friedl Pfeifer helped open the first chairlift on nearby Aspen Mountain on January 12, 1947.

Description

Midnight Mine and Little Annie Trail begins at the intersection of Central #24: Aspen Mountain Trail and FR 118 at the summit of Aspen Mountain. Bear right at the summit near the gondola station and gate onto FR 118 (FR 123 branches off to the left).

The main trail, Midnight Mine Road (FR 118), is rated a 2 for difficulty because sections of the road are not frequently maintained. For the first half-mile, the trail is narrow and descends through a corridor of trees. Along this short section before reaching the Hidden Treasure Hiking Trailhead, there is little room for passing on-

View from the trail across Castle Creek Valley

coming vehicles. Along the remainder of the length of Midnight Mine Trail, sections of shelf road can be narrow, but passing oncoming vehicles is not an issue because there are plenty of pullouts.

The road descends steeply in sections and switchbacks down the northwest face of Aspen Mountain. Although the trail mostly travels through stands of evergreen and aspen trees, which are quite scenic in fall, breaks in the trees reveal views west across Castle Creek Valley to the impressively steep Aspen Highlands ski runs on the slopes of Lodge Peak.

After about a mile and a half, the Little Annie Spur diverges from the main trail and descends the south slope of Aspen Mountain. The spur is a wide and well-maintained road that switchbacks down into Castle Creek Valley past several tailings piles and old mining claims and ends at the intersection with Central #26: Taylor Pass Trail (Castle Creek Road or CR 15), approximately 4 miles north of Ashcroft ghost town.

Be aware that both the main trail and spur are heavily used for all sorts of outdoor recreation, including mountain biking, hiking, as well as riding dirt bikes and ATVs. The route is also a popular snowmobiling trail in winter with a large parking and staging area located near the lower end of FR 118, less than a mile from the intersection of Central #26: Taylor Pass Trail (Castle Creek Road or CR 15).

Current Road Information
White River National Forest
Aspen Ranger District
806 West Hallam
Aspen, CO 81611
(970) 925-3445

Map References
USFS   White River National Forest
Maptech CD:
    Colorado Springs/Ski Areas/Central
Benchmark's *Colorado Road & Recreation Atlas,* p. 86
Colorado Atlas & Gazetteer, p. 46
The Roads of Colorado, p. 93
Trails Illustrated, #127

Route Directions

▼0.0   At the summit of Aspen Mountain and the intersection with Central #24: Aspen Mountain Trail, zero trip meter and proceed southwest past gondola station through gate and bear right past FR 123 onto FR 118.

1.4▲   Trail ends at summit of Aspen Mountain and intersection with Central #24: Aspen Mountain Trail.
       GPS: N39°09.11' W106°49.15'

▼0.5   **SO** Hidden Treasure Hiking Trail on right.
0.9▲   **SO** Hidden Treasure Hiking Trail on left.

▼1.2   **BL** Road on right.
0.2▲   **BR** Road on left.

▼1.3   **TR** T-intersection.
0.1▲   **TL** Road on left.
       GPS: N39°08.14' W106°49.57'

▼1.4   **SO** Little Annie Spur on left. Zero trip meter.
0.0▲   Proceed northeast on FR 118.
       GPS: N39°08.08' W106°49.57'

Castle Creek

The trail runs through aspen stands

Little Annie Spur

▼0.0 **TL** Proceed southeast on Little Annie Road.

3.1▲ **TL** Spur ends at main trail. Zero trip meter and proceed west on FR 118.

▼1.7 **BR** Intersection signed Lower Hurricane Road (dead end) on left.

1.4▲ **BL** Intersection signed Lower Hurricane Road (dead end) on right.

▼3.1 Spur ends at intersection with Central #26: Taylor Pass Trail (Castle Creek Road or CR 15).

0.0▲ Spur begins at intersection with Central #26: Taylor Pass Trail (Castle Creek Road or CR 15), approximately 4 miles north of Ashcroft ghost town. Zero trip meter and proceed northeast on the Little Annie Spur of Central #25: Midnight Mine and Little Annie Trail.
GPS: N39°06.41′ W106°49.88′

Continuation of Main Trail

▼0.0 Proceed west on FR 118.

4.2▲ **SO** Little Annie Spur on right. Zero trip meter.
GPS: N39°08.08′ W106°49.57′

▼0.1 **SO** Track on right is a cut through to Central #24: Aspen Mountain Trail. Proceed north on FR 118.

4.1▲ **SO** Track on right is a cut through to Central #24: Aspen Mountain Trail.
GPS: N39°08.17′ W106°49.66′

▼1.8 **SO** Tailings piles and old mine workings on left and right.

2.4▲ **SO** Tailings piles and old mine workings on left and right.
GPS: N39°08.89′ W106°49.80′

▼3.4 **SO** Driveway on right.

0.8▲ **SO** Driveway on left.

▼4.0 **SO** Cross over Castle Creek.

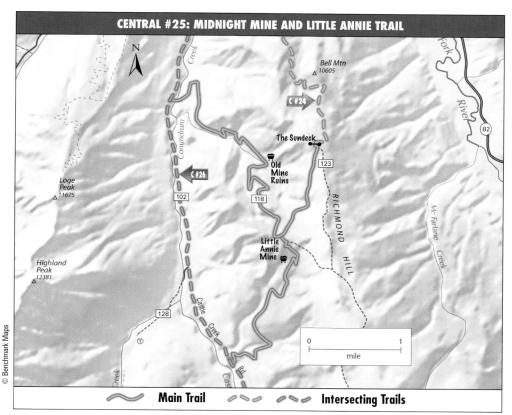

Main Trail ∿∿∿   ⌀⌀⌀ **Intersecting Trails**

0.2▲   **SO**   Cross over Castle Creek.

▼4.2   Trail ends at intersection with Central #26: Taylor Pass Trail, approximately 2.7 miles south of Colorado 82 on Castle Creek Road (CR 15). Midnight Mine signed Rd 15-A.

0.0▲   Trail begins at the intersection with

Central #26: Taylor Pass Trail, approximately 2.7 miles south of Colorado 82 on Castle Creek Road (CR 15). Zero trip meter and proceed southeast on Midnight Mine Road (FR 118), signed Rd 15-A.

GPS: N39°09.63' W106°50.89'

View from the trail across Castle Creek Valley

© Benchmark Maps

Taylor Pass Trail

STARTING POINT Intersection of Central #27: Reno Divide Trail (FR 759) and Taylor River Road (CR/FR 742)

FINISHING POINT Aspen

TOTAL MILEAGE 25.5 miles

UNPAVED MILEAGE 15.0 miles

DRIVING TIME 2.5 hours

ROUTE ELEVATION 7,800 to 11,928 feet

USUALLY OPEN Early July to late September

DIFFICULTY RATING 6

SCENIC RATING 9

Special Attractions

- Very challenging 4WD trail.
- Taylor Lake, an attractive alpine lake near the summit.
- A challenging creek crossing.
- Spectacular summit views.
- Aspen viewing in the fall.

History

Taylor Pass was officially named in 1940 for mining pioneer Jim Taylor, who prospected the area as early as 1860. The pass road was instrumental in making Ashcroft, where the first ore discoveries in the Roaring Fork Valley had been made in 1879, an important early supply center for mining in the area. The road is one of three formed in the wake of the major ore discoveries in the inaccessible Roaring Fork Valley in 1879 and 1880, as interests in Buena Vista, Crested Butte, and Leadville vied for access to the new area.

In 1880, Taylor Pass Road was built by Stevens and Company, owned by H. B. Gillespie, to haul freight into the area from Taylor Park and Buena Vista. Subsequently, the same company ran stagecoaches along the route. In 1881, a telegraph line was run over the pass.

Although the Taylor Pass route to Crested Butte was easier than the Pearl Pass route, which opened in 1882, neither were satisfactory, as freight wagons had to be "snubbed" (that is, taken apart and hauled over in pieces) to cross the pass.

When rich ore was discovered in Aspen in 1880, it became apparent that Aspen was likely to eclipse Ashcroft as the center of the mining activity in the valley. Local business interests were quick to organize the Twin Lakes and Roaring Fork Toll Company to construct a road over what is now known as Independence Pass to the smelters and railhead at Leadville. This road opened in 1881 and proved by far the most successful

Summit of Taylor Pass

of the three. The need for all of the roads passed in 1887, when the Denver & Rio Grande Railroad reached Aspen, followed by the Colorado Midland Railroad the following year.

The township of Dorchester was established well after the initial flurry of activity that resulted from the discoveries in the Roaring Fork Valley. In 1900, gold was discovered in the Italian Mountains, and Dorchester became the main mining camp in the area. Despite initial optimism that swelled the population to more than 1,000, the mines were never very successful. The harsh winters made operating the mines difficult and costly. Nonetheless, some of the mines were operated year-round despite the ever-present danger of snow slides. On one occasion, 15 were reported in a single day. Activity lingered on until World War I, helped by production of lead and zinc, but shortly afterward the mines were closed and the remaining residents moved away.

Ashcroft was settled shortly after silver strikes in 1879. Initially, the town was known as Castle Forks but was soon renamed Ashcroft. In its early days the town served as the gateway to Aspen for travelers coming over Taylor Pass or Cottonwood Pass. Established at about the same period as Aspen, Ashcroft seemed likely to become the more successful of the two. The Ashcroft post office was established in 1880. The town had

Ashcroft today

five hotels, a newspaper, a school, a jail, a doctor, a bowling alley, several stores, and many saloons.

Two factors led to the decline of Ashcroft. One was the completion of Independence Pass, which opened accessibility to nearby Aspen. Then, in 1887, the Denver & Rio Grande completed a railway line into Aspen, which encouraged Ashcroft's residents to migrate to Aspen.

Description
The start of this 4WD route can be reached either from Crested Butte by way of the Central #27: Reno Divide Trail or from

Bridge over Castle Creek near Ashcroft ghost town

Tincup or Buena Vista by connecting with Taylor River Road (CR 742) at Taylor Park Reservoir.

The route commences heading west on CR 742, a well-maintained passenger vehicle road. The turnoff to Taylor Pass (FR 761) is a little more than 2 miles after the town site of Dorchester. From this point, the road is 4WD, although initially it is just a bumpy road through the forest.

At the 1.6-mile point in from CR 742, the trail formerly ran in the creek for about a hundred yards, requiring negotiation of the rocky streambed in water up to bumper

The trail where it enters White River National Forest

level. However, the forest service rerouted the creek and leveled the road somewhat. This section had been the most difficult part of the road, particularly when water obscured large boulders.

A couple of miles farther on, after reaching timberline, the road splits into a number of alternative routes past Taylor Lake and up the final ascent to the summit. The one detailed in the directions below is the easiest and most scenic. It proceeds around the southern and western sides of Taylor Lake.

From the summit of the pass, you enter the White River National Forest. Two roads lead down to Aspen: Express Creek Road and Richmond Hill Road (FR 123). The directions follow the quicker and easier Express Creek Road via the ghost town of Ashcroft.

The initial descent is a steep, very narrow shelf road, and the gravel road surface

Narrow, rocky section of trail climbing to Taylor Pass from the north

can be loose and slippery. We recommend that you engage first or second gear in low range to avoid locking the brakes and proceed slowly. The steep descent, in two stages, lasts for about half a mile. The views from the summit and during the descent along Express Creek are magnificent. At timberline, the road enters a dense aspen forest as it continues to descend to Castle Creek Road, about one-quarter of a mile north of the ghost town of Ashcroft.

In 1974, the Aspen Historical Society leased Ashcroft's town site from the U.S. Forest Service in order to preserve the historic remains. Although some of the buildings you see there today are original, others were brought in to replace deteriorated ones so that tourists can safely explore the resurrected ghost town.

From this point, the road is paved all the way into Aspen.

Narrow, steep shelf section near the pass

A view of Taylor Lake from the pass

The refreshing waters of Taylor Lake in midsummer

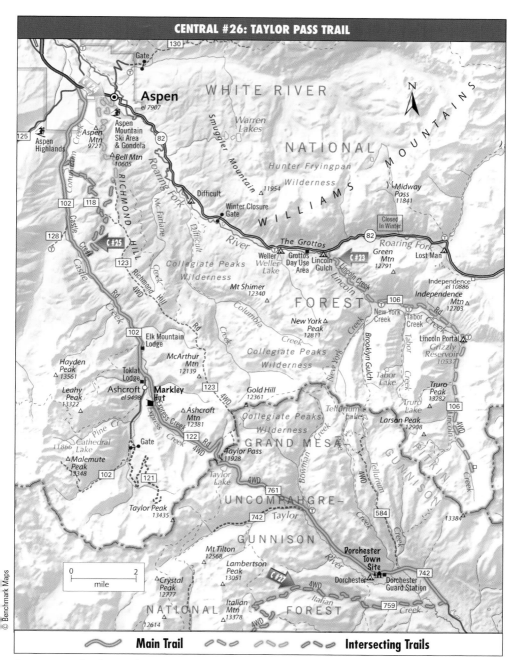

Main Trail ~~~ **Intersecting Trails**

© Benchmark Maps

Current Road Information

Grand Mesa, Uncompahgre & Gunnison
National Forests
Gunnison Ranger District
216 North Colorado
Gunnison, CO 81230
(970) 641-0471

Map References

USFS   Gunnison National Forest; White
River National Forest
Maptech CD:
Colorado Springs/Ski Areas/Central
Benchmark's *Colorado Road & Recreation
Atlas*, p. 86

Colorado Atlas & Gazetteer, pp. 46, 59
The Roads of Colorado, p. 93
Trails Illustrated, #127, #131

Route Directions

▼0.0   At intersection of Central #27: Reno Divide Trail (FR 759) and Taylor River Road (CR/FR 742), zero trip meter and proceed northwest. This intersection is 11 miles north of Taylor Park Reservoir. Note: Sign here reads "Dead end."

5.6▲   End at intersection with Central #27: Reno Divide Trail (FR 759).
     GPS: N 38°57.24' W 106°37.26'

▼1.8   SO   Tellurium Creek Road on right.
3.8▲   SO   Tellurium Creek Road on left.

▼2.4   SO   Track on left to Old Dorchester Guard Station.
3.2▲   SO   Track on right to Old Dorchester Guard Station.

▼2.6   SO   USFS Dorchester Campground turnoff on left.
3.0▲   SO   USFS Dorchester Campground turnoff on right.

▼2.9   SO   Fishing Access Road on left.
2.7▲   SO   Fishing Access Road on right.

▼5.5   SO   Cattle guard.
0.1▲   SO   Cattle guard.

▼5.6   TR   Onto Taylor Pass Road (FR 761). Zero trip meter.
0.0▲   Proceed on FR 742.
     GPS: N 38°59.73' W 106°42.17'

▼0.0   Proceed onto FR 761.
3.4▲   TL   Intersection: FR 761 and Taylor River Road (FR 742). Zero trip meter.

▼1.4   SO   Cross through creek.
2.0▲   SO   Cross through creek.

▼1.5   BR   Fork in road.
1.9▲   BL   Fork in road.

▼1.6   SO   Road follows the path of the old creek

bed. Note: In the summer of 1997, the creek was diverted from this section to the east side of the road.

1.8▲   SO   Road follows the path of the old creek bed.

▼2.9   SO   Cross through creek.
0.5▲   SO   Cross through creek.

▼3.4   TL   Fork in road with sign to Taylor Pass Divide Road. 761.1A on left; FR 761.1 to the right. Zero trip meter.
0.0▲   Proceed on FR 761.
     GPS: N 39°01.04' W 106°44.92'

▼0.0   Proceed along 761.1A.
1.4▲   TR   Fork in road. Zero trip meter.

▼0.1   SO   Taylor Lake on right.
1.3▲   SO   Taylor Lake on left.

▼0.5   SO   Ponds on left.
0.9▲   SO   Ponds on right.

▼0.6   BR   Fork in road. Follow sign to Taylor Pass.
0.8▲   SO   Follow sign to "Taylor Pass Road #761, 1 mile."
     GPS: N 39°00.71' W 106°45.42'

▼0.7   SO   Cross through creek.
0.7▲   SO   Cross through creek.

▼1.4   BL   Taylor Pass. Zero trip meter.
0.0▲   BR   Proceed from summit on the track to the southwest, which descends from the left-hand side of the "Taylor Pass" sign, entering Gunnison National Forest.
     GPS: N 39°01.21' W 106°45.32'

▼0.0   BL   Proceed on the track (FR 122) that descends from the right-hand side of the "Taylor Pass" sign, entering White River National Forest. Follow Express Creek Road (FR 122) toward Ashcroft.
4.6▲   BR   Taylor Pass. Zero trip meter.

▼0.6   SO   Bridge over Express Creek.
4.0▲   SO   Bridge over Express Creek.

▼2.2　SO　Cross through creek.
2.4▲　SO　Cross through creek.

▼2.7　SO　Track on left to Markley Hut.
1.9▲　SO　Track on right to Markley Hut.
　　　　　GPS: N 39°02.21′ W 106°47.26′

▼4.0　SO　Cross through creek.
0.6▲　SO　Cross through creek.

▼4.2　SO　Private track on left.
0.4▲　SO　Private track on right.

▼4.4　SO　Bridge over Castle Creek.
0.2▲　SO　Bridge over Castle Creek.

▼4.6　TR　Intersection with Castle Creek Road. The restored ghost town of Ashcroft is just to the left. Zero trip meter.
0.0▲　　　Continue toward Taylor Pass on Express Creek Road.
　　　　　GPS: N 39°03.63′ W 106°48.03′

▼0.0　　　Proceed north along Castle Creek Road toward Aspen.
3.8▲　TL　Intersection: Castle Creek Road (FR 102) and Express Creek Road (CR 15C). The restored ghost town of Ashcroft is 0.4 miles south. Zero trip meter.

▼3.8　SO　Central #25: Midnight Mine and Little Annie Trail spur on right. Zero trip meter.
0.0▲　　　Proceed south on Castle Creek Road.
　　　　　GPS: N39°06.41′ W106°49.88′

▼0.0　　　Proceed north on Castle Creek Road toward Aspen.
4.0▲　SO　Central #25: Midnight Mine and Little Annie Trail spur on left. Zero trip meter.

▼4.0　SO　Central #25: Midnight Mine and Little Annie Trail on right. Zero trip meter.
0.0▲　　　Proceed south on Castle Creek Road.
　　　　　GPS: N39°09.63′ W106°50.89′

▼0.0　　　Proceed north on Castle Creek Road toward Aspen.

2.7▲　SO　Central #25: Midnight Mine and Little Annie Trail on left. Zero trip meter.

▼2.7　TR　Intersection with CR 13. Then almost immediately is the intersection with Colorado 82. Aspen is to the right. End of trail.
0.0▲　　　At the intersection of Colorado 82 and CR 13 in Aspen, zero trip meter and proceed southwest. Almost immediately turn left onto Castle Creek Road.
　　　　　GPS: N 39°11.74′ W 106°50.39′

The rocky section on the southern end of the trail

Reno Divide Trail

STARTING POINT Intersection of Colorado 135 and Cement Creek Road (FR 740)

FINISHING POINT Intersection of Central #26: Taylor Pass Trail (CR/FR 742) and Italian Creek Road (FR 759)

TOTAL MILEAGE 26.3 miles

UNPAVED MILEAGE 25.8 miles

DRIVING TIME 4 hours

ROUTE ELEVATION 8,595 to 12,015 feet

USUALLY OPEN Mid-June to mid-October

DIFFICULTY RATING 4

SCENIC RATING 8

Special Attractions

- Very scenic, varied, and moderately difficult 4WD trail.
- Access from Crested Butte to Taylor Pass.
- Good backcountry camping sites.

History

In 1879, prospectors crossed Pearl Pass into the Roaring Fork Valley and discovered ore near Ashcroft. In the following year, more rich ore was discovered near Aspen. By this time, the area was teeming with miners.

In 1880, a company was formed to build a road over Independence Pass from Leadville to Aspen in order to provide access to Leadville's railhead and smelters. At the same time, the pack trail over Taylor Pass, which had been used by prospectors since the previous year, was upgraded to a wagon road to provide access from Taylor Park and Buena Vista. The opening of Taylor Pass Road spurred the desire of those in Crested Butte to gain access to the new mining area. The road over Reno Divide was built to forge a stage route connection to Taylor Pass Road.

The Denver & Rio Grande Railroad spur reached Crested Butte from Gunnison in 1881. By that time, Aspen was the center of a silver boom, following the first rich ore discoveries in the Roaring Fork Valley in 1879 and the further major discoveries the following year. Crested Butte was only 24 miles from Aspen and 16 miles from Ashcroft, and the railroad was determined to expand access to its new railhead from the Roaring Fork Valley. This prompted the development of Pearl Pass Road in 1882. Although more direct, this route was extremely difficult, requiring wagons to be snubbed over the pass (that is, taken apart

Aspens along an easy section of road near the beginning of the trail

The trail following beside Cement Creek

and hauled over in pieces). Pearl Pass Road operated for only three years.

The toll road over Independence Pass from Leadville opened in 1881 and proved to be far more successful than either of the southern routes. With the arrival in Aspen of the Denver & Rio Grande Railroad in 1887 and the Colorado Midland Railroad in 1888, the two southern roads became obsolete.

Description

This route provides access from Crested Butte to Taylor Pass Road, which leads across the Continental Divide into Aspen. It provides an alternative 4WD route to the more difficult Pearl Pass.

The route starts at the intersection of Colorado 135 and Cement Creek Road (FR 740), about 7 miles south of Crested Butte. For the first 9 miles of the route, Cement Creek Road travels alongside the creek in a very picturesque setting. The valley alternates between very wide sections and very narrow sections: The walls close in to form a canyon just wide enough for the

creek and the road to squeeze through and then open up to panoramic views. The road through this section is easily traveled by a 2WD vehicle.

Immediately after the turn onto FR 759, the road starts to climb. Although there are some sections of shelf road, they are lined with trees and are not intimidating. The surface of the road is sound and is maintained by the Gunnison 4-Wheelers Club.

After passing through the gate at the 3.6-mile point on FR 759, the road begins to deteriorate. For about the next 4 miles, the road is rough and can be very muddy after rain. Even under normal conditions, the road has muddy sections scarred with potholes, but it should not present too great an obstacle for a 4WD vehicle. This is the most difficult part of the journey.

Shortly after passing above timberline, you will encounter a steep-sided but narrow, small creek crossing along an off-camber section of the track. Having negotiated this crossing in a Suburban, we can attest to it being passable in a full size SUV.

The road flattens out and travels along

an open alpine ridge past the Stewart and Star Mines. The views of the Italian Creek Valley and the Taylor River Valley are spectacular.

As the road descends, it is a bit rough, rocky, and muddy in sections, but the surface is generally sound and should not pose any problems under normal conditions.

From the gate just after the Lilly Pond Trailhead, the road (in dry conditions) is easily navigable in a car. However, after rain it can be very muddy. There are numerous backcountry camping spots along this section.

Current Road Information

Grand Mesa, Uncompahgre & Gunnison National Forests
Gunnison Ranger District
216 North Colorado
Gunnison, CO 81230
(970) 641-0471

Italian Creek Road

Map References

USFS   Gunnison National Forest
Maptech CD:
    Colorado Springs/Ski Areas/Central
Benchmark's *Colorado Road & Recreation*
    Atlas, p. 86
Colorado Atlas & Gazetteer, pp. 58, 59
The Roads of Colorado, pp. 93, 109
Trails Illustrated, #131

Route Directions

▼0.0		At intersection of Colorado 135 and Cement Creek Road (FR 740), zero trip meter and proceed east.
8.8▲		End at intersection with Colorado 135.
		GPS: N 38°48.27' W 106°53.39'
▼0.2	SO	Cross bridge.
8.6▲	SO	Cross bridge.
▼0.5	SO	Unpaved.
8.3▲	SO	Paved.
▼1.7	SO	Farris Creek Trailhead on left.
7.1▲	SO	Farris Creek Trailhead on right.
▼3.2	SO	Track to USFS Summer Home Group on right.
5.6▲	SO	Track to USFS Summer Home Group on left.
▼3.5	SO	USFS Cement Creek Campground.
5.3▲	SO	USFS Cement Creek Campground.
▼4.5	SO	Seasonal closure gate.
4.3▲	SO	Seasonal closure gate.
▼7.7	SO	Bridge.
1.1▲	SO	Bridge.
▼7.9	SO	Cross over Cement Creek.
0.9▲	SO	Cross over Cement Creek.
▼8.6	SO	Cross through small creek.
0.2▲	SO	Cross through small creek.
▼8.8	BR	Intersection on right with FR 759 (Italian Creek Road) toward Reno Divide. Cement Creek Road continues straight ahead. Zero trip meter.

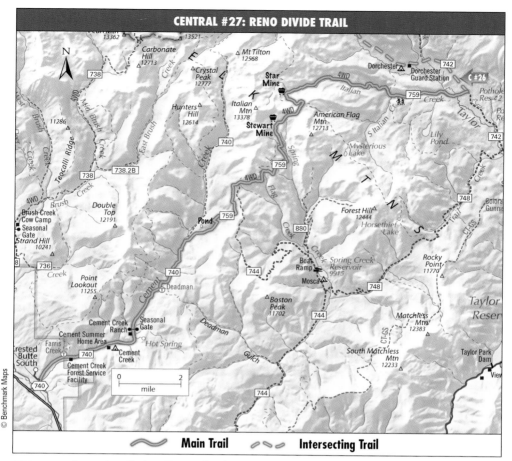

~~~ **Main Trail**   ∽∾ **Intersecting Trail**

0.0▲		Proceed south along Cement Creek Road.
		GPS: N 38°53.07' W 106°47.42'

▼0.0		Proceed along FR 759.
9.2▲	**TL**	Intersection. Italian Creek Road and Cement Creek Road. Zero trip meter.

▼1.3	**SO**	Cabin ruins on left.
7.9▲	**SO**	Cabin ruins on right.

▼3.6	**SO**	Track on right. Gate. Track on left. Proceed through gate (leaving it as you found it). Follow FR 759.
5.6▲	**SO**	Track on right. Proceed through gate (leaving it as you found it). Follow FR 759. Track on left.
		GPS: N 38°54.46' W 106°45.76'

▼5.4	**SO**	Cross through small, muddy creek.

3.8▲	**SO**	Cross through small, muddy creek.

▼5.7	**SO**	Cross through small creek.
3.5▲	**SO**	Cross through small creek.

▼6.5	**SO**	Pond on left and track on right (closed to motorized vehicles).
2.7▲	**SO**	Track on left (closed to motorized vehicles). Pond on right.

▼6.9	**SO**	Cross through creek.
2.3▲	**SO**	Cross through creek.

▼7.5	**BR**	Track on left.
1.6▲	**BL**	Track on the right is a difficult alternative track that rejoins the road at the gate at mileage point 5.6 ahead.
		GPS: N 38°55.97 W 106°44.36'

▼**7.7**   **SO** Cross through creek with steep sides.
1.5▲   **SO** Cross through creek with steep sides.

▼**7.8**   **SO** Cross through small creek.
1.3▲   **SO** Cross through small creek.

▼**8.1**   **SO** Stewart Mine and track to it on left.
1.1▲   **SO** Stewart Mine and track to it on right.

▼**8.4**   **SO** Stewart Mine cabin ruins on right.
0.8▲   **SO** Stewart Mine cabin ruins on left.

▼**8.8**   **BL** Track on right.
0.4▲   **BR** Track on left.
          GPS: N 38°56.54' W 106°43.59'

▼**8.9**   **BL** Fork in road. Right fork leads to
                   overlook and returns to main road in
                   short distance.
0.3▲   **BR** Fork in road. Left fork leads to
                   overlook and returns to main road in
                   short distance.

▼**9.2**   **BL** Fork in road. Star Trailhead on the
                   right. Zero trip meter at sign.
0.0▲   Continue along main track.
          GPS: N 38°56.87' W 106°43.41'

▼**0.0**   Proceed toward Taylor Road.
8.3▲   **BR** Fork in road. Star Trailhead on the left.
                   Zero trip meter at sign.

▼**0.8**   **SO** Track on right.
7.4▲   **SO** Track on left.

▼**1.0 SO/BL** Cabin ruins on left. Cross through
                   small creek; then bear left past a
                   track on the right.
7.3▲ **BR/SO** Track on the left. Cross through a
                   small creek; then cabin ruins on right.

▼**1.1**   **SO** Cross through two small creeks.
7.2▲   **SO** Cross through two small creeks.

▼**1.2**   **BL** Mine ruins on right on private
                   property. Follow sign toward Taylor
                   Park.
7.1▲   **BR** Mine ruins on left. Follow sign to
                   Cement Creek.

▼**1.4**   **TR** Intersection. Private road on the left.
6.9▲   **TL** Private road is straight ahead.

▼**2.0**   **SO** Track on right. Follow sign to Taylor
                   Park.
6.3▲   **SO** Follow sign to Cement Creek.

Creek crossing near Stewart Mine

▼2.7	SO	Cross through creek.
5.6▲	SO	Cross through creek.
▼4.6	SO	Cross through creek.
3.7▲	SO	Cross through creek.
▼5.3	SO	Dorchester walking trail on left.
3.0▲	SO	Dorchester walking trail on right.
▼5.5	SO	Lilly Pond walking trail on right.
2.8▲	SO	Lilly Pond walking trail on left.

GPS: N 38°57.20′ W 106°40.17′

▼5.6	SO	Gate.
2.7▲	SO	Gate.
▼7.8	SO	Cross bridge over Taylor River.
0.5▲	SO	Cross bridge over Taylor River.
▼8.3		End at intersection with Taylor River Road (CR/FR 742). Taylor Reservoir is to the right and Central #26: Taylor Pass Trail is to the left.
0.0▲		At intersection of Taylor River Road (CR/FR 742) and Italian Creek Road (FR 759), zero trip meter and proceed west along Italian Creek Road.

GPS: N 38°57.24′ W 106°37.26′

A rustic signpost and cabin in the distance

Schofield Pass and Devil's Punchbowl Trail

STARTING POINT Mount Crested Butte
FINISHING POINT Marble
TOTAL MILEAGE 21.2 miles
UNPAVED MILEAGE 20.1 miles
DRIVING TIME 3.5 hours
ROUTE ELEVATION 8,000 to 10,707 feet
USUALLY OPEN Late July to mid-September
DIFFICULTY RATING 6
SCENIC RATING 10

Special Attractions

- Famous and dangerous 4WD trail along an old stagecoach route.
- Historic mill on Crystal River.
- Ghost towns of Gothic and Crystal and town site of Schofield.
- Can be combined with Kebler Pass Road (CR 12) to form a loop.

History

Schofield Pass was named for Judge B. F. Schofield, who founded the town of Schofield. Ute Indians used the pass, and they led the first white men across it. Prospectors traveled the pass frequently

Gothic

Emerald Lake

Waterfall near Schofield town site

during the 1870s, although the first big strikes in the area did not occur until around 1880. In the mid-1870s, the Hayden survey party crossed Schofield Pass and plotted it on its map.

By the early 1880s, the cities of Marble, Crystal, Schofield, and Gothic were all at their peak. The pass road was heavily used but was never improved beyond a rough, narrow wagon road. Nonetheless, a stage ran from Crested Butte to Crystal for a number of years. This small road's political apogee came when it was traveled by President Ulysses S. Grant during his visit to many of the mining camps in the area, accompanied by John Routt, the last appointed governor of the territory and the first elected governor of the state.

The township of Gothic was established in 1879 with the discovery of gold and silver ores in the area. Within four months, nearly 200 buildings had been erected, including a hotel, three stores, a butcher shop, a barbershop, and a saloon. Millions of dollars' worth of gold and silver ores were extracted from the hills. At its peak, the bustling mining city had a population of around 8,000.

Gothic gained a reputation as a very wild town with lots of drinking, gambling, and prostitution. When, on his trip through the area in 1880, Ulysses S. Grant asked to see a wild mining town, he was shown Gothic. He reportedly drove his own stage into town and arrived to a riotous celebration.

Gothic's first mayor was elected by a roll of dice between two men. The winner was Garwood Judd, one of the town's saloon keepers. After gold and silver played out, fortunes receded quickly; by 1884, most of the residents had left town. Garwood Judd remained there by himself until his death in 1930, earning himself the reputation of "the man who stayed." He was proud of his title and even nailed a plaque engraved with the phrase over his door. His ashes were scattered around the town.

Schofield was platted in August 1879 by B. F. Schofield and his party. Prospectors discovered silver in the area as early as 1872, but their fear of Indians deferred permanent settlement for several years. A smelter was built in 1880 and a mill in 1881. By 1882, the town had a population of about 400 and the usual amenities of a hotel, a restaurant (whose staff had trouble boiling water because of the altitude), a

A useful reminder to check your brakes

general store, a blacksmith shop, and a barbershop.

When former president Ulysses S. Grant and former governor Routt visited Schofield, the residents of Schofield

Crossing Crystal River above the treacherous section of the trail

thought that if they could sell shares in one of the local mines to Grant, they could boast that the president owned a mine in Schofield. When that failed, they tried to unsuccessfully "lose" shares to Grant in a poker game—to no avail. Finally, they brought out a big barrel of whiskey, hoping to get Grant drunk and just give him the mining shares! Needless to say, Grant was impressed with Schofield's hospitality, but it is unclear whether he ended up with any claim.

Unfortunately, the ore found around Schofield was poor in quality. Although miners did find some good galena, the inaccessible location and high transportation costs drained off their profits. These factors, coupled with the immense problems of eight-month winters dumping as much as 40 feet of snow, led to the demise of Schofield. The post office closed in 1885.

Crystal began as a silver mining camp in 1880. Early prospectors named the town after the crystal-like quartz they found along the creek. In the mid-1880s, Crystal had a population of about 500, a newspaper, a general store, many private homes, several saloons, and the Crystal Club (a men's club), which still stands in town.

The trail to Crystal was arduous, leading from Crested Butte over Schofield Pass. The difficulty of traversing this trail made it economically impossible to transport anything but the richest ores in or out of Crystal. Eventually, a better road was constructed, connecting the town with Carbondale.

Although Crystal survived the silver crash of 1893, its population was reduced to a small number of residents. The much-photographed Crystal Mill remains standing on the outskirts of town along the Crystal River. The mill was built by G. C. Eaton

The start of the infamous section above the Crystal River

An embedded rock that makes the road even more hazardous

and supplied power to the local mines. A waterwheel turned an air compressor to supply air for drilling and power for a stamp mill and sawmill.

Special Note on the Difficulty of This Road

The road through Crystal River Canyon down to the area known as the Devil's Punchbowl is known as one of the most dangerous 4WD roads in Colorado. The road's reputation is well deserved in light of the alarming number of fatalities that have occurred on it. The most tragic was in 1970, when seven members of one family perished when their Suburban plunged from the shelf road down a 200-foot drop-off and into the river. Many accidents have taken additional lives in the years since. Seven vehicles slipped off the road in the summer of 1997, and at least one of these accidents resulted in fatalities.

It is hard to dispute statistics like these, but most experienced four-wheelers will be puzzled by such a record. Certainly the road is very narrow and drops off precipitously into the river, but the surface is sound, and the road is no narrower, nor the drop more frightening, than that of many other 4WD roads in the state. Undoubtedly most accidents here must be caused by a combination of factors: the driver's inexperience, the onset of fear when committed beyond the point of turning back, and perhaps even carelessness or a failure to appreciate the very small margin for error.

Another potential hazard is caused by having to cross the river immediately before starting down the canyon. Even in late summer, the water is likely to be bumper deep and will thoroughly soak your brakes. Therefore, follow the recommendation of the large sign erected by the forest service and check that your brakes are working properly before proceeding down the canyon. Also, do not be tempted to get out of your vehicle halfway down the canyon to take a photo and leave your vehicle reliant on the Park gear position.

Dead Horse Mill on the Crystal River

As is the case with all the more difficult roads in this book, you should not attempt this route until you have traveled many other less difficult roads and are certain that you will not become flustered by the steep drop-off only a foot or so from your wheels. Less experienced drivers are well advised not to attempt this route in a full-sized vehicle.

In spite of the risk it involves, this is a very rewarding trail. If you decide to give it a go, remember to take it very slowly and carefully.

Description

The route starts in the ski resort of Mount Crested Butte. It follows a well-maintained gravel road to Gothic, now the home of the Rocky Mountain Biological Survey, which studies the wide variety of regional flora and fauna. A few well-preserved old buildings still stand. Set in a beautiful area, the town is experiencing a revival as a summer tourist and residential area.

The summit of Schofield Pass lies beyond Emerald Lake. The low, wooded summit does not offer the views that are associated with most pass summits. The road to the pass is suitable for a passenger car. From that point on until about 2 miles out of Marble, stream crossings and rocky sections necessitate a high-clearance vehicle.

About a mile after the summit, the town site of Schofield lies in an open meadow beside the South Fork of the Crystal River. About a mile farther, you cross through a wide section of the South Fork of the Crystal River. In the later part of summer, this is unlikely to be more than bumper deep, but the streambed contains some large rocks.

Upon exiting the river, the road curves and immediately starts the narrow, steep descent down Crystal River Canyon. Shortly after commencing the downhill run, you are confronted with a large, embedded rock in the center of the road. You have the choice of squeezing past on the side of the rock wall or on the side of the drop-off. The road suffers from snow and rock slides, and it is not unusual to find it impassable—or at least requiring some clearance work.

At the bottom of the canyon are the Devil's Punchbowl and, fewer than 2 miles farther, the township of Crystal. The powerhouse overhanging the Crystal River, called the Dead Horse Mill or the Crystal Mill, is about a quarter of a mile past Crystal on the left. The road continues past the very scenic Beaver Lake and on into Marble.

Although most years this road is open for about eight weeks, sometimes the snow does not melt and the road is closed all summer.

Current Road Information

White River National Forest
Sopris Ranger District
620 Main Street
Carbondale, CO 81623
(970) 963-2266

Map References

USFS   Gunnison National Forest; White River National Forest
Maptech CD:
      Colorado Springs/Ski Areas/Central; Grand Junction/Western Slope
Benchmark's *Colorado Road & Recreation Atlas,* p. 85
Colorado Atlas & Gazetteer, pp. 45, 46, 58
The Roads of Colorado, p. 92
Trails Illustrated, #128, #131, #133

Route Directions

▼0.0		In Mt. Crested Butte, where the Grand Butte Hotel walkway crosses over Gothic Road, zero trip meter and proceed north along Gothic Road.
10.6▲		End in Mt. Crested Butte town center.
		GPS: N 38°53.97' W 106°57.97'
▼1.1	SO	End of pavement. Follow main road.
9.5▲	SO	Paved. Follow main road.
		GPS: N 38°54.77' W 106°57.74'
▼1.7	SO	Cattle guard. Enter National Forest (FR 317) and proceed toward Gothic.
8.9▲	SO	Leave National Forest and proceed toward Crested Butte. Cattle guard.
▼3.3	SO	Cattle guard.
7.3	SO	Cattle guard.

▼4.7   **SO** Bridge over East River.
5.9▲   **SO** Bridge over East River.

▼5.0   **SO** Bridge.
5.6▲   **SO** Bridge.

▼5.1   **SO** Gothic ghost town: general store and visitor center.
5.4▲   **SO** Gothic ghost town.

▼5.7   **SO** Track on right to Judd Falls, Trailriders, and Cooper Creek

Trailheads.

4.9▲   **SO** Track on left to Judd Falls, Trailriders, and Cooper Creek Trailheads.

▼6.5   **SO** Turnoff to USFS Avery Peak Picnic Grounds on right.
4.1▲   **SO** Turnoff to USFS Avery Peak Picnic Grounds on left.

▼6.7   **SO** Seasonal gate and bridge.
3.9▲   **SO** Bridge and seasonal gate.

▼7.0   **SO** USFS Gothic Campground on left;

Lizard Lake

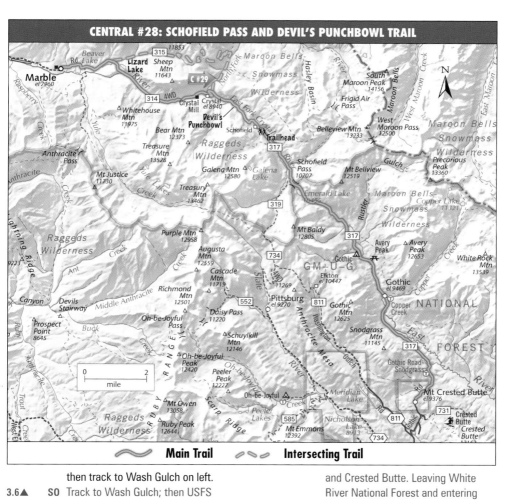

~~~ Main Trail   ⌒⌒ Intersecting Trail

		then track to Wash Gulch on left.
3.6▲	SO	Track to Wash Gulch; then USFS Gothic Campground on right.
▼7.6	SO	Track to Rustler Gulch on right.
3.0▲	SO	Track to Rustler Gulch on left.
▼8.0	SO	Track on left.
2.6▲	SO	Track on right.
▼8.8	SO	Track on left.
1.8▲	SO	Track on right.
▼9.8	SO	Track on left to Emerald Lake.
0.8▲	SO	Track on right to Emerald Lake.
▼10.6	SO	Schofield Pass summit. Paradise Basin track on left; trailhead to Gothic on right. Zero trip meter.
0.0▲		Continue on main road toward Gothic

		and Crested Butte. Leaving White River National Forest and entering Gunnison National Forest on FR 317.
		GPS: N 39°00.93' W 107°02.80'
▼0.0		Continue straight ahead toward Marble. Leaving Gunnison National Forest and entering White River National Forest.
4.4▲	SO	Schofield Pass summit. Paradise Basin track on right; trailhead to Gothic on left. Zero trip meter.
▼0.7	SO	Baroni Mine portal on right; then cross through creek.
3.7▲	SO	Cross through creek. Baroni Mine portal on left.
▼1.1	SO	Track on left to North Pole Basin.
3.3▲	SO	Track on right to North Pole Basin.

▼1.5   SO   Bridge over South Fork of Crystal River.

2.9▲   SO   Bridge over South Fork of Crystal River.

▼1.7   SO   Tracks on right.

2.7▲   SO   Tracks on left.

▼2.3   SO   Track on left to waterfall just off the road. Cross bridge with waterfall on right.

2.1▲   SO   Waterfall on left; cross bridge. Track on right to waterfall just off the road.

▼2.5   SO   Cross over river.

1.9▲   SO   Cross over river.

▼2.7   SO   Cross through wide creek.

1.7▲   SO   Cross through wide creek.

    GPS: N 39°02.70' W 107°04.36'

▼2.8   SO   Tight squeeze past one large rock.

1.6▲   SO   Tight squeeze past one large rock.

▼2.8-3.2 SO   Very narrow and rocky descent.

1.2-1.6▲ SO   Very narrow and rocky ascent.

▼3.2   SO   Narrow bridge over Crystal River.

1.2▲   SO   Narrow bridge over Crystal River.

    GPS: N 39°02.99' W 107°04.67'

▼4.4   BL   Intersection. Right goes to Central #29: Lead King Basin Trail. Zero trip meter.

0.0▲   Continue on main track toward Schofield Pass, Gothic, and Crested Butte.

    GPS: N 39°03.56' W 107°05.77'

▼0.0   Continue toward Crystal on FR 314.

4.3▲   BR   Intersection. Left goes to Central #29: Lead King Basin Trail. Zero trip meter.

▼0.5   SO   Crystal township.

3.8▲   SO   Crystal township.

▼0.6   SO   Cross over Crystal River.

3.7▲   SO   Cross over Crystal River.

▼0.7   SO   Crystal Mill on left.

3.6▲   SO   Crystal Mill on right.

    GPS: N 39°03.56' W 107°06.22'

▼2.9   SO   Track on left.

1.4▲   SO   Track on right.

▼3.9   SO   Lizard Lake on right.

0.4▲   SO   Lizard Lake on left.

    GPS: N 39°04.19' W 107°09.21'

▼4.2   SO   Bridge over Lost Trail Creek.

0.1▲   SO   Bridge over Lost Trail Creek.

▼4.3   BL   Intersection with Central #29: Lead King Basin Trail (FR 315) on right. Left to Marble. Zero trip meter.

0.0▲   Continue along main road.

    GPS: N 39°04.49' W 107°09.50'

▼0.0   Proceed toward Marble.

1.9▲   BR   Intersection with Central #29: Lead King Basin Trail (FR 315) on left. Zero trip meter.

▼0.6   SO   Road on right.

1.3▲   SO   Road on left.

▼1.2   SO   Beaver Lake on left.

0.7▲   SO   Beaver Lake on right.

▼1.5   TL   Stop sign.

0.4▲   TR   Stop sign.

▼1.6   TR   Intersection.

0.3▲   TL   Intersection.

▼1.7   SO   Bridge.

0.2▲   SO   Bridge.

▼1.8   TL/TR   Onto 1st Street; then right onto State Street.

0.1▲   TL/TR   Onto 1st Street; then right onto Main Street (CR 3/FR 315).

▼1.9   End in front of Marble Community Church on State Street.

0.0▲   On State Street in Marble, go to the Marble Community Church. Zero trip meter and proceed east.

    GPS: N 39°04.25' W 107°11.30'

Lead King Basin Trail

STARTING POINT Intersection of Central #28: Schofield Pass and Devil's Punchbowl Trail (FR 314) and FR 315

FINISHING POINT Intersection of FR 315 and FR 314

TOTAL MILEAGE 7.7 miles

UNPAVED MILEAGE 7.7 miles

DRIVING TIME 1.75 hours

ROUTE ELEVATION 8,592 to 10,800 feet

USUALLY OPEN Late July to mid-September

DIFFICULTY RATING 5

SCENIC RATING 8

Special Attractions

■ Abundant wildflowers in early summer.
■ The challenging, narrow, and rocky section at the east end of the route.

Description

This trail is a side road of Schofield Pass Road. It commences 3.7 miles west of Crystal township and 1.9 miles east of Marble and finishes 0.5 miles east of Crystal township.

Initially, FR 315 ascends from the road running alongside the Crystal River (FR 314) through pine and aspen forest. The road is bumpy with embedded rock and drainage channels cut across it but is not difficult in dry conditions. Sections of black soil can become very boggy after rain.

A series of switchbacks is encountered in an uphill section, but the surface is firm, and the only difficulty is caused by wheel ruts worn by other vehicles.

At about the 7-mile point the road gets considerably more difficult, especially in a full-size vehicle, as you follow the creek cascading down into the valley. Clearances between trees and rocks are tight. The route is more difficult if attempted from east to west rather than in the direction we have described.

The area is justly famous for the wildflowers that carpet the basin in July and August, and numerous aspen provide color later in the season.

Current Road Information

White River National Forest
Sopris Ranger District
620 Main Street
Carbondale, CO 81623
(970) 963-2266

Map References

USFS White River National Forest
Maptech CD:
    Colorado Springs/Ski Areas/Central
Benchmark's *Colorado Road & Recreation Atlas,* p. 85
Colorado Atlas & Gazetteer, p. 46
The Roads of Colorado, p. 92
Trails Illustrated, #128

A gentle, scenic section surrounded by aspen stands and pine trees

Route Directions

▼0.0   At the intersection of FR 314 and FR 315 between Marble and Crystal, zero trip meter and follow sign toward Lead King Basin.

7.7▲   End at intersection with Central #28: Schofield Pass and Devil's Punchbowl Trail (FR 314) between Marble and Crystal.
         GPS: N 39°04.49′ W 107°09.50′

▼0.4   **SO**   Private track on left to Colorado Outward Bound School.

7.3▲   **SO**   Private track on right to Colorado Outward Bound School.

▼0.7   **SO**   North Lost Creek Trailhead on left. Cross through North Lost Creek.

7.0▲   **SO**   Cross through North Lost Creek. North Lost Creek Trailhead on right.

▼1.8   **SO**   Cross over creek.

5.9▲   **SO**   Cross over creek.

▼2.0   **BL**   Fork in road. Continue on FR 315.

5.7▲   **BR**   Fork in road. Continue on FR 315.
         GPS: N 39°04.68′ W 107°07.46′

▼2.3   **SO**   Cross through creek.

5.4▲   **SO**   Cross through creek.

▼3.7   **BR**   Track on left.

4.0▲   **BL**   Track on right.

▼4.0   **SO**   Cross through creek; then track on left.

3.7▲   **SO**   Track on right. Cross through creek.

▼4.1   **SO**   Track on left.

3.6▲   **SO**   Track on right.

▼6.1   **SO**   Cross through creek.

1.6▲   **SO**   Cross through creek.

▼6.2   **SO**   Cross through creek.

1.5▲   **SO**   Cross through creek.

▼6.3   **SO**   Trailhead parking area on left.

1.4▲   **SO**   Trailhead parking area on right.

▼6.5   **SO**   Track on left crosses through creek.

1.2▲   **SO**   Track on right crosses through creek.

▼6.6   **BR**   Cross bridge over creek. Bear right at each of two intersections.

1.1▲   **BL**   Bear left at each of two intersections. Cross bridge over creek.

▼6.7   **SO**   Cross through creek.

1.0▲   **SO**   Cross through creek.

Lost Lake

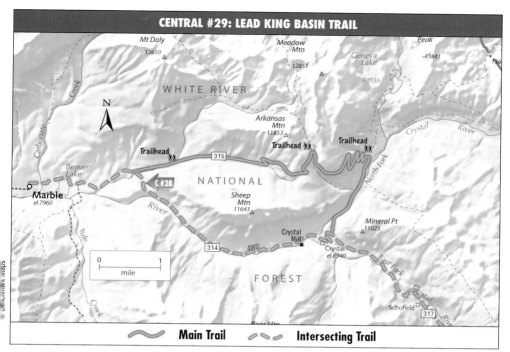

Main Trail   **Intersecting Trail**

▼7.7   End at intersection with FR 314. Marble and Crystal to the right. Schofield Pass, Crested Butte, and Gothic to the left.

0.0▲   At intersection of Central #28: Schofield Pass and Devil's Punchbowl Trail (FR 314) and FR 315, zero trip meter and proceed along FR 315.

GPS: N 39°03.56' W 107°05.77'

As the trail ascends it gets rougher and more eroded

Old Monarch Pass Road

STARTING POINT Intersection of US 50 and
FR 237 (1 mile east of Monarch Pass)

FINISHING POINT Intersection of Central #35:
Tomichi Pass Trail (FR 888) and FR 237

TOTAL MILEAGE 10.3 miles

UNPAVED MILEAGE 10.3 miles

DRIVING TIME 30 minutes

ROUTE ELEVATION 8,900 to 11,375 feet

USUALLY OPEN Early June to November

DIFFICULTY RATING 1

SCENIC RATING 7

Special Attractions

- Access to a network of 4WD trails.
- An alternative to the main highway, US 50.

History

In 1878, 11 years before finding gold near Wagon Wheel Gap and establishing the town that was to bear his name, Nicholas Creede found silver on the east side of Monarch Pass; within months, 3,000 prospectors had arrived. The discovery led to the establishment of several towns in the area, including Maysville, Garfield (originally called Junction City), and Monarch (called Chaffee City until 1884). In the same year, silver, gold, and lead were dis-covered in the Tomichi Valley on the west side of Monarch Pass.

In 1880, the Denver & Rio Grande Railroad built a spur line from Salida to Monarch, which continued to operate in summers until 1982. Also in 1880, a wagon road was built to serve as a stage route. This route travels from the ski area and connects with Old Monarch Pass Road. Today it is sometimes referred to as the Old, Old Monarch Pass Road. It had been open as a 4WD road but has now been closed by the forest service.

In the 1920s, Old Monarch Pass Road was opened, crossing the pass about 1 mile south of the original route. Although it was designed as a motor vehicle road, it was never paved but is still well maintained.

Following much debate about whether Marshall Pass or Monarch Pass should be used as the route for US 50, the present Monarch Pass Road was constructed in 1939. The ski area opened in the same year. When it opened, Charles Vail, the state highway engineer, named the pass after himself and had "Vail Pass" signs placed at the summit. Local residents expressed their objections to this unilateral decision by obliterating the signs with black paint. Many years later, his wish was more permanently granted along I-70.

View from above the summit of Old Monarch Pass

Description

Old Monarch Pass Road (FR 237) provides a good alternative route between US 50 from the east of Monarch Pass through to the 4WD roads in the Tomichi Valley. It commences 1 mile east of the present summit, and the entrance is well marked. The road is graded, wide, and easy for a passenger vehicle to negotiate. There are some sections with steep drop-offs, but in dry conditions these do not pose any serious problems.

The route follows a high-voltage power line through dense pine forest with only occasional stands of aspens and few expansive mountain views. It is not an unusually scenic route, and the best views are at the highest point, near the main pass.

Current Road Information

Grand Mesa, Uncompahgre, & Gunnison National Forests
Gunnison Ranger District
216 North Colorado
Gunnison, CO 81230
(970) 641-0471

Map References

USFS   Gunnison National Forest
Maptech CD:
  Colorado Springs/Ski Areas/Central;
  Alamosa/Pueblo/South Central
Benchmark's *Colorado Road & Recreation Atlas,* p. 98
Colorado Atlas & Gazetteer, pp. 59, 69
The Roads of Colorado, p. 110
Trails Illustrated, #130 (incomplete), #139

View to the southeast of the Monarch Crest Tram on top of Monarch Mountain

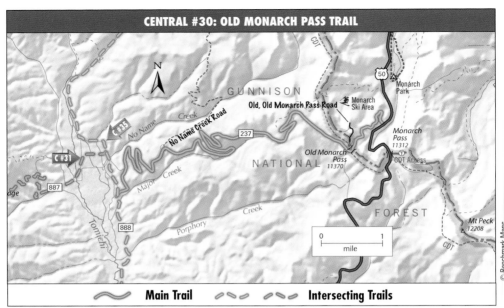

~~~ **Main Trail** ⟋⟍⟋ ⟋⟍⟋ **Intersecting Trails**

Route Directions

▼0.0   From US 50, turn onto Monarch Pass Road (FR 237). Zero trip meter and proceed west.

10.3▲   End at intersection with US 50.
     GPS: N 38°30.27' W 106°19.65'

▼0.2   SO   Road on right dead-ends in 0.3 miles.
10.1▲   SO   Road on left dead-ends in 0.3 miles.

▼1.1   SO   Track on right.
9.2▲   SO   Track on left.

▼1.3   SO   Monarch Pass summit. Vandals had removed the plaque from the summit marker when we were there.
9.0▲   SO   Monarch Pass summit.
     GPS: N 38°29.90' W 106°20.25'

▼2.8   SO   Campsites on left.
7.5▲   SO   Campsites on right.

Good backcountry campsite with a creek near the trail

| ▼3.3 | SO | Campsites on left. |
| 7.0▲ | SO | Campsites on right. |

| ▼4.6 | SO | Track on left. |
| 5.7▲ | SO | Track on right. |

▼7.6	SO	Track marked to Galena Gulch and No Name Creek on right. Note: This trail is gated about 3 miles in at GPS: N 38°30.84′ W 106°23.09′. There are ruins of an old mine where the track is blocked.
2.7▲	SO	Track marked to Galena Gulch and No Name Creek on left.
		GPS: N 38°29.88′ W 106°23.76′

| ▼8.8 | SO | Short track on left to campsites with attractive views. |
| 1.5▲ | SO | Short track on right to campsites with attractive views. |

▼10.3		End at intersection with Central #35: Tomichi Pass Trail (FR 888).
0.0▲		At intersection of Central #35: Tomichi Pass Trail (FR 888) and FR 237, zero trip meter and proceed along FR 237 toward Old Monarch Pass.
		GPS: N 38°29.16′ W 106°24.58′

Black Sage Pass Road

STARTING POINT Intersection of Central #35: Tomichi Pass Trail (FR 888) and FR 887

FINISHING POINT Intersection of Central #32: Waunita Pass Road (FR 763) and FR 887

TOTAL MILEAGE 7.0 miles

UNPAVED MILEAGE 7.0 miles

DRIVING TIME 30 minutes

ROUTE ELEVATION 8,970 to 9,745 feet

USUALLY OPEN Early July to late October

DIFFICULTY RATING 1

SCENIC RATING 7

Special Attractions

■ Easy road through gentle, attractive countryside.

■ Access to a network of 4WD trails.

History

The Hayden survey party traveled this route between Pitkin and Whitepine. When silver was discovered near Pitkin in the late 1870s, this route provided a lower, more undulating, albeit longer, entryway to the area. By 1880, a stagecoach and numerous freight wagons were using this road daily.

In 1882, the Denver, South Park & Pa-

Sign marking the summit of Old Monarch Pass

Summit of Black Sage Pass

cific Railroad opened the line to Pitkin through the Alpine Tunnel. The route remained in use to deliver freight from Pitkin. By this time, the resort of Waunita Hot Springs was very popular and also needed stagecoaches and freight wagons to ferry tourists and supplies.

Subsequently, the pass was used principally for access between Whitepine and Gunnison. The stage way station at the summit of the pass continued to operate into the late 1890s.

Description
The road is accessible to passenger cars under dry conditions. It provides an easy drive through attractive ranchland and a gentle ascent to a forested summit before the scenery widens out into an open valley.

The route connects with a number of other routes in this book. To the east is Old Monarch Pass Road, and to the north are Tomichi Pass, Hancock Pass, and the Alpine Tunnel.

Current Road Information
Grand Mesa, Uncompahgre & Gunnison National Forests
Gunnison Ranger District
216 North Colorado
Gunnison, CO 81230
(970) 641-0471

Map References
USFS   Gunnison National Forest
Maptech CD:
    Colorado Springs/Ski Areas/Central;
    Alamosa/Pueblo/South Central
Benchmark's *Colorado Road & Recreation Atlas*, p. 98
Colorado Atlas & Gazetteer, pp. 59, 69
The Roads of Colorado, p. 109
Trails Illustrated, #139

Route Directions

▼0.0		At intersection of Central #35: Tomichi Pass Trail (FR 888) and FR 887, zero trip meter and proceed west along FR 887 toward Waunita Hot Springs.
3.5▲		End at intersection with Central #35: Tomichi Pass Trail (FR 888).
		GPS: N 38°30.10′ W 106°25.26′

▼1.1	SO	Cattle guard.
2.4▲	SO	Cattle guard.

▼1.5	SO	Track on left to campsites.
2.0▲	SO	Track on right to campsites.

▼2.2	SO	Track on right.
1.3▲	SO	Track on left.

▼3.5	SO	Summit of Black Sage Pass. Zero trip meter. Cross cattle guard. Short side

View from the summit of Black Sage Pass

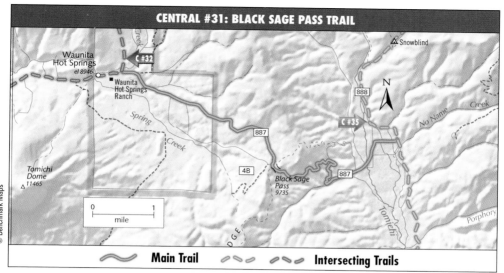

Waunita
Hot Springs
el 8946

C #32

Waunita
Hot Springs
Ranch

△ Snowblind

888

N

Spring

Creek

Creek

C #35

No Name

887

Tomichi
Dome
△ 11465

4B

Black Sage
Pass
9735

887

Tomichi

Porphory

RIDGE

0   1
mile

~~ **Main Trail**   ◌◞◞   ◞◞◌ **Intersecting Trails**

road on left dead-ends in 1.2 miles.
Remain on FR 887.

0.0▲   Continue along FR 887.

GPS: N 38°29.46' W 106°27.11'

▼0.0   Continue toward Waunita Hot Springs
        and Pitkin.

3.5▲ SO Track on right. Cross cattle guard.
          Summit of Black Sage Pass. Zero trip
          meter.

▼1.7 SO Cattle guard.
1.8▲ SO Cattle guard.

▼3.3 TL Intersection with FR 774 on right.
0.2▲ TR Intersection with FR 774 straight on.
          Remain on FR 887.

GPS: N 38°30.81' W 106°29.61'

▼3.5   End at intersection with Central #32:
        Waunita Pass Road.

0.0▲   At intersection of FR 887 and FR 763,
        zero trip meter and proceed east on
        FR 887.

GPS: N38°30.82' W106°29.90'

Dirt bikes on the western end of Black Sage Pass Road

Waunita Pass Road

STARTING POINT Pitkin

FINISHING POINT Intersection of CR/FR 887 and US 50

TOTAL MILEAGE 19.0 miles

UNPAVED MILEAGE 19.0 miles

DRIVING TIME 1 hour

ROUTE ELEVATION 9,190 to 10,303 feet

USUALLY OPEN Year-round

DIFFICULTY RATING 1

SCENIC RATING 6

Special Attractions

■ Easy road through gentle, attractive countryside.

■ Access to a network of 4WD trails.

History

With the rich ore discoveries in the Monarch Pass area and on through the Tomichi Valley in 1878, stages and freight operations made regular journeys between Salida and Pitkin across Monarch, Black Sage, and Waunita Passes.

In 1880, the Denver & Rio Grande Railroad built a spur line from Salida to Monarch; and in 1882, the Alpine Tunnel railroad was opened by the Denver, South Park & Pacific Railroad, providing a railroad to Pitkin.

Waunita Pass Road continued to be used for freight to the Tomichi Valley silver mining area. The route also provided access between Pitkin and the resort facilities at Waunita Hot Springs. However, the road was in decline from the time of the railroad.

The road passes the site of Bowerman where in 1903 J. C. Bowerman struck gold at the Independent Mine and started a rush into the area. Although newspapers heavily promoted the strike, it is doubtful that the coverage was justified by the true extent of the discovery.

Bowerman told people that his find was so rich that even a single blast could yield thousands of dollars. However, the first shipment from the Bowerman mine was postponed many times, and he became secretive about the true assay of his mine and even fenced off the property. In the end, it

A sketch of Waunita Hot Springs Resort in 1916 showing hotel, cottages, post office, tennis courts, and bathhouses

View of the rolling hills surrounding Waunita Pass Road

took more than a year for him to make the first shipment, by which time a boomtown had been incorporated. By then, however, the initial enthusiasm was already on the wane.

Description

The route is generally accessible to passenger vehicles, passing through gentle valley scenery along Hot Springs Creek, then through pine and aspen forest before reaching the pass and dropping down into Pitkin.

The town site of Bowerman is on private property.

Current Road Information

Grand Mesa, Uncompahgre & Gunnison National Forests
Gunnison Ranger District
216 North Colorado
Gunnison, CO 81230
(970) 641-0471

Map References

USFS   Gunnison National Forest
Maptech CD:
    Colorado Springs/Ski Areas/Central;
    Alamosa/Pueblo/South Central
Benchmark's *Colorado Road & Recreation Atlas,* p. 98

Waunita Hot Springs Resort today

Colorado Atlas & Gazetteer, pp. 59, 69
The Roads of Colorado, p. 109
Trails Illustrated, #139

Route Directions

▼0.0   From the Pitkin City Hall building at Main and 4th Streets in Pitkin, zero trip meter and proceed southwest.

10.7▲   End at the Pitkin City Hall building at Main and 4th Streets in Pitkin.

            GPS: N 38°36.48' W 106°31.15'

▼0.1   **TL**   Intersection with 2nd Street on left.
10.6▲   **TR**   Onto Main Street.

▼0.2   **TR**   Onto State Street.
10.5▲   **TL**   Onto 2nd Street.

▼0.3   **TL**   Onto 1st Street.
10.4▲   **TR**   Onto State Street.

▼0.4   **BR**   Fork with FR 763 on right.
10.3▲   **BL**   Fork with 1st Street on left.

▼0.6   **SO**   Bridge over Quartz Creek.
10.1▲   **SO**   Bridge over Quartz Creek.

▼1.5   **SO**   Cattle guard; then Gunnison National Forest sign.

▼9.2▲   **SO**   Cattle guard.

▼3.4   **SO**   Track on right.
7.3▲   **SO**   Track on left.

▼3.8   **SO**   Track on left.
6.9▲   **SO**   Track on right.

▼4.8   **SO**   Summit of Waunita Pass. Road to Wiley Gulch on left and FR 698 on right.
5.9▲   **SO**   FR 698 on left and Wiley Gulch road on right. Summit of Waunita Pass.

            GPS: N 38°34.68' W 106°30.56'

▼6.6   **SO**   Two small tracks on left.
4.1▲   **SO**   Two small tracks on right.

▼6.9   **SO**   Site of Bowerman (private property).
3.8▲   **SO**   Site of Bowerman (private property).

            GPS: N 38°33.75' W 106°30.69'

▼8.6   **SO**   Wiley Gulch on left.
2.1▲   **SO**   Wiley Gulch on right.

▼10.7   **TR**   Intersection. Track on the left is Central #31: Black Sage Pass Road. Zero trip meter.

Waunita Hot Springs Reservoir

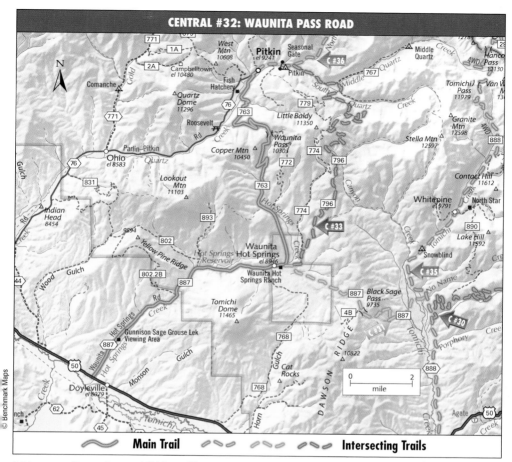

~ **Main Trail** ~ ~ ~ **Intersecting Trails**

0.0▲		Proceed toward Pitkin on FR 763.
		GPS: N 38°30.82' W 106°29.90'
▼0.0		Proceed toward Waunita Hot Springs on FR 887.
8.3▲	**TL**	T-intersection. Straight on is Central #31: Black Sage Pass Road. Zero trip meter.
▼0.2	**SO**	Cattle guard.
8.1▲	**SO**	Cattle guard.
▼0.5	**SO**	Waunita Hot Springs Ranch Resort on right.
7.8▲	**SO**	Waunita Hot Springs Ranch Resort on left.
▼2.4	**SO**	Track to Waunita Hot Springs Reservoir on right.
5.9▲	**SO**	Track to Waunita Hot Springs Reservoir on left.
▼2.5	**SO**	Track on right.
5.8▲	**SO**	Track on left.
▼2.6	**SO**	Great Horse Gulch track on right.
5.7▲	**SO**	Great Horse Gulch track on left.
▼2.9	**SO**	Short track on left.
5.4▲	**SO**	Short track on right.
▼3.5	**SO**	Bridge over Hot Springs Creek.
4.8▲	**SO**	Bridge over Hot Springs Creek.
▼8.3		Cattle guard and end at intersection with US 50.
0.0▲		At intersection of US 50 and CR/FR 887, zero trip meter and proceed north on 887.
		GPS: N 38°27.39' W 106°37.02'

Middle Quartz Creek Trail

STARTING POINT Intersection of Central #31: Black Sage Pass Road (FR 887) and Central #32: Waunita Pass Road

FINISHING POINT Intersection of Central #36: Cumberland Pass Trail (FR 765) and FR 767

TOTAL MILEAGE 12.4 miles

UNPAVED MILEAGE 12.4 miles

DRIVING TIME 1.25 hours

ROUTE ELEVATION 9,025 to 11,000 to feet

USUALLY OPEN Mid-June to late November

DIFFICULTY RATING 5

SCENIC RATING 7

Special Attractions

- 4WD alternative to Waunita Pass Road.
- Access to a network of 4WD roads.
- Good camping along Middle Quartz Creek.

Middle Quartz Creek Trail winding through a stand of aspens

Description

Middle Quartz Creek Road is part of the network of forest roads on the eastern side of Central #32: Waunita Pass Road. It crosses the same minor ridgeline separating the waters of Hot Springs Creek and Quartz Creek as Waunita Pass, which is about two miles to the west.

The route is a less-used alternative to Central #32: Waunita Pass Road and warrants a 4WD vehicle. It is part of a network of 4WD roads that allow exploration deep into Gunnison National Forest in areas such as Stridiron Gulch, Wiley Gulch, Canyon Creek, and the south and middle forks of Quartz Creek.

While the track is rough in spots, it should cause little difficulty in dry conditions. It offers more solitude than the more heavily used Central #32: Waunita Pass Road and travels though aspen and pine forest. The scenery is attractive but lacks the spectacular views of other trails.

The area around Middle Quartz Creek offers good backcountry camping and fishing. It is surrounded with areas that offer scenic and historic day trips: historic and attractive Pitkin nearby to the west, Cumberland Pass and Tincup to the north, Brittle Silver Basin and Alpine Tunnel to the east, and Black Sage and Old Monarch Passes to the south.

Current Road Conditions

Gunnison National Forest
Gunnison Ranger District
216 North Colorado
Gunnison, CO 81230
(970) 641-0471

Map References

USFS   Gunnison National Forest
Maptech CD:
   Colorado Springs/Ski Areas/Central;
   Alamosa/Pueblo/South Central
Benchmark's *Colorado Road & Recreation Atlas*, p. 98
Colorado Atlas & Gazetteer, pp. 59, 69
The Roads of Colorado, p. 109
Trails Illustrated, #139

Route Directions

▼0.0   From T-intersection of Central #31: Black Sage Pass Trail (FR 887) and FR 774 to Middle Quartz Creek, zero trip meter and proceed east along FR 774.

12.7▲   End at T-intersection with Central #31: Black Sage Pass Trail (FR 887). Central #32: Waunita Pass Road is straight on 0.2 miles.

    GPS: N 38°30.81' W 106°29.61'

▼0.3 **BL** Track on right dead-ends.
12.4▲ **BR** Track on left dead-ends.

▼0.7 **BR** FR 774 on left. Follow FR 769.
12.0▲ **BL** FR 774 on right. Follow FR 769.

▼1.4 **SO** Waunita hiking trail (TR 497) on right.
11.3▲ **SO** Waunita hiking trail (TR 497) on left.

    GPS: N 38°31.60' W 106°28.88'

▼2.4 **SO** Track on right.

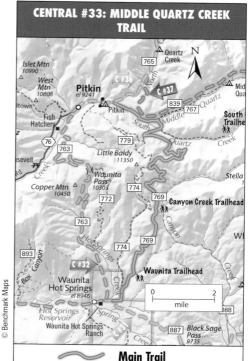

CENTRAL #33: MIDDLE QUARTZ CREEK TRAIL

© Benchmark Maps

Main Trail

Intersection of FR 774 and FR 769 near the beginning of the trail

10.3▲	SO	Track on left.

▼2.9	SO	Track on right (unmarked).
9.8▲	SO	Track on left (unmarked).

▼3.3	BR	Intersection. Sign on right points to Hicks Gulch behind and Buffalo Fork straight ahead. Sign on the left marks track to Stridiron Creek.
9.4▲	BL	Intersection. Hicks Gulch straight. Track to Stridiron Creek on right.
		GPS: N 38°32.80′ W 106°28.13′

▼3.4	SO	Track on right.
9.3▲	SO	Track on left.

▼4.9	BL	Fork in the road. Canyon Creek Trail is to the right. Follow road left toward Middle Quartz Creek.
7.8▲	BR	Canyon Creek Trail is to the left.
		GPS: N 38°34.06′ W 106°28.23′

▼6.6	SO	Track on right, then track on left. Remain on FR 769.
6.0▲	SO	Track on left, then track on right. Remain on FR 769.
		GPS: N 38°34.67′ W 106°27.86′

▼7.1	BR	Track on left.
5.6▲	BL	Track on right.
		GPS: N 38°34.80′ W 106°28.36′

Significantly eroded section of trail

The trail is rocky for most of its length

Creek crossing at the end of the trail

▼7.8   **TR**   Fork in the road, FR 769 to the right; FR 779 to the left.

4.9▲   **BL**   Remain on FR 769. FR 779 on the right.

GPS: N 38°35.22' W 106°28.25'

▼10.0   **TR**   Intersection with FR 769 to the right; FR 779 to the left.

2.7▲   **TL**   Remain on FR 769. FR 779 on the right.

GPS: N 38°35.71' W 106°28.55'

▼10.6   **SO**   Cross over creek.

2.1▲   **SO**   Cross over creek.

▼10.8   **SO**   Track on right leads to South Quartz Trailhead walking track.

1.9▲   **SO**   Track on left leads to South Quartz Trailhead walking track.

▼11.0   **TL**   Cross through creek; then intersection with Middle Quartz Creek Road (FR 767). Middle Quartz Creek Campground to the right and Pitkin to the left.

1.7▲   **TR**   Intersection with FR 769; then cross through creek.

GPS: N 38°36.19' W 106°28.07'

▼12.7   End at intersection with Central #36: Cumberland Pass Trail (FR 765). Pitkin is to the left and Tincup to the right.

0.0▲   At intersection of Central #36: Cumberland Pass Trail (FR 765) and FR 767, zero trip meter and proceed east along FR 767.

GPS: N 38°36.72' W 106°29.68'

Hancock Pass Trail

STARTING POINT St. Elmo

FINISHING POINT Intersection with Central #37: Alpine Tunnel Road (FR 839) and FR 888

TOTAL MILEAGE 9.3 miles

UNPAVED MILEAGE 9.3 miles

DRIVING TIME 1.25 hours

ROUTE ELEVATION 9,980 to 12,250 feet

USUALLY OPEN Early July to October

DIFFICULTY RATING 4 (5 if traveling toward St. Elmo)

SCENIC RATING 9

Special Attractions

- St. Elmo township and the sites of Hancock and Romley.
- Spectacular summit views of Brittle Silver Basin.
- Hiking trail to the east portal of the Alpine Tunnel.
- Moderately difficult 4WD route.
- Access to a network of 4WD trails.

History

The history of the Hancock Pass crossing is poorly documented, perhaps because of the confusion between this pass and Williams Pass, which is located a couple of miles farther north. Hancock Pass was used as a mining route in the 1880s but has never been an important commercial route. It was not officially named until 1962. Much of the route on the east side of the pass follows the old Denver, South Park & Pacific railway grade toward the Alpine Tunnel.

This trip originates at one of the most photographed and best-preserved ghost towns in Colorado: St. Elmo.

The route passes the town site of Romley founded in the late 1870s for the workers of the nearby Mary Murphy and Pat Murphy Mines.

The Mary Murphy Mine was by far the biggest mine in the Alpine District. It is said to be named after a kind nurse in Denver who once cared for the prospector who discovered the mine. The Mary Murphy grew so large that it supported Romley, St.

St. Elmo's main street around 1880

St. Elmo today

Elmo, and Hancock, making the region quite prosperous.

When the Denver, South Park & Pacific Railroad came through Romley in 1881, a 5,000-foot tramway was built to transfer ore to the railroad cars. In 1908, tragedy struck when sparks from a train engine kindled a fire that reduced most of Romley to ashes. When the town was rebuilt, the buildings were painted bright red with white trim, although nobody knows why!

The Mary Murphy Mine, which continued to operate until 1926, is located on the road to Pomeroy Lakes (Central #43). In 1982, the mining company destroyed the buildings that remained in the deserted town.

The Denver, South Park & Pacific Railroad established the town of Hancock in 1880 to support the construction of the Alpine Tunnel. It was named for the Hancock Placer, the first claim in the area. Most of the hundreds of workers employed to build the tunnel lived in Hancock. With five general stores, a hotel, several saloons and restaurants, and two sawmills cutting lumber for the tunnel and railroad, the town supported a population of close to 1,000.

After the Alpine Tunnel was completed in 1881, Hancock became a station on the line to Pitkin. Main Street faced the railroad tracks. The population declined substantially when the tunnel was completed, but many workers were still needed to keep the tracks clear of heavy snow. Large crews labored constantly throughout winter months.

Hancock's population continued to dwindle when many of the area mines closed down, but the big decline occurred after 1910 when the Alpine Tunnel caved in. Hancock became a true ghost town. All the buildings have now collapsed, although the structures and foundations are clearly visible in the meadow. The last to fall away was a saloon, and the remains of it and other buildings are still evident.

Description
Romley is located about 2.5 miles from St. Elmo. Shortly past Romley is the turnoff for the road to Pomeroy Lakes, which goes past the Mary Murphy Mine.

The Allie Belle Mine building in 1950

The precarious position of the building today

Old log cabin remains on Hancock Pass Trail

A rock has crashed into one of the cabins near the Allie Belle Mine

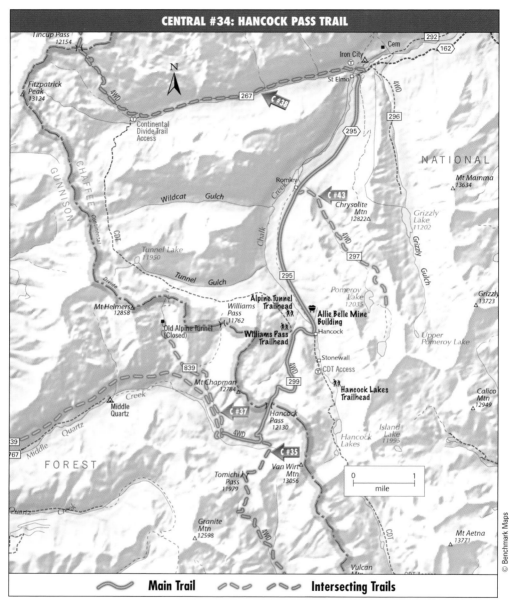

∿	**Main Trail**	⌒⌒◦	⌒⌒◦	**Intersecting Trails**

© Benchmark Maps

At the 4.8-mile point is one of the most precarious-looking structures you are likely to see. The building, which looks as though it will slide into the middle of the road at any moment, once stored ore produced by the Allie Belle Mine while it was waiting to be loaded into rail trucks. Despite appearances, the building has been cantilevered this way for years and is presumably quite sound. A number of other mine buildings are located above this structure. A huge rock has rolled down the hill and crashed through the back wall of a miners' cabin—we hope not while he was in residence!

Not far past the leaning storage shed lies the town site of Hancock.

Just past Hancock, there is a parking lot at the start of the hiking trail to the Atlantic railway station, which was located at the eastern end of the Alpine Tunnel. Before 1992, this road was open to vehicles, but a landslide blocked it that year, leaving as the only access a 2.5-mile hike along the old railway grade.

Shortly after the parking lot there is an intersection. Turn right and continue on the trail to Hancock Pass. Bear left to a 1.4-mile road to Hancock Lakes Trailhead (GPS coordinates: N38°37.18′ W 106° 21.29′). A half-mile walk from the trailhead are the picturesque Hancock Lakes.

Until this intersection, the route is an easy 2WD road and suitable for passenger vehicles. However, from this point on, the road becomes progressively tougher and is rated 4WD.

The summit of the pass provides a spectacular view of Brittle Silver Basin and the ridge of 13,000-foot peaks beyond. The Tomichi Pass shelf road is clearly visible, clinging to the southern ridge surrounding the basin.

From the summit, the remaining mile of road descends steeply into Brittle Silver Basin. For the last hundred yards, loose rocks make getting traction a little difficult, especially if you are going uphill toward the pass.

Current Road Information

Grand Mesa, Uncompahgre & Gunnison National Forests
Gunnison Ranger District
216 North Colorado
Gunnison, CO 81230
(970) 641-0471

Map References

USFS   Gunnison National Forest; San Isabel National Forest
Maptech CD:
      Colorado Springs/Ski Areas/Central
Benchmark's *Colorado Road & Recreation Atlas,* p. 98
Colorado Atlas & Gazetteer, p. 59
The Roads of Colorado, p. 110
Trails Illustrated, #130

Route Directions

▼0.0   At Miner's Exchange general store in St. Elmo, zero trip meter and proceed east out of St. Elmo on CR 162.

5.7▲   End at Miner's Exchange general store in St. Elmo.

GPS: N 38°42.23′ W 106°20.65′

Hancock Lakes

▼0.3　**TR**　Onto CR/FR 295 toward Hancock.

5.4▲　**TL**　Onto CR 162 toward St. Elmo.

▼0.8　**SO**　San Isabel National Forest Service board sign on right.

4.9▲　**SO**　San Isabel National Forest Service board sign on left.

▼2.4　**SO**　Cross through creek.

3.3▲　**SO**　Cross through creek.

▼2.5　**SO**　Romley on right.

3.2▲　**SO**　Romley on left.

▼3.1　**BR**　Road forks.

2.6▲　**SO**　Track on right.

▼3.3　**SO**　Central #43: Pomeroy Lakes and Mary Murphy Mine Trail is on left.

2.4▲　**SO**　Track on right to Pomeroy Lakes and Mary Murphy Mine.

　　　　GPS: N 38°40.38′ W 106°21.95′

▼4.8　**SO**　Old ore storage house for the Allie Belle Mine on left, a precariously perched building overhanging the road.

0.9▲　**SO**　Ore storage house for the Allie Belle Mine on right.

　　　　GPS: N 38°39.08′ W 106°22.07′

▼5.5　**SO**　Hancock town site.

0.2▲　**SO**　Hancock town site.

　　　　GPS: N 38°38.40′ W 106°21.64′

▼5.6　**BL**　Cross over creek; then fork in road. Follow sign to Hancock Pass and Hancock Lakes. Track on right is parking for walking track to the Alpine Tunnel east portal.

0.1▲　**BR**　Left is parking area. Bear right toward Hancock; then cross over creek.

▼5.7　**TR**　U-turn onto FR 299 toward Hancock Pass. (SO goes to Hancock Lakes Trailhead.) Zero trip meter.

0.0▲　　　Proceed toward Hancock.

　　　　GPS: N 38°38.27′ W 106°21.63′

▼0.0　　　Proceed along FR 299.

3.6▲　**TL**　U-turn left goes to Hancock. Right goes to Hancock Lakes. Zero trip meter.

▼1.5　**SO**　Track on right to mine.

2.1▲　**SO**　Track on left to mine.

▼1.9-2.0 **SO**　Mine portals on right along the road.

1.6-1.7▲ **SO**　Mine portals on left along the road.

▼2.0　**SO**　Hancock Pass sign is slightly before the summit. After crest, road is now named FR 266.

1.6▲　**SO**　Hancock Pass sign is slightly past the summit. After crest, road is now named FR 299.

　　　　GPS: N 38°37.31′ W 106°22.44′

▼2.9　**SO**　Rough and rocky shallow crossing through creek. Remains of old cabin on right.

0.7▲　**SO**　Remains of old cabin on left. Cross through creek.

▼3.0　**TR**　Intersection. Left to Tomichi Pass (FR 888) and right to Pitkin.

0.6▲　**BL**　Intersection. FR 888 continues to Tomichi Pass. Follow road to Hancock Pass (FR 266).

　　　　GPS: N 38°36.69′ W 106°22.69′

▼3.6　　　End at intersection with Central #37: Alpine Tunnel Road (FR 839).

0.0▲　　　At intersection of Central #37: Alpine Tunnel Road (FR 839) and FR 888, zero trip meter and proceed along FR 888.

　　　　GPS: N 38°36.83′ W 106°23.37′

The descent from Hancock Pass looking toward Tomichi Pass

Tomichi Pass Trail

STARTING POINT Intersection of Central #34: Hancock Pass Trail (FR 266) and FR 888

FINISHING POINT Intersection of FR 888 and US 50

TOTAL MILEAGE 15.9 miles

UNPAVED MILEAGE 12.1 miles

DRIVING TIME 2 hours

ROUTE ELEVATION 8,600 to 12,020 feet

USUALLY OPEN Early July to October

DIFFICULTY RATING 5

SCENIC RATING 9

Special Attractions

- A challenging 4WD trail.
- Wonderful summit views of Brittle Silver Basin and Hancock Pass Trail.
- Town sites of Tomichi and Whitepine.
- Access to a network of 4WD trails.

History

"Tomichi" is the Ute word for hot water, a reference to the many hot springs in the area.

The main access to the mining areas of Tomichi and Whitepine was southeast to Monarch via Old Monarch Pass or west to Gunnison via Black Sage Pass. From the late 1870s, this entire area was teeming with miners, and Tomichi Pass Road was built to provide access north from the mining settlements of Tomichi and Whitepine to the Denver, South Park & Pacific Railroad and the towns of Pitkin and, via Hancock Pass, St. Elmo. However, the route was too high and difficult to be developed much beyond a pack trail, although wagons did use it when road and weather conditions allowed.

Tomichi was laid out because of silver finds in the area in 1880. Before long, the town's population swelled to nearly 1,500. A smelter was constructed to serve the Magna Charta Tunnel, the best producing silver mine in the area, and the other local mines. Unfortunately, it was destroyed by fire in 1883. The silver crash in 1893 drastically reduced the town's population. All the nearby mines were closed except the Eureka, which operated until 1895. In 1899, a huge avalanche struck the town, destroying all the buildings and mine machinery. Five or six people were killed, and all survivors abandoned the site.

Prospectors began arriving in Whitepine in 1879, and the town was founded in 1880 and thrived throughout the 1880s. Its population reached about 3,000, but despite high expectations, none of the area mines produced much, and with the silver crash of 1893, the town was doomed. By the following year, Whitepine was virtually deserted.

Whitepine Cemetery

Akron Mine remains

The town saw a brief resurgence of activity in 1901 and staged a more lasting comeback when lead, zinc, and copper were mined during World Wars I and II, mainly at the Akron Mine. The Akron Mine hit a high point in 1948, when it reached production of 100 tons per day. In 1946, Whitepine opened a ski area with an 1,800-foot rope tow, but after just two years the tow was dismantled and moved. Whitepine is now primarily a summer residence, with many reconstructed miners' cabins.

The Whitepine and Tomichi stage line serviced the two towns with regular stages to Sargents from 1881. At Sargents, passengers could connect with the Denver & Rio Grande Railroad, which reached town that year following the completion of the line across Marshall Pass.

Description

Tomichi Pass Trail remains one of the more difficult roads in the area. On the north

Sign near the cemetery hints of the rough ascent to Tomichi Pass

Rocky intersection of Tomichi Pass Trail and Hancock Pass Trail

side of the pass, the road crosses a plank bridge over boggy ground before climbing a very narrow shelf that can be blocked by talus slides. It may be necessary to clear the road in order to pass safely. The road is certainly better suited to a smaller 4WD vehicle, but we have traveled it both ways in a Suburban, so it is possible to safely negotiate it in a full-sized vehicle. The wrecked 4WD vehicle below the road serves as a cautionary billboard for the reckless.

The summit provides a wonderful view back to Hancock Pass Trail. On the south side of the pass, the road begins a long, fairly gentle descent, with narrow sections where passing another vehicle is difficult. The road surface is rough but is mainly embedded rock and provides a sound footing. People who are afraid of heights will be pleased to know that drop-offs along this road are mostly restricted to the immediate vicinity of the summit of the pass.

View of the Tomichi Pass Trail from Hancock Pass

A log bridge over a muddy section of Tomichi Pass Trail

Once the road descends below timberline, it becomes smoother and easier. About 3 miles after the pass, the road goes through the old Tomichi Cemetery. This heavily forested site is all that remains of the Tomichi township.

From Whitepine, the road may be negotiated in a passenger vehicle.

Current Road Information

Grand Mesa, Uncompahgre & Gunnison
National Forests
Gunnison Ranger District
216 North Colorado
Gunnison, CO 81230
(970) 641-0471

Map References

USFS   Gunnison National Forest
Maptech CD:
    Colorado Springs/Ski Areas/Central;
    Alamosa/Pueblo/South Central
Benchmark's *Colorado Road & Recreation
    Atlas,* p. 98
Colorado Atlas & Gazetteer, pp. 59, 69
The Roads of Colorado, p. 110
Trails Illustrated, #130, #139

Route Directions

▼0.0   From intersection of FR 266 and FR 888, zero trip meter and proceed along FR 888 toward Tomichi.

15.9▲   End at intersection with Central #34: Hancock Pass Trail (FR 266). Straight ahead leads to Central #37: Alpine Tunnel Road.
    GPS: N 38°36.69' W 106°22.69'

▼0.3 **SO** Interesting mine with several old buildings, an old boiler, and open portal.
15.6▲ **SO** Interesting mine with several old buildings, an old boiler, and open portal.
    GPS: N 38°36.62' W 106°22.46'

▼0.8 **SO** Plank bridge over boggy area.
15.1▲ **SO** Plank bridge over boggy area.

▼1.1 **SO** Summit of Tomichi Pass.
14.8▲ **SO** Summit of Tomichi Pass.
    GPS: N 38°36.20' W 106°22.95'

▼1.3 **SO** Walking trail on right to Canyon Creek, South Quartz, Horseshoe Creek.
14.6▲ **SO** Walking trail on left to Canyon Creek, South Quartz, Horseshoe Creek.

▼1.9 **SO** Cross through creek.
14.0▲ **SO** Cross through creek.

▼2.0 **SO** Cross through creek.
13.9▲ **SO** Cross through creek.

▼2.4 **SO** Cross through creek.
13.5▲ **SO** Cross through creek.

▼2.6 **SO** Cross through creek.
13.3▲ **SO** Cross through creek.

▼2.9 **SO** Cross through creek.
13.0▲ **SO** Cross through creek.

▼3.4 **SO** Cross through creek.
12.5▲ **SO** Cross through creek.

▼4.0 **SO** Tomichi Cemetery on left. Bear right at intersection with FR 888.1C.
11.9▲ **SO** Tomichi Cemetery on right. Bear left at FR 888.1C.
    GPS: N 38°34.26' W 106°22.19'

CENTRAL #35: TOMICHI PASS TRAIL

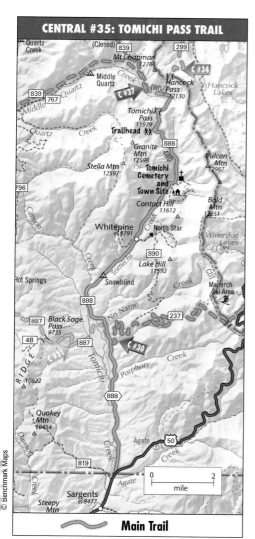

Main Trail

▼4.1   **SO**   Cross through creek.
11.8▲   **SO**   Cross through creek.

▼4.2   **SO**   Track on left.
11.7▲   **SO**   Track on right.

▼4.3   **SO**   Track on left.
11.6▲   **SO**   Track on right.

▼4.4   **TL**   Track on right is a dead end. Turn toward Whitepine.
11.5▲   **TR**   Track on left is a dead end. Turn toward Tomichi Pass.
      GPS: N 38°34.06' W 106°22.44'

▼6.1   **SO**   Bridge over Tomichi Creek.
9.8▲   **SO**   Bridge over Tomichi Creek.

▼6.5   **SO**   Town of Whitepine.
9.4▲   **SO**   Town of Whitepine.
      GPS: N 38°32.59' W 106°23.57'

▼6.8   **SO**   Mine and mill on left.
9.1▲   **SO**   Mine and mill on right.

▼8.4   **SO**   USFS Snowblind Campground on left.
7.5▲   **SO**   USFS Snowblind Campground on right.

▼10.0   **SO**   Intersection with Central #31: Black Sage Pass Road (FR 887) to the right.
5.9▲   **SO**   Intersection with Central #31: Black Sage Pass Road (FR 887) to the left.
      GPS: N 38°30.11' W 106°25.25'

▼11.4   **SO**   Central #30: Old Monarch Pass Trail on left.
4.5▲   **SO**   Central #30: Old Monarch Pass Trail on right.

▼12.1   **SO**   Road becomes paved.
3.8▲   **SO**   Pavement ends.

▼15.9   End at intersection with US 50.
0.0▲   At intersection of US 50 and FR 888, zero trip meter and proceed along FR 888 toward Whitepine.
      GPS: N 38°25.40 W 106°24.36'

Only a few headstones remain at Tomichi Cemetery

© Benchmark Maps

Cumberland Pass Trail

STARTING POINT Tincup
FINISHING POINT Pitkin
TOTAL MILEAGE 15.7 miles
UNPAVED MILEAGE 15.2 miles
DRIVING TIME 1.5 hours
ROUTE ELEVATION 9,190 to 12,015 feet
USUALLY OPEN Early July to late September
DIFFICULTY RATING 3
SCENIC RATING 10

Special Attractions

- The historic and attractive town of Tincup, one of the wildest towns of the old West.
- Tincup Cemetery.
- Access to a multitude of side roads near the summit.
- Spectacular, panoramic summit views.
- Bon Ton Mine, with its deserted cabins and mine buildings.

History

The main road was built in 1882, upgrading an earlier pack trail. Until this time, Tincup had received the majority of its supplies across the gentler slopes of Cotton-

Sign at the summit of Cumberland Pass

wood Pass. However, when the Denver, South Park & Pacific Railroad reached Pitkin in 1882, it became necessary to have a good freight route from Tincup to Quartz, the major depot established by the railroad 2.5 miles north of Pitkin.

Description

The main road over Cumberland Pass is one of the highest 2WD roads in the United States. This 4WD road takes an alterna-

A footbridge to the Protestant knoll of Tincup Cemetery

Boot Hill section of Tincup Cemetery

tive, more direct, but slower route from Tincup to the north side of the pass.

The route leaves Tincup and travels past the old cemetery, which consists of four grassy knolls. One was for Catholics, one for Protestants, and another for Jews; the fourth—and largest—is the Boot Hill section, which was reserved as the final resting place for those who died with their boots on and guns blazing. The size of Boot Hill is a reflection of Tincup's notoriety as one of the wildest towns of the old West.

This route turns off from the main Cumberland Pass Road at the 0.3-mile point. The turnoff is unmarked and not easily noticed. As it climbs toward the pass, the road passes numerous abandoned mines, rusting mining machinery, and decaying cabins as it winds through the pine trees. Although it is narrow in sections and has some loose surfaces, the road provides no particular difficulty in dry conditions.

As the road ascends above timberline, magnificent panoramic views open up, and numerous 4WD trails crisscross the area. Staying on the correct trail can be tricky in this section; fortunately, the summit is visible, and most trails allow you to head in that direction. Because so many people use these roads, it is especially important to Tread Lightly! and remain on the trails open to 4WD vehicles.

At the summit, the high peaks of the Sawatch Range dominate the skyline to the east, the Elk Mountains are in the distance to the west, and the Willow Creek Valley is to the north, with the main 2WD road to Tincup visible as it descends into the valley.

The descent toward Pitkin is along a well-maintained 2WD road. It passes through the remains of the Bon Ton Mine, which has numerous old cabins. The mine commenced operations around 1910 but found its greatest success when it switched to molybdenum production.

Five miles past the Bon Ton is the turnoff for the Alpine Tunnel and Tomichi and Hancock Passes.

Current Road Information

Grand Mesa, Uncompahgre & Gunnison National Forests
Gunnison Ranger District
216 North Colorado
Gunnison, CO 81230
(970) 641-0471

Map References

USFS   Gunnison National Forest

Maptech CD:

   Colorado Springs/Ski Areas/Central

Benchmark's *Colorado Road & Recreation Atlas*, pp. 86, 98

Colorado Atlas & Gazetteer, p. 59

The Roads of Colorado, p. 109

Trails Illustrated, #130

Route Directions

▼0.0		Start at intersection of Mirror Lake Road (FR 267) and Cumberland Pass Road (FR 765) in Tincup. Zero trip meter and proceed south.
4.9▲		End at intersection with Mirror Lake Road (FR 267), which is also Central #38: Tincup Pass Trail.
		GPS: N 38°45.27′ W 106°28.77′

▼0.1	SO	Cross bridge.
4.8▲	SO	Cross bridge.

▼0.2	SO	FR 765.2A to Tincup Cemetery on left.
4.7▲	SO	FR 765.2A to Tincup Cemetery on right.

▼0.3	TL	Turn onto unmarked turnoff on left, FR 765.2B.
4.6▲	TR	Turn onto FR 765 toward Tincup.
		GPS: N 38°44.98′ W 106°28.83′

▼2.1	TL	Intersection.
2.8▲	TR	Intersection.
		GPS: N 38°43.57′ W 106°28.73′

▼2.3	SO	Private cottages on left.
2.6▲	SO	Private cottages on right.
		GPS: N 38°43.37′ W 106°28.78′

▼2.5	BL	Track on right.
2.4▲	BR	Track on left.
		GPS: N 38°43.19′ W 106°28.70′

▼2.6	SO	Mine on left, building ruins, and

Log cabin ruins near the Bon Ton Mine

Other old cabins at the Bon Ton Mine

tailings dump. Then bear right at track on left. Then turn left and right through an S-turn.

2.3▲ TR/TL S-turn; then bear left at track on right. Then continue past mine on right, building ruins and tailings dump.

GPS: N 38°43.12' W 106°28.70'

▼2.7 SO Track on left. Abandoned mine machinery.

2.2▲ SO Track on right. Abandoned mine machinery.

GPS: N 38°43.04' W 106°28.71'

▼2.9 BL Fork in road.

2.0▲ BR Track on left.

GPS: N 38°42.87' W 106°28.68'

Bon Ton Mine

▼3.0   **BL**   Fork in road.
1.9▲   **BR**   Fork in road.

▼3.1 **SO/BR**   Track on right to several cabin ruins. Then bear right at fork in road.
1.8▲ **BL/BR**   Track on right. Track on left to cabin ruins.
     GPS: N 38°42.75′ W 106°28.65′

▼3.2   **SO**   Track on right. Track on left.
1.7▲   **SO**   Track on left. Track on right.

▼3.4   **BR**   Fork in road; then continue straight on past track on right.
1.5▲   **SO**   Track on left; then bear left at fork in road.
     GPS: N 38°42.47 W 106°28.70′

▼3.5   **BL**   Track on right.
1.4▲   **BR**   Track on left.

▼4.1   **BR**   Fork in road.
0.8▲   **BL**   Fork in road.

▼4.5   **BR**   Fork in road.
30 yds▲   **BL**   Fork in road.

▼30 yds   **BL**   Fork in road.
0.4▲   **BR**   Fork in road.

▼4.9   **TL**   Cumberland Pass summit and intersection with Cumberland Pass Road. Zero trip meter at summit marker.
0.0▲   Proceed along 765.2B.
     GPS: N 38°41.37′ W 106°29.03′

▼0.0   Continue south on FR 765 toward Pitkin.
7.9▲   **TR**   Cumberland Pass summit. Zero trip meter at summit marker and shortly after turn right onto 4WD track (FR 765.2B).

▼0.6   **SO**   4WD track on right.
7.3▲   **SO**   4WD track on left.

▼0.9   **SO**   4WD track on right.
7.0▲   **SO**   4WD track on left.

▼1.0   **UT**   Track on right.
6.9▲   **UT**   Track on left.

▼1.3   **SO**   4WD track on left.
6.6▲   **SO**   4WD track on right.

▼2.8   **SO**   Bon Ton Mine on left and cluster of old mine buildings.
5.1▲   **SO**   Bon Ton Mine on right and cluster of old mine buildings.
     GPS: N 38°40.97′ W 106°28.80′

The summit of Cumberland Pass

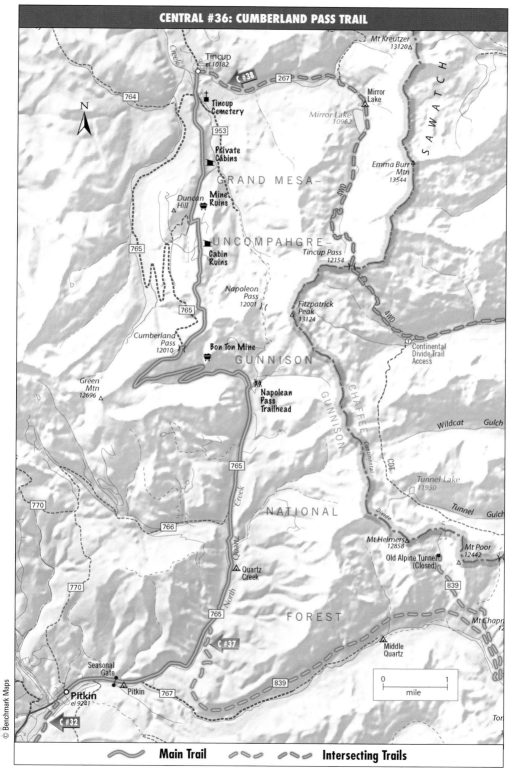

Main Trail ~~~ ~~~ **Intersecting Trails**

© Benchmark Maps

▼4.0   SO   Track on left leads to Napoleon Pass Trailhead.
3.9▲   SO   Track on right leads to Napoleon Pass Trailhead.

▼4.9   SO   Tracks on right and left.
3.0▲   SO   Tracks on left and right.

▼5.3   SO   Cross North Quartz Creek.
2.6▲   SO   Cross North Quartz Creek.

▼5.5   SO   Track on right.
2.4▲   SO   Track on left.

▼5.9   SO   FR 766 to Hall's Gulch on right.
2.0▲   SO   FR 766 to Hall's Gulch on left.
GPS: N 38°39.07' W 106°28.15'

▼6.6   SO   Track on left to Mosquito Creek.
1.3▲   SO   Track on right to Mosquito Creek.

▼6.9   SO   USFS Quartz Campground on left.
1.0▲   SO   USFS Quartz Campground on right.

▼7.9   SO   Town site of Quartz. Central #37: Alpine Tunnel Road (FR 839) on left. Zero trip meter.
0.0▲   Proceed along FR 765 toward Cumberland Pass.
GPS: N 38°37.49' W 106°28.52'

▼0.0   Proceed along FR 765 toward Pitkin.
2.9▲   SO   Town site of Quartz. Central #37: Alpine Tunnel Road (FR 839) on right. Zero trip meter.

▼1.5   SO   FR 767 on left.
1.4▲   SO   FR 767 on right.

▼1.9   SO   Seasonal gate; then USFS Pitkin Campground on left.
1.0▲   SO   USFS Pitkin Campground on right; then seasonal gate.

▼2.4   TR   Stop sign at intersection of State and 9th Streets in Pitkin. Silver Plume General Store.
0.5▲   TL   Onto FR 765.

▼2.5   TL   Onto Main Street.
0.4▲   TR   Onto 9th Street.

▼2.9   End at Pitkin City Hall at intersection of Main Street (CR 76) and 4th Street.
0.0▲   In front of the Pitkin City Hall at the intersection of Main Street (CR 76) and 4th Street, zero trip meter and proceed northeast along Main Street.
GPS: N 38°36.50' W 106°31.14'

The panoramic view afforded as the trail crosses a meadow near the summit

Alpine Tunnel Road

STARTING POINT Intersection of Alpine Tunnel Road (FR 839) and Central #36: Cumberland Pass Trail (FR 765) at Quartz town site

FINISHING POINT Alpine Station

TOTAL MILEAGE 9.5 miles (one-way)

UNPAVED MILEAGE 9.5 miles

DRIVING TIME 45 minutes (one-way)

ROUTE ELEVATION 11,180 to 11,597 feet

USUALLY OPEN Early July to September

DIFFICULTY RATING 1

SCENIC RATING 10

Special Attractions

- The restored Alpine Station.
- The Palisades section of the old railroad grade.
- Railroad water tanks.
- Town sites of Quartz and Woodstock and the site of the Sherrod Loop.

History

Two railroads waged a battle to be the first to connect the Gunnison area to Denver. The Denver & Rio Grande Railroad chose Marshall Pass as its route, so the owner of the Denver, South Park & Pacific Railroad, former governor John Evans, financed a project to tunnel through the Sawatch Range.

Inside the Alpine Tunnel in 1975

A tunnel through the Continental Divide seemed a shorter and more strategic route. Bids were opened to build the Alpine Tunnel in 1879. The bore through the mountain was to be 1,800 feet long. However, the railroad underestimated the severity of the weather, the geologic rock formations at the site, and the difficulty of

A long snowshed that was located near Alpine Station, circa 1882

Alpine Station, circa 1885

Alpine Tunnel Station

working at the 11,600-foot altitude, with wind gusts to 50 miles per hour and temperatures at 40 degrees below zero.

In 1880, work began, and 500 laborers worked day and night. Work camps were established at each end of the tunnel. Severe weather conditions and poor working conditions created and exacerbated gigantic labor problems. Workers walked off the site in droves when they experienced the high winds and freezing temperatures they were expected to endure. The railroad recruited workers from the East and Midwest by offering free transportation to Colorado. More than 100,000 men were employed, and many worked only a day or two before leaving. Sometimes the entire crew threatened to quit en masse.

The tunnel was bored by July 1881, almost a year behind schedule (which had allowed only six months to complete the project). When the competing Denver & Rio Grande reached Gunnison in early August, the discouraged Denver, South Park & Pacific Railroad company halted the Alpine Tunnel project for about six months. Finally, work continued, and the first train passed through the tunnel in December 1881.

The Alpine Station was developed at the west, or Pacific, end of the tunnel, with a bunkhouse where track workers lived, a storehouse, and a section house. The section house included a kitchen, a dining room, a pantry, and several bedrooms. A large stone engine house was built at the station in 1881. Aside from holding six engines, the engine house also contained a large coal bin and a water tank with a 9,516-gallon capacity, a turntable, and a locomotive service area. In 1883, a telegraph office was constructed.

Snowsheds were erected at each end of the tunnel bore to protect the rails. The shed on the Atlantic side was 150 feet in length, and the one on the Pacific side was 650 feet.

Train service through the Alpine Tunnel began in June 1882. The completed project was considered an engineering marvel. At 16 places on the western descent, walls were laid to provide a shelf for rail construction. The most spectacular shelf is at the Palisades, a mile below the tunnel, where a stone wall 450 feet long, 30 feet high, and 2 feet thick was built from hand-cut stones without mortar. You can see this wall along the drive to the Alpine Tunnel. Over 500,000 feet of California redwood were used to reinforce the tunnel, as workers found loose rock and decomposed granite instead of self-supporting granite. The total cost of the tunnel was more than $250,000.

Many problems plagued the Alpine Tunnel during its period of operation. In March 1884, a train whistle caused a severe

Crossing the Palisades

snow slide that swept away the town of Woodstock and killed 13 of its residents. The town was not rebuilt. In 1906, a fire destroyed the wood buildings at Alpine Station; even the stone buildings were demolished when they collapsed from the intense heat of the blaze. In 1910, several people lost their lives when the tunnel caved in. The tunnel was never reopened. Rails were first removed in November 1918; however, the rails in the tunnel itself remain in place. Eventually the railroad property was sold.

Description

This historic route is an easy 2WD road that is popular with tourists and has plenty of pull-offs to enable passing where the road is narrow. The only concern is that it has very steep drop-offs in some sections.

This route starts at the town site of Quartz, approximately 3 miles northeast of Pitkin on Cumberland Pass Road (FR 765) at the Alpine Tunnel Road turnoff (FR 839). The town was originally founded in 1879 as a mining camp, but it was the arrival of the Denver, South Park & Pacific Railroad in 1882 that spurred its development. It was a major service depot for the railroad.

The remnants of the Midway water tank lie nearly 3 miles along the route. The tank was so named because it is at the halfway point between Pitkin and the Alpine Tunnel. The tank, which collapsed and has been removed from the base structure, used to hold 47,500 gallons.

A little more than 2 miles farther is the Tunnel Gulch water tank, which has been restored by the Mile High Jeep Club. This 30,000-gallon tank replaced the Woodstock tank. The route continues past the town site of Woodstock. The stone base of the old Woodstock railway water tank is all that remains.

The Sherrod Loop is marked by an information board. The loop was a horseshoe section of track that enabled the trains to turn 228 degrees to remain on the sunnier

The remains of the stone engine house

south side of the valley. The snow on the north slope was 10 to 20 feet deep and typically did not melt until the summer.

About 1.25 miles after the turnoff to Hancock Pass, you drive across the Palisades, which clings to the cliff face.

The route finishes at a parking area, a short walk from Alpine Station. The telegraph station has been restored, and you can see the ruins of the stone engine house and section house. Volunteers have reconstructed the station platform and relaid 120 feet of the original Denver, South Park & Pacific rails. A further short walk takes you to the tunnel entrance, which is completely blocked by a rock slide.

Current Road Information

Grand Mesa, Uncompahgre & Gunnison National Forests
Gunnison Ranger District
216 North Colorado
Gunnison, CO 81230
(970) 641-0471

Map References

USFS Gunnison National Forest
Maptech CD:
    Colorado Springs/Ski Areas/Central
Benchmark's *Colorado Road & Recreation Atlas,* p. 98
Colorado Atlas & Gazetteer, p. 59
The Roads of Colorado, pp. 109, 110
Trails Illustrated, #130

Route Directions

▼0.0   From the T-intersection of Alpine Tunnel Road (FR 839) and Central #36: Cumberland Pass Trail (FR 765) at the site of Quartz, zero trip meter and proceed east toward the Alpine Tunnel.

7.3▲   End at intersection with Central #36: Cumberland Pass Trail.
GPS: N 38°37.47' W 106°28.52'

▼3.2   SO   Remains of Midway water tank on left. Only base is left standing.

4.1▲   SO   Remains of Midway water tank on

The railroad embankment leading to the collapsed southern end of the Alpine Tunnel

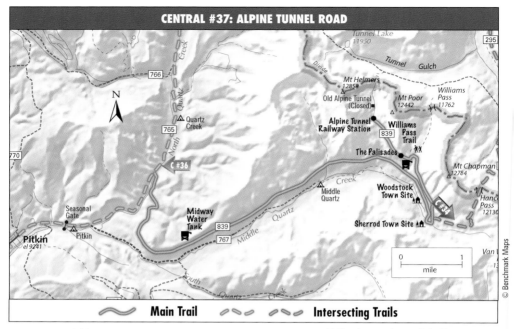

| ~ **Main Trail** | ◠◡◠ ◠◡◠ **Intersecting Trails** |

right.

▼6.4   **SO**   Tunnel Gulch water tank on left.

0.9▲   **SO**   Tunnel Gulch water tank on right.

▼7.0   **SO**   Town site of Woodstock on right.

0.3▲   **SO**   Town site of Woodstock on left.

▼7.2   **SO**   Town site of Sherrod and Sherrod Loop on right.

0.1▲   **SO**   Town site of Sherrod and Sherrod Loop on left.

▼7.3   **TL**   Intersection with FR 888 (Central #34: Hancock Pass Trail). Zero trip meter.

0.0▲   At intersection of FR 888 (Central #34: Hancock Pass Trail) with FR 839 (Alpine Tunnel Road), zero trip meter and proceed toward Quartz and Pitkin on FR 839.

GPS: N 38°36.83′ W 106°23.36′

▼0.0   Continue on FR 839 toward Alpine Station.

▼0.1   **SO**   South Park Railroad marker on right and Gunnison National Forest.

▼0.2   **SO**   Track on left to private cabin.

▼0.9   **SO**   Williams Pass Road sign on right.

▼1.3   **SO**   Palisades marker on left. Elevation 11,300 feet.

▼2.2   Public toilets, picnic tables, and gate. It is a short walk to the Alpine Station buildings beyond the gate.

GPS: N 38°38.29′ W 106°24.45′

Tunnel Gulch water tank

Tincup Pass Trail

STARTING POINT St. Elmo
FINISHING POINT Tincup
TOTAL MILEAGE 12.4 miles
UNPAVED MILEAGE 12.4 miles
DRIVING TIME 1.25 hours
ROUTE ELEVATION 9,980 to 12,154 feet
USUALLY OPEN Early July to October
DIFFICULTY RATING 3
SCENIC RATING 8

Special Attractions

- The historic and attractive towns of St. Elmo and Tincup.
- Very attractive scenery, including the summit views and Mirror Lake.
- Access to a network of 4WD trails.
- Excellent backcountry campsites.

History

Tincup Pass was first used by the Indians and then as a pack trail. A wagon road was built following the flood of silver prospectors into the area in 1879. By 1880, the pass was an established freight route, with wagon service run by Witowski and Dunbar's Hack Line. In 1881, it was developed further and became a toll road; soon three stage lines were running daily stages over the pass. The route was surveyed for a number of railroads, and a tunnel was even started under the pass, but the project was soon abandoned. The pass road was used during World War I to train the cavalry. In 1954, prison laborers upgraded the road.

Tincup was established after the Gold Cup Mine was discovered in 1879; the town was first named Virginia City but its name was changed in 1882. People flooded into Tincup, which in its heyday became the second largest town in Gunnison County. It was notorious as one of the wildest and roughest mining camps in Colorado. Its saloons and gambling parlors operated night and day. Drunkenness and shootings were casual occurrences.

Tincup was ruled by the underworld with organized crime in control of all city offices, many saloons, gaming halls, and the brothels, which seemed to flourish in the

Tincup in 1906

early mining camps. When the first marshal started work in 1880, he was told to see nothing, do nothing, and hear nothing; his first arrest would be his last. He lasted only a few months; when he was not paid, he quit. The second marshal occasionally rounded up a few drunks, put them in jail, and then released them. The third marshal decided to harass a saloon owner one night and didn't live long enough to regret it. The fourth marshal went insane and killed himself. The fifth marshal was shot and killed.

Tincup managed to survive through the silver crash of 1893 with its gold and silver production. The town continued into the twentieth century only to end dramatically in a fire that burned it to the ground in 1906. The fire started in a store that sold kerosene. As the flames spread, they destroyed everything in one city block. The town was rebuilt, but it never fully recovered. In 1913, a second fire severely damaged several other buildings.

After the Gold Cup Mine closed in 1917, Tincup declined rapidly, and in 1918 the post office closed.

Description

The route starts from the western edge of St. Elmo, a famous ghost town that looks as if it were created by Hollywood, and immediately starts the climb toward the pass. Initially, the road follows the North Fork of Chalk Creek, passing numerous backcountry campsites.

The road is reasonably wide but quite rough, although the surface is sound. As the road progresses, it becomes rockier, but the rocks are embedded, so the surface remains solid. The road travels through pine and spruce forest.

The summit offers beautiful views of the Arkansas River Valley and the Taylor Park area. Mirror Lake can be glimpsed in the foreround as you look west toward Tincup.

About 3 miles west of the summit, the road travels along the edge of Mirror Lake, a popular fishing spot. Nearby, there is a U.S. Forest Service campground. There are also numerous very good backcountry campsites between Mirror Lake and Tincup.

From Mirror Lake, the road is easily negotiated by a passenger vehicle.

Tincup Town Hall, built in 1906

Tincup

Current Road Information

Grand Mesa, Uncompahgre & Gunnison
National Forests
Gunnison Ranger District
216 North Colorado
Gunnison, CO 81230
(970) 641-0471

Map References

USFS   Gunnison National Forest; San
       Isabel National Forest
Maptech CD:
       Colorado Springs/Ski Areas/Central
Benchmark's *Colorado Road & Recreation
       Atlas,* p. 86
Colorado Atlas & Gazetteer, p. 59

Mirror Lake

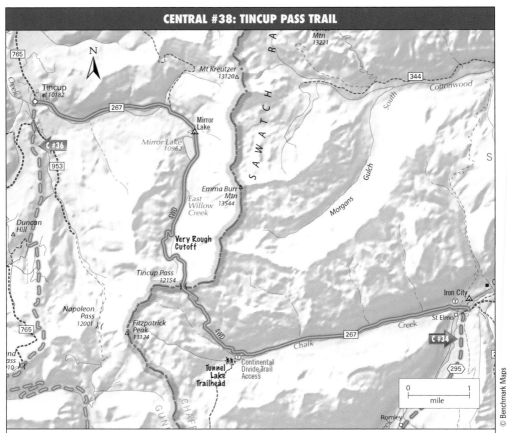

~~~ **Main Trail** ⟋⟍⟋ ⟋⟍⟋ **Intersecting Trails**

The Roads of Colorado, pp. 109, 110
Trails Illustrated, #129, #130

Route Directions

▼0.0		In front of the Miner's Exchange in St. Elmo, zero trip meter and proceed west.
9.3▲		End in front of the Miner's Exchange in St. Elmo.
		GPS: N 38°42.23' W 106°20.65'

▼0.1	**TR**	At Tincup sign; then cross bridge over North Fork of Chalk Creek.
9.2▲	**TL**	Onto St. Elmo's main street.

▼0.2	**BR**	Fork in road.
9.1▲	**BL**	Track on right.

▼0.4	**SO**	Poplar Gulch Trailhead on right.
8.9▲	**SO**	Poplar Gulch Trailhead on left.

▼0.8	**SO**	Cattle guard.
8.5▲	**SO**	Cattle guard.

▼1.8	**SO**	Cross over creek.
7.5▲	**SO**	Cross over creek.

▼3.0	**SO**	Track on right.
6.3▲	**SO**	Track on left.

▼3.9	**SO**	Tunnel Lake walking trail on left.
5.4▲	**SO**	Tunnel Lake walking trail on right.
		GPS: N 38°41.54' W 106°24.80'

▼4.6	**SO**	Cross through creek.
4.7▲	**SO**	Cross through creek.

▼6.1	**SO**	Tincup Pass summit. Enter Gunnison National Forest; then cattle guard.
3.2▲	**SO**	Cattle guard; then enter San Isabel

National Forest. Tincup Pass summit.

GPS: N 38°42.57' W 106°26.00'

▼6.7   **BL**   Old alternative route is straight ahead.

2.6▲   **BR**   More difficult alternative route rejoins on left.

▼7.5   **SO**   More difficult alternative route rejoins on right.

1.8▲   **BR**   More difficult alternative route on left.

▼8.8   **SO**   Cross through creek at head of Mirror Lake.

0.5▲   **SO**   Cross through creek at head of Mirror Lake.

▼9.3   **SO**   Tincup side of Mirror Lake and angler parking on left. Zero trip meter.

0.0▲   **BL**   Follow track around the left side of Mirror Lake toward Tincup Pass.

GPS: N 38°44.78' W 106°25.81'

▼0.0   Proceed along Mirror Lake Road (FR 267).

3.1▲   **BL**   Mirror Lake and angler parking on right. Zero trip meter.

▼0.1   **SO**   Track to USFS Mirror Lake Campground on left.

3.0▲   **SO**   Track to USFS Mirror Lake Campground on right.

▼0.4   **SO**   Timberline Trailhead on right.

2.7▲   **SO**   Timberline Trailhead on left.

▼0.9   **SO**   Cross over East Willow Creek.

2.2▲   **SO**   Cross over East Willow Creek.

▼2.9   **BL**   Fork in road. Entering Tincup.

0.2▲   **BR**   Leaving Tincup.

▼3.1   End in Tincup at intersection with Cumberland Pass Road (FR 765).

0.0▲   At intersection of Mirror Lake Road (FR 267) and Cumberland Pass Road (FR 765) in Tincup, zero trip meter and proceed toward Mirror Lake.

GPS: N 38°45.27' W 106°28.77'

The trail near the summit of Tincup Pass

Mount Antero Trail

STARTING POINT Intersection of CR 162 and Baldwin Creek Road (FR 277)

FINISHING POINT Mount Antero

TOTAL MILEAGE Approximately 6.5 miles (one-way)

UNPAVED MILEAGE Approximately 6.5 miles

DRIVING TIME 1.75 hours (one-way)

ROUTE ELEVATION 9,400 to 14,269 feet

USUALLY OPEN Mid-June to late September

DIFFICULTY RATING 5

SCENIC RATING 9

Special Attractions

■ A very challenging and famous 4WD trail.

■ Wonderful alpine scenery.

■ Access to a network of 4WD trails.

History

Mount Antero is named for Chief "Graceful Walker" Antero of the Uintah band of the Ute Indians. Antero was one of the signatories to the Washington Treaty of 1880, which revised the terms of the Brunot Treaty signed seven years earlier and led to the Ute losing nearly all their land. Antero was a force for peace during the period of very problematic relations between the Ute and the whites in the late 1860s and 1870s. In 1869, John Wesley Powell spent the winter with Antero and Chief Douglas (who was later held responsible for the Meeker Massacre) and learned to speak the Ute language.

While Mount Antero was doubtless examined by prospectors in the late 1870s as silver was being discovered all around, it proved to have little silver to offer. In fact, not a single claim was staked. What the prospectors did not notice, or failed to appreciate, was that Mount Antero offered a fortune in gemstones.

In 1884, a prospector named Nathaniel D. Wanemaker discovered a number of blue aquamarines in the area. He constructed a small stone cabin high on the south side of the mountain. It is said that he discovered $600 worth of gems in his first summer and continued to prospect for gems for many years.

Mount Antero has proved extraordinarily rich in aquamarines, topaz, and clear

Crossing Baldwin Creek

Crossing a talus bed

and smoky quartz crystals. The aquamarines range in color from pale blue-green to deep blue. Some of the clear crystals from Mount Antero are huge; a 7-inch specimen is on display at the Harvard Mineralogical Museum and another was cut into a 6-inch-diameter sphere and displayed at the 1893 Columbian Exposition. The more common smoky quartz crystals weigh as much as 50 pounds.

The most recent mining on Mount Antero has been for beryllium, a lightweight, corrosion-resistant, rigid, steel gray metallic element that melts only at extremely high temperatures. Beryllium is a prized aerospace structural material, as a moderator and reflector in nuclear reactors, and in a copper alloy used for springs, electrical contacts, and non-sparking tools. In the 1950s, the access road on the mountain's south shoulder was constructed by the company mining the beryllium.

Description

The Mount Antero route starts at the intersection of the road between Nathrop and St. Elmo (CR 162) and FR 277. The turnoff is 12 miles west of US 285 along CR 162 and 3.3 miles east of St. Elmo.

FR 277 ascends steeply right from the point of departure from CR 162. It is a rough, rocky shelf road through the pine and aspen forest but offers some very good views back into the valley and the township of Alpine. The track is narrow and has some very steep drop-offs. Pull-offs for passing other vehicles are only just adequate in some sections. High clearance is definitely required, but if you carefully select your line, the rocks are not large enough to cause vehicle damage.

Some good news: Once you have completed the first 2 miles, you are past the most difficult section of the route.

At the 2.7-mile point, you cross through

The trail climbing Mount Antero above timberline

Baldwin Creek, which has a firm base and is usually only about a foot deep. From the creek crossing, the road again climbs a couple of loose talus slopes before emerging above timberline. The road then commences a series of narrow switchbacks before winding around the south face and continuing up the east face. Passing opportunities are limited in this section, so it pays to watch for oncoming vehicles and plan ahead.

At the 3.8-mile point, there is an intersection. The track on the right leads to a dead end. This is the last chance to turn around before the end of the road, and the next section is more difficult than anything encountered until this point. (Note: The difficulty rating for this route is based on stopping here.) We recommend that if you wish to see the last half mile of the road, you walk it.

Current Road Information

Pike & San Isabel National Forests
Salida Ranger District
325 West Rainbow Boulevard
Salida, CO 81201
(719) 539-3591

Map References

USFS   San Isabel National Forest
Maptech CD:
    Colorado Springs/Ski Areas/Central
Benchmark's *Colorado Road & Recreation
    Atlas,* p. 99
Colorado Atlas & Gazetteer, p. 59
The Roads of Colorado, p. 110
Trails Illustrated, #130

Route Directions

▼0.0   From CR 162 (3.3 miles east of St. Elmo), turn onto Baldwin Creek Road (FR 277) toward Mt. Antero and zero

The trail switchbacks above treeline

Parked near Mount White with Mount Antero in the background

Main Trail

© Benchmark Maps

trip meter.

GPS: N 38°42.60' W 106°17.46'

▼1.1   **SO**   Track on right is Central #42: Boulder Mountain Trail.

▼2.7   **TL**   Central #41: Baldwin Lakes Trail is straight ahead (FR 277.2). Zero trip meter.

GPS: N 38°40.99' W 106°16.32'

▼0.0   Cross through Baldwin Creek and continue on FR 278 toward Mt. Antero.

▼0.2   **SO**   Cross through creek.

▼0.3   **SO**   Track on left.

▼1.5   **SO**   Cross through creek.

▼3.3   **BL**   Central #40: Browns Lake Trail (278.2) on right. Remain on 278.A.

GPS: N 38°39.70' W 106°15.43'

▼3.4   **SO**   Intersection with 278.B on right, which climbs Mt. White, providing spectacular views all around, especially looking back at Mt. Antero and into the valley to the south.

▼3.8   **BL**   Track on right. Park and walk remaining section.

GPS: N 38°39.74' W 106°14.94'

The narrow, loose descent

Browns Lake Trail

STARTING POINT Intersection of Central #39: Mount Antero Trail (FR 278A) and FR 278.2

FINISHING POINT Browns Creek Trailhead

TOTAL MILEAGE 3.3 miles (one-way)

UNPAVED MILEAGE 3.3 miles

DRIVING TIME 45 minutes (one-way)

ROUTE ELEVATION 2,800 to 11,400 feet

USUALLY OPEN Mid-June to late September

DIFFICULTY RATING 4

SCENIC RATING 10

Special Attractions

- The extremely scenic Browns Lake.
- Part of a network of 4WD trails near the summit of Mount Antero.

Description

The 4WD trail to Browns Lake, a side road from the Mount Antero road, sees much less traffic than that more famous route.

After turning off the Mount Antero road, you cross an alpine meadow before commencing the rocky descent down into Browns Creek Valley. The road enters the timberline and wends its way through the pine forest with rather tight clearance between the trees.

The trail proceeds past the remains of a mining camp, including the ruins of a miners' cabin. Proceeding toward the trailhead and the end of the 4WD road, you'll enjoy picture-postcard views of Browns Lake, located in the valley at an altitude of 11,286 feet.

The road is moderately difficult, with sections of narrow switchbacks, loose surface rock, and some tight clearances, but the solitude and the scenery make it all worthwhile.

Current Road Information

Pike & San Isabel National Forests
Salida Ranger District
325 West Rainbow Boulevard
Salida, CO 81201
(719) 539-3591

The trail approaching Browns Lake

Browns Lake

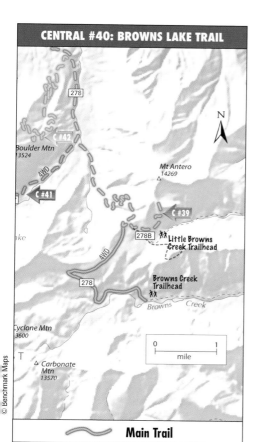

CENTRAL #40: BROWNS LAKE TRAIL

Main Trail

Map References

USFS   San Isabel National Forest
Maptech CD:
    Colorado Springs/Ski Areas/Central
Benchmark's *Colorado Road & Recreation
    Atlas*, p. 99
Colorado Atlas & Gazetteer, p. 60
The Roads of Colorado, p. 110
Trails Illustrated, #130

Route Directions

▼0.0   At intersection of Central #39: Mt.
            Antero Trail (FR 278.A) and trail to
            Browns Lake (FR 278.2), zero trip
            meter and proceed along FR 278.2
            into the valley.
            GPS: N 38°39.70′ W 106°15.43′

▼1.9   SO   Cabin ruins on right.
▼2.0   SO   Cabin ruins on left.
▼2.5   SO   Cross through creek.
▼3.3   Track ends at Browns Creek
            Trailhead.
            GPS: N 38°38.63′ W 106°14.70′

Beautiful Browns Lake in the distance

Baldwin Lakes Trail

STARTING POINT Intersection of Central #39: Mount Antero Trail (FR 278) and Baldwin Creek Road (FR 277)

FINISHING POINT Parking area at Baldwin Lakes

TOTAL MILEAGE 2.9 miles (one-way)

UNPAVED MILEAGE 2.9 miles

DRIVING TIME 1 hour (one-way)

ROUTE ELEVATION 10,880 to 12,200 feet

USUALLY OPEN Mid-June to late September

DIFFICULTY RATING 5

SCENIC RATING 7

Special Attractions

- Challenging 4WD trail.
- Scenic views of Baldwin Lakes.

Description

The Baldwin Lakes route is a very rough and rocky side road to the Mount Antero road. The talus roadbed is slippery, and sharp rocks make a flat tire a continual threat.

The first section of road travels along the creek, past open meadows and many backcountry camping spots. As it continues up to the first lake, you travel through the pine forest, emerging to cross huge talus rock slides and then re-entering the forest. About 2 miles along the road, the surface

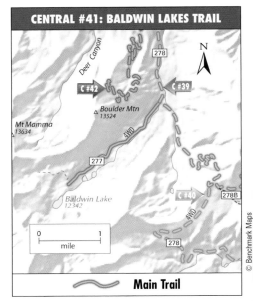

CENTRAL #41: BALDWIN LAKES TRAIL

© Benchmark Maps

~~~~~ **Main Trail**

rock becomes mostly embedded in the soil and more stable. There is a fairly steep section where the melting snow drains across the trail, making it boggy and somewhat slippery when you are going uphill. The last section of the road has large embedded rocks to negotiate before you reach the small parking area.

Views of Baldwin Creek Valley, the high alpine bowl encircled by steep valley walls, and the lakes cradled in its base combine to make the journey very scenic.

A rough, loose section of the trail

The scenic Baldwin Creek Valley

Current Road Information
Pike & San Isabel National Forests
Salida Ranger District
325 West Rainbow Boulevard
Salida, CO 81201
(719) 539-3591

Map References
USFS   San Isabel National Forest
Maptech CD:
    Colorado Springs/Ski Areas/Central

Benchmark's *Colorado Road & Recreation*
   Atlas, p. 99
Colorado Atlas & Gazetteer, p. 59
The Roads of Colorado, p. 110
Trails Illustrated, #130

Route Directions

▼0.0   From the intersection of FR 278 and FR 277.2, at the small parking area beside Baldwin Creek crossing, zero

Baldwin Lakes

trip meter and proceed toward Baldwin Lakes.

GPS: N 38°40.97′ W 106°16.34′

▼0.2   **SO**   Remains of log cabin.

▼0.9   **BR**   Fork in road.

▼1.5   **BL**   Fork in road. Follow lower track (FR 277). Track on right goes to old mine farther up the mountain.

GPS: N 38°40.14′ W 106°17.45′

▼2.2   **BR**   Small parking area on left with view of the lakes and a walking track.

GPS: N 38°39.69′ W 106°18.10′

▼2.9   Small parking/turnaround area. From this point, the track becomes more difficult than our rating indicates. Large embedded rocks make impact with the underside of the vehicle likely.

GPS: N 38°39.95′ W 106°18.36′

Boulder Mountain Trail

STARTING POINT Intersection of Central #41: Baldwin Lakes Trail (FR 277) and Boulder Mountain Road

FINISHING POINT Mine shaft and cabin ruins near the top of the mountain

TOTAL MILEAGE 4.8 miles (one-way)

UNPAVED MILEAGE 4.8 miles

DRIVING TIME 1.25 hours (one-way)

ROUTE ELEVATION 9,950 to 12,800 feet

USUALLY OPEN Mid-June to late September

DIFFICULTY RATING 5

SCENIC RATING 8

Special Attractions

- Challenging 4WD trail.
- Spectacular alpine views.

Description

This route, another side road to the Mount Antero Trail, is also rough and rocky but

Baldwin Lakes

A relatively easy section of Boulder Mountain Trail

A switchback on Boulder Mountain Trail

less so than the Mount Antero road. The challenge of this road is that it is narrow with very high drop-offs. To make matters more interesting, especially if you have a full-sized vehicle, small pine trees grow on the inside edge of the track, pushing you perilously close to the edge. To add to the excitement, sections of the road are significantly off-camber!

The road carries less traffic than others in the area, which is fortunate because there are sections where the only way to get

The mine at the end of the trail

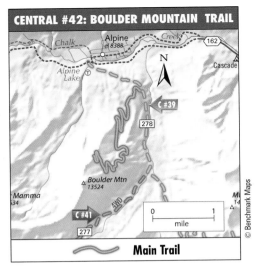

CENTRAL #42: BOULDER MOUNTAIN TRAIL

Main Trail

© Benchmark Maps

ruins of an old mine cabin and an open mine portal set into the bare talus slope.

Current Road Information

Pike & San Isabel National Forests
Salida Ranger District
325 West Rainbow Boulevard
Salida, CO 81201
(719) 539-3591

Map References

USFS San Isabel National Forest
Maptech CD:
    Colorado Springs/Ski Areas/Central
Benchmark's *Colorado Road & Recreation
    Atlas*, p. 99
Colorado Atlas & Gazetteer, p. 59
The Roads of Colorado, p. 110
Trails Illustrated, #130

Route Directions

▼0.0   From the 1.1-mile mark on Central
         #39: Mt. Antero Trail (Baldwin Creek
         Road), zero trip meter and make a
         sharp right turn onto an unmarked,
         rocky track.
         GPS: N 38°42.21′ W 106°16.47′

▼0.9 SO Campsites off to the left and right.
         Then cabin ruins and track on left.
▼4.8   Top of track. Mine shaft and ruins.
         GPS: N 38°41.20′ W 106°17.32′

around an oncoming vehicle is for one vehicle to reverse a good distance. Remember that the vehicle going uphill has the right-of-way, but common sense should always prevail. Because of the steep talus slopes, you have to stop often and clear rubble off the road.

On the way up, the route affords some wonderful, panoramic views across to the Mount Antero road and the adjoining mountain peaks, but when you reach the mine at the top, the view is truly spectacular—across the Chalk Creek Valley, Alpine Lake, and the township of Alpine.

At the end of the trail are the windswept

Mining ruins at the end of the trail

Pomeroy Lakes and Mary Murphy Mine Trail

STARTING POINT Intersection of Central #34: Hancock Pass Trail (FR 295) and FR 297.1

FINISHING POINT Parking area at Pomeroy Lakes

TOTAL MILEAGE 2.7 miles (one-way)

UNPAVED MILEAGE 2.7 miles

DRIVING TIME 1 hour (one-way)

ROUTE ELEVATION 10,500 to 12,035 feet

USUALLY OPEN Mid-June to late September

DIFFICULTY RATING 5

SCENIC RATING 7

Special Attractions

- Remains of the Mary Murphy Mine.
- A varied, challenging, short 4WD trail.
- Pomeroy Lakes in their barren, scenic, alpine setting.

History

According to legend, Dr. A. E. Wright, who discovered the Mary Murphy Mine in the mid-1870s, named it after a nurse who cared for him when he was taken to the hospital in Denver. If Mary was a nurse with whom Wright was smitten, it is not

Looking across Chalk Creek at log cabin ruins

clear who the adjoining Pat Murphy Mine was named after. One thing is certain: The Mary Murphy Mine was enormously successful and was the main engine of the local economy. It supported the towns of St. El-

Mary Murphy Mine tram support

mo, Romley, and Hancock. When the mine closed in 1926, it spelled the end for these towns and also for the remaining section of the old Alpine Tunnel railroad. The tracks were torn up within the year.

Description

This route starts along the road to Hancock that follows the Alpine Tunnel railroad grade.

After turning onto FR 297, the road passes many remains of the Mary Murphy Mine, located high above the road on the mountainside. Towers used by the tramway, which extended over 2 miles into Pomeroy Gulch from the railway grade, are still clearly evident as you drive along the initial section of the road. There are also a number of buildings where the tramway deposited the ore that it carried down from the top of the mountain.

Until this point the road is suitable for 2WD vehicles, but as the route proceeds along FR 297.2, the road becomes high-clearance 4WD only.

Continuing toward the lake, you pass a number of good backcountry camping sites and a grave on the side of the road that dates back to 1884.

The road gets progressively rockier and more rutted and eroded before reaching the parking area near the lakes, merely 2.7 miles from the start.

Current Road Information

Pike & San Isabel National Forests
Salida Ranger District
325 West Rainbow Boulevard
Salida, CO 81201
(719) 539-3591

Map References

USFS   San Isabel National Forest
Maptech CD:
    Colorado Springs/Ski Areas/Central
Benchmark's *Colorado Road & Recreation Atlas,* pp. 98, 99

Mill remains

Colorado Atlas & Gazetteer, p. 59
The Roads of Colorado, p. 110
Trails Illustrated, #130

Route Directions

▼0.0   At the intersection of Central #34: Hancock Pass Trail (FR 295) with sign to Mary Murphy Mine and Pomeroy Lakes, zero trip meter and proceed along FR 297.1.
GPS: N 38°40.38′ W 106°21.95′

▼0.2   SO   Rocky ascent. Mine ruins on right.
▼0.3   SO   Cabin on left. Cross over creek.
▼0.6   SO   Track on left.
▼0.7   SO   Mary Murphy Mine headquarters on right. Mine and tailings on left.
▼0.8   SO   Tracks on left.
▼0.9   SO   Gated track on left goes to Mary Murphy Mine ruins. Zero trip meter.
GPS: N 38°39.95′ W 106°21.34′

▼0.0   BR   Continue on FR 297.2 to Pomeroy Lakes.
▼0.2   SO   Track on right.
▼0.5   SO   Short track on left to mine ruins up the hill. Cross through creek.
▼0.7   SO   Grave on right (date: 1857-1884).
▼0.8   SO   Track on left.
▼1.0   TL   Track on right and straight ahead to

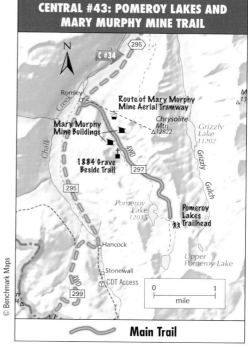

CENTRAL #43: POMEROY LAKES AND MARY MURPHY MINE TRAIL

© Benchmark Maps

Main Trail

campsites.

▼1.2   SO   Cross through creek.
▼1.8   End at Pomeroy Lakes and parking area.
GPS: N 38°38.90′ W 106°20.34′

Pomeroy Lake

Marshall Pass Poncha Creek Trail

STARTING POINT Intersection of Central #45: Marshall Pass Railway Grade Road and FR 203

FINISHING POINT Marshall Pass

TOTAL MILEAGE 8.1 miles

UNPAVED MILEAGE 8.1 miles

DRIVING TIME 1.25 hours

ROUTE ELEVATION 8,595 to 10,846 feet

USUALLY OPEN Mid-June to late September

DIFFICULTY RATING 3

SCENIC RATING 8

Special Attractions

- 4WD alternative to the railroad grade route to Marshall Pass.
- Very good views, especially near the summit.
- Access to good backcountry campsites, fishing, and many hiking trails.

Description

This route is narrower, rougher, and scenically more varied than the main road to Marshall Pass, which follows the old rail-road grade (Central #45). However, while not suitable for passenger vehicles, it offers little difficulty to a 4WD vehicle.

The trail begins at the intersection of Central #45: Marshall Pass Railway Grade Road and FR 203.

FR 203 gets progressively narrower and rougher, although it remains suitable for passenger vehicles in dry conditions. After Starvation Creek, creek crossings and the rougher road make a high-clearance vehicle necessary.

FR 203 offers numerous undeveloped campsites beside Poncha Creek for the first 6 miles after its intersection with CR/FR 200. From this point, the trail starts its ascent toward the pass, and camping possibilities become scarce. Eventually, the road departs from the creek to make the final climb through a series of alpine meadows, offering spectacular views before reaching the pass.

There are some very good backcountry campsites and numerous fishing spots beside Poncha Creek. For those who prefer more of the comforts of home, the particularly scenic O'Haver Lake offers a developed U.S. Forest Service campground with access for RVs and camper trailers. A num-

Old railway bridge over Poncha Creek

The foundations of one of Mears's old railroad bridges

ber of hiking trails run through the area, including the Colorado Trail and the Continental Divide Trail.

Current Road Information

Pike & San Isabel National Forests
Salida Ranger District
325 West Rainbow Boulevard
Salida, CO 81201
(719) 539-3591

Map References

USFS   Gunnison National Forest
Maptech CD:
　　　Alamosa/Pueblo/South Central
Benchmark's *Colorado Road & Recreation Atlas*, p. 99
Colorado Atlas & Gazetteer, p. 70
The Roads of Colorado, p. 110
Trails Illustrated, #139

A beaver dam that has created a pool beside the trail

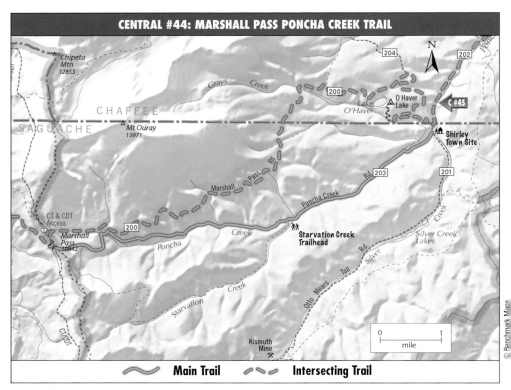

Main Trail   **Intersecting Trail**

Route Directions

▼0.0   Trail begins at the intersection of Central #45: Marshall Pass Railway Grade Road (FR 200) and FR 203. Zero trip meter and proceed toward Poncha Creek on FR 203.

8.1▲   **TR**   Trail ends at the intersection with Central #45: Marshall Pass Railway Grade.
      GPS: N 38°25.37' W 106°08.45'

▼0.8   **SO**   Track on right. Beaver Creek sign.
7.3▲   **SO**   Track on left. Beaver Creek sign.

▼1.0   **BR**   Signpost reads "Via Poncha Creek 7– FR 203." Intersection. Numerous good backcountry camping spots are found all along Poncha Creek.

7.1▲   **BL**   Intersection.
      GPS: N 38°24.92' W 106°08.31'

▼3.4   **SO**   Trailhead for Starvation Creek walking trail.
4.7▲   **SO**   Trailhead for Starvation Creek walking trail.

▼3.6   **SO**   Track on right is 0.25 miles in length with additional camping spots.
4.5▲   **SO**   Track on left.

▼4.6   **SO**   Cross over Tent Creek.
3.5▲   **SO**   Cross over Tent Creek.

▼5.1   **SO**   Track on left down to Poncha Creek and numerous campsites down below the road.
3.0▲   **SO**   Track on right.

▼5.5   **SO**   Cross over creek. Slightly farther, there's a short track on the right and four campsites.
2.6▲   **SO**   Track on left; then cross over creek.
      GPS: N 38°23.70' W106°12.50

▼6.8   **SO**   Cross over Ouray Creek
1.3▲   **SO**   Cross over Ouray Creek.

▼6.9   **SO**   Camping on right and left in grassy areas; then cross over Poncha Creek.
1.2▲   **SO**   Cross over Poncha Creek.

ATV rider on the trail

▼7.0 SO Open meadow on left with scenic
          views of valley and Sangre de Cristo
          mountain range to the east. No
          vehicle access.
1.1▲ SO Open meadow on right with scenic
          views.

▼7.1 SO Track on left to campsite.
1.0▲ SO Track on right to campsite.

▼7.5 SO 4WD track on left (203.1A) to
          Starvation Creek walking trail. This
          side trip leads 1.6 miles to TR 1408,
          which loops back to Marshall Pass
          after 6.6 miles. At the 1.8-mile point
          there is a scenic overlook—GPS: N
          38°22.96' W 106°13.19'.
0.6▲ SO Track on right to scenic overlooks.
          GPS: N 38°23.53' W 106°14.22'

▼8.0 TL Intersection with Central #45:
          Marshall Pass Railway Grade Road
          (FR 200). Track on left is the Colorado
          Trail.
0.1▲ TR FR 200 continues straight ahead.
          GPS: N 38°23.50' W 106°14.75'

▼8.1   Summit of Marshall Pass. Central

#45: Marshall Pass Railway Grade
Road (FR 200) continues to Sargents.
0.0▲ Summit of Marshall Pass. Zero trip
      meter.
      GPS: N 38°23.50' W 106°14.85'

Rocky section of the trail

Marshall Pass Railway Grade Road

STARTING POINT Mears Junction at US 285 and FR 200, 5 miles south of Poncha Springs

FINISHING POINT Sargents

TOTAL MILEAGE 29.7 miles

UNPAVED MILEAGE 29.7 miles

DRIVING TIME 1.25 hours

ROUTE ELEVATION 8,420 to 10,846 feet

USUALLY OPEN Late May to mid-October

DIFFICULTY RATING 1

SCENIC RATING 7

Special Attractions

- Easy, scenic road along a historic railroad grade.
- Developed campground and good fishing at picturesque O'Haver Lake.
- Provides a loop route between Marshall Pass and Mears Junction, when combined with Central #44: Marshall Pass Poncha Creek Trail.
- Steam train water tank in Sargents.

History

This pass is named for Lieutenant William L. Marshall, who discovered it while on the Wheeler survey expedition in 1873. Reportedly, he was suffering from a toothache and sought a quicker route back to Denver and relief from a dentist!

In 1877, Otto Mears constructed a wagon road to Gunnison across the pass from his Poncha Pass toll road. It served as a stagecoach route until the opening of the railroad and was used by President Grant in 1880. Mears sold the road to the Denver & Rio Grande Railroad. The Denver & Rio Grande was embroiled in a classic railroad battle during the early 1880s in its race to be first to link the Arkansas Valley and the Gunnison Basin area. The Denver, South Park & Pacific Railroad chose a route that

Denver & Rio Grande train climbing the grade to Marshall Pass in 1900

Aspens beside the old railroad grade in early fall

necessitated the construction of the famous Alpine Tunnel (Central #37).

With the aid of 23 snowsheds to protect it from the elements, a Denver & Rio Grande narrow gauge railway won the battle by using the Marshall Pass route. Operations commenced in 1881 and continued until 1953. The tracks were dismantled in 1955. A post office, located at the station at the top of the pass, continued to operate until 1952. President William H. Taft was probably the most famous passenger to cross the pass by train.

Located on the western end of the trail is Sargents. The town was established in the late 1870s and was named for Joseph Sargent who had been employed at the Los Piños Indian Agency and had established a ranch in the area in 1879. Initially the settlement was known as Marshalltown, but the name was changed in 1882. The town never grew very large and in the late 1880s had a population of only about 150.

Description
This route follows the old railroad grade and is easier than the alternative route via Poncha Creek (Central #44). The route is unpaved but wide and well graded. It is suitable for RVs and trailers making their way to the campground at O'Haver Lake or across Marshall Pass on CR 200.

O'Haver Lake offers good fishing and a developed forest service campground with access for RVs and camper trailers. A number of hiking trails run through the area, including the Colorado Trail and the Continental Divide Trail.

The trail starts at Mears Junction, which is the intersection of US 285 and CR/FR 200. Once the junction of two of Otto Mears's toll roads, the intersection is located about 5 miles south of Poncha Springs and 2.4 miles north of Poncha Pass. West of the pass, the journey runs through gentle, rolling countryside and ranchland with many stands of aspens adding color in fall. At Sargents, there is an old wooden water tank that used to service the steam locomotives that chugged up Marshall Pass from 1881 to 1953.

Current Road Information
Pike & San Isabel National Forests
Salida Ranger District
325 West Rainbow Boulevard
Salida, CO 81201
(719) 539-3591

O'Haver Lake

Map References

USFS   Gunnison National Forest; San
    Isabel National Forest
Maptech CD:
    Alamosa/Pueblo/South Central
Benchmark's *Colorado Road & Recreation
    Atlas*, p. 99
Colorado Atlas & Gazetteer, pp. 69, 70
The Roads of Colorado, p. 102
Trails Illustrated, #139

Route Directions

▼0.0   At Mears Junction, zero trip meter
          and turn from US 285 onto CR/FR 200
          heading west across cattle guard.
3.1▲   Cross cattle guard and end at
          intersection with US 285.
          GPS: N 38°26.89' W 106°06.40'

▼1.3   **SO** Cattle guard.

A small pond beside the trail

Another of the many stands of aspen along the route

1.8▲	TL	Cattle guard.

▼2.2	TR	Shirley town site. Public toilets on left. Turn right onto CR/FR 202.
0.9▲	TL	Turn left onto CR/FR 200. Shirley town site and public toilets on right.

▼3.1	TR	Intersection with CR/FR 200. O'Haver Lake is straight ahead, with fishing access and developed camping. Central #44: Marshall Pass Poncha Creek Trail to the left. Zero trip meter.
0.0▲		Proceed east on FR 202 toward Mears Junction.

GPS: N 38°25.37' W 106°08.45'

▼0.0		Proceed northeast on FR 200.
10.2▲	TL	Intersection with FR 202. O'Haver Lake is to the right. Central #44: Marshall Pass Poncha Creek Trail is straight ahead. Zero trip meter.

▼1.7	SO	Track on right is CR 204.
8.5▲	SO	Track on left is CR 204.

▼2.4	SO	O'Haver Lake on left below road.
7.8▲	SO	O'Haver Lake on right below road.

▼3.9	SO	Cross over Gray's Creek.

6.3▲	SO	Cross over Gray's Creek.

▼6.8	SO	Cross over Tent Creek.
3.4▲	SO	Cross over Tent Creek.

▼7.2	SO	Track on right.
3.0▲	SO	Track on left.

An old railroad cutting

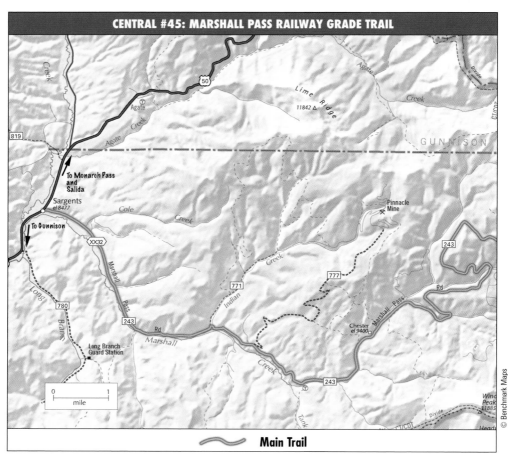

© Benchmark Maps

〜〜 **Main Trail**

▼9.0　SO　Old railway embankment across Ouray Creek.

1.2▲　SO　Old railway embankment across Ouray Creek.

▼9.9　SO　Hiking trail on right.

0.3▲　SO　Hiking trail on left.

▼10.0　SO　Marshall Pass Trailhead sign and public toilets on left.

0.2▲　SO　Marshall Pass Trailhead sign and public toilets on right.

▼10.2　SO　Road on left is Central #44: Marshall Pass Poncha Creek Trail. Track on left is the Colorado Trail. Zero trip meter.

0.0▲　　　Proceed north on FR 200.

　　　　　GPS: N 38°25.37' W 106°08.45'

▼0.0　　　Proceed northeast on FR 200.

16.4▲　BL　Track on right is the Colorado Trail; then Central #44: Marshall Pass Poncha Creek Trail on right. Zero trip meter.

▼0.1　SO　Summit of Marshall Pass.

16.3▲　SO　Track on left; then enter San Isabel National Forest; then cattle guard. Summit of Marshall Pass. Proceed west across cattle guard onto FR 243; then track on right.

　　　　　GPS: N 38°23.50' W 106°14.85'

▼0.2　SO　Seasonal gate.

16.2▲　SO　Seasonal gate.

▼1.0　SO　Track on left.

15.4▲　SO　Track on right.

▼1.3　SO　Track on left.

15.1▲　SO　Track on right.

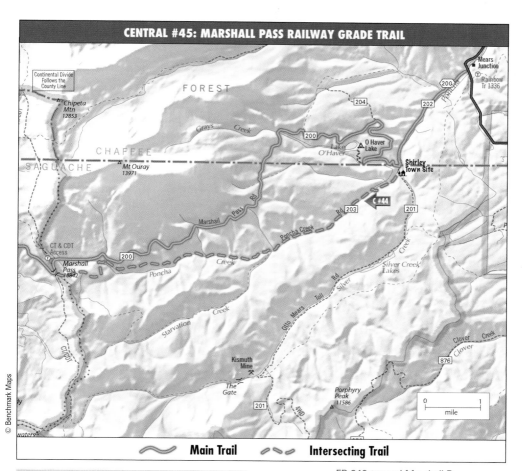

~~~ **Main Trail**   ⌒⌒⌒ **Intersecting Trail**

▼3.9   **SO**   Track on left for hiking, horses, and snowmobiles.

12.5▲   **SO**   Track on right for nonmotorized vehicles.

▼4.3   **SO**   Cattle guard.

12.1▲   **SO**   Cattle guard.

▼6.0   **SO**   Cross Millswitch Creek. Two tracks (closed) on left.

10.4▲   **SO**   Two tracks (closed) on right. Cross Millswitch Creek.

▼8.2   **SO**   Track on right to site of Chester.

8.2▲   **SO**   Track on left to site of Chester.
        GPS: N 38°22.28′ W 106°18.45′

▼11.0   **TL**   Seasonal gate. Intersection with road on right.

5.4▲   **TR**   Intersection and seasonal gate. Take FR 243 toward Marshall Pass.
        GPS: N 38°22.20′ W 106°20.62′

▼11.5   **SO**   Cattle guard.

4.9▲   **SO**   Cattle guard. Entering National Forest sign.

▼12.0   **SO**   Sign: "Indian Creek." Road on right is CR 35 W. (You are on CR XX 32.)

4.4▲   **SO**   CR 35 W on left goes to a network of 4WD tracks and the Pinnacle Mine.

▼16.4   End at intersection with US 50 in Sargents.

0.0▲   At intersection of US 50 and CR XX 32 (FR 243) in Sargents, zero trip meter and proceed along the county road toward Marshall Pass.
        GPS: N 38°24.46′ W 106°24.90′

Hayden Pass Trail

STARTING POINT Villa Grove
FINISHING POINT Intersection of Hayden
 Creek Road (CR 6) and US 50
TOTAL MILEAGE 15.8 miles
UNPAVED MILEAGE 14.4 miles
DRIVING TIME 1.5 hours
ROUTE ELEVATION 6,590 to 10,870 feet
USUALLY OPEN Early July to mid-October
DIFFICULTY RATING 3
SCENIC RATING 7

Special Attractions

- One of the few 4WD trails in the Sangre de Cristo range.
- Varied 4WD route with good views, particularly of the San Luis Valley.
- Can be combined with Central #47 across Medano Pass to form a loop.

History

This pass was another used by the Ute to cross between the San Luis Valley and the Arkansas River to the northeast. In 1874, a wagon road was built across the pass, and Ferdinand Hayden noted this road when his survey party crossed it in 1875. The pass is officially named for an early settler of the Wet Mountain Valley, Lewis Hayden.

By the late 1870s, Hayden Pass was a popular route to Villa Grove—an important supply center at that time to the main route west via Cochetopa Pass and to the mining area of Bonanza, some 17 miles northwest. It connected to the network of toll roads built by Otto Mears over the Cochetopa, Los Piños, and Poncha Passes. Mears built one of his first toll roads between Villa Grove and Bonanza, alongside Kerber Creek.

Villa Grove, established in 1870 as Garibaldi, was nestled in a grove of trees. In 1872, the name was changed to Villagrove, which was subsequently broken into two words. A narrow gauge spur line of the Denver & Rio Grande Railroad terminated at Villa Grove prior to being extended to Alamosa in 1890.

Description

The route heads east from Villa Grove, but the turnoff is unmarked except for a "Villa Grove Common" sign. The road initially travels through the ranchland of the San Luis Valley before starting its ascent toward the pass.

The route is easy to navigate but has a few sections, mainly on the east side, that are steep and quite rough and require high clearance. It travels through pine forest most of the way but provides some good views along the route, particularly the sweeping views back across the San Luis Valley.

The route passes Rainbow Trail, a 55-mile hiking trail, and two U.S. Forest Service campgrounds before reaching US 50 at Coaldale, 4.1 miles west of Cotopaxi and 20 miles south of Salida.

Current Road Information

Pike & San Isabel National Forests
Salida Ranger District
325 West Rainbow Boulevard
Salida, CO 81201
(719) 539-3591

The trail as it starts the ascent to the pass

Looking toward Coaldale from near the summit

Map References

USFS   Rio Grande National Forest; San
   Isabel National Forest
Maptech CD:
   Alamosa/Pueblo/South Central
Benchmark's *Colorado Road & Recreation
   Atlas,* pp. 99, 100
Colorado Atlas & Gazetteer, pp. 70, 71
The Roads of Colorado, p. 127

Route Directions

▼0.0   At intersection of US 285 and CR LL
         57 (FR 970) in Villa Grove, zero trip
         meter and proceed east along LL 57.

6.9▲   End at intersection with US 285 in
         Villa Grove.
         GPS: N 38°14.96' W 105°56.92'

▼0.1   SO Cattle guard and sign to Hayden Pass.

The road on the east side of Hayden Pass

6.8▲	SO	Cattle guard.

▼1.6	SO	Cross over San Luis Creek.
5.3▲	SO	Cross over San Luis Creek.

▼2.7	SO	Cattle guard. CR 60 MM on left.
4.2▲	SO	CR 60 MM on right. Cattle guard.

▼2.8	SO	Track on right.
4.1▲	SO	Track on left.

▼4.1	SO	Track on left.
2.8▲	SO	Track on right.

▼4.2	SO	Track on right.
2.7▲	SO	Track on left.

▼4.6	SO	Enter Rio Grande National Forest.
2.3▲	SO	Leave Rio Grande National Forest.

GPS: N 38°16.84′ W 105°52.30′

▼6.9	SO	Summit of Hayden Pass. Zero trip meter.
0.0▲		Continue. Enter Rio Grande National Forest. Name of road changes to FR 970.

GPS: N 38°17.60′ W 105°50.95′

▼0.0		Continue. Enter San Isabel National Forest. Name of road changes to FR 64.
8.9▲	SO	Summit of Hayden Pass. Zero trip meter.

An expansive view on the east side of the pass

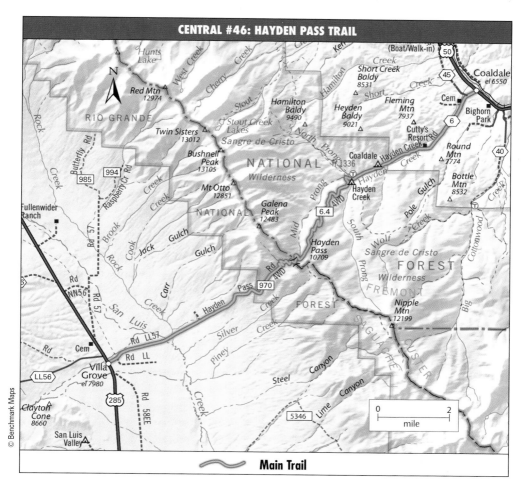

~~~ **Main Trail**

▼1.1   **SO**   Track on left.
7.8▲   **SO**   Track on right.

▼1.5   **SO**   Cabin on right.
7.4▲   **SO**   Cabin on left.

▼1.9   **SO**   Track on left.
7.0▲   **SO**   Track on right.

▼2.0   **SO**   Track on left.
6.9▲   **SO**   Track on right.

▼2.8   **SO**   Track on left.
6.1▲   **SO**   Track on right.

▼4.1   **TR**   Intersection. San Isabel National Forest Campground entrance and Rainbow Trail walking track straight ahead. Turn onto CR 6 (FR 006) toward Coaldale.

4.8▲   **TL**   Intersection. San Isabel National Forest Campground entrance and Rainbow Trail walking track. Turn onto FR 64.
GPS: N 38°19.79' W 105°49.36'

▼5.4   **SO**   USFS Coaldale Campground on right.
3.5▲   **SO**   USFS Coaldale Campground on left.

▼8.6   **SO**   Paved road on left.
0.3▲   **SO**   Paved road on right.

▼8.9   End at intersection with US 50.
0.0▲   Intersection: US 50 and CR 6, at Coaldale. Sign: "NF Access Hayden Creek." Zero trip meter and proceed south along CR 6 (FR 006), also called Hayden Creek Road.
GPS: N 38°22.06' W 105°45.11'

Medano Pass and Great Sand Dunes Trail

STARTING POINT Intersection of Colorado 69 and FR 559

FINISHING POINT Tollbooth for Great Sand Dunes National Park & Preserve on Colorado 150

TOTAL MILEAGE 21.6 miles

UNPAVED MILEAGE 20.1 miles

DRIVING TIME 2 hours

ROUTE ELEVATION 7,706 to 9,940 feet

USUALLY OPEN Late May to late October

DIFFICULTY RATING 4

SCENIC RATING 10

Special Attractions

■ The spectacular Great Sand Dunes National Park & Preserve with much more scenic access than the paved roads.

■ Four-wheel driving through sand and numerous creek crossings.

■ Historic pass route that can be combined with Central #46 across Hayden Pass to form a loop.

History

Medano means "sand hill" in Spanish, and the pass was also known as Sandhill Pass.

In 1807, Zebulon Pike crossed the pass after his famous attempt to climb the 14,000-foot peak that bears his name. By the 1850s, the pass was much used by fur traders and the mountain men heading for the San Juan region of Colorado. Captain John Gunnison even considered using it as a railroad route as early as 1853. In that same year, the Frémont expedition party crossed the pass but viewed the sand as too great an obstacle for a successful wagon route.

In 1866, a band of Ute attacked and killed settlers near La Veta, a small settlement 35 miles southeast of Medano Pass. They retreated over the pass but were captured by Kit Carson and Chief Ouray.

The route has never been developed for use by wagons or as a railroad and remains much as it has always been.

Description

This route commences at the intersection of Colorado 69 and FR 559, 23 miles south of Westcliffe and 9 miles west of Gardener. For nearly the first 7 miles, the road is 2WD as it travels through the Wolf Springs Ranch.

From the intersection with FR 412, it becomes a 4WD road and begins to switchback its way toward the pass. It is narrow and rough but presents no great problem as the surface is sound. The forest service has cut numerous channels across the road to protect it from erosion.

From the summit, the scenery on the descent changes, with interesting rock formations and numerous creek crossings. These are shallow enough (12 to 18 inches) that they should not pose any problem for a 4WD vehicle; rather, they add some variety to the trail. Use caution if it has rained recently, as the road can become boggy.

Increasing patches of sand herald the Great Sand Dunes National Park & Pre-

A section of trail alongside the towering sand dunes

serve, one of Colorado's natural wonders. Before entering the park & preserve, the main route is intersected by a number of side roads, along many of which the sand can be a greater obstacle than it is on this section of the main road.

After entering the Great Sand Dunes National Park & Preserve, the road travels beside the towering sand dunes, providing a much better view of them than that from the paved roads most visitors use. In places, the sand dunes are as close as 75 yards from the trail. There are a number of pull-offs, but be careful as the sand can be treacherous. It is a short walk to the creek and across to the face of the dunes.

As the road travels deeper into the park, the sand gets progressively worse, and you may need to deflate your tires to about 20 pounds. You may reinflate your tires at an air compressor station, which is open during the peak season months. At other times, or if it is not available, inquire at the Visitor Center for assistance.

Signs warn you of the most difficult section, where the sand is deep and loose, and steady momentum is required to avoid getting stuck. Shortly after this, you encounter the paved road (Colorado 150) that carries most visitors to the national park.

Current Road Information
Great Sand Dunes National Park and Preserve
11999 US 50
Mosca, CO 81146
(719) 378-6300

Map References
USFS   San Isabel National Forest
Maptech CD:
   Alamosa/Pueblo/South Central
Benchmark's *Colorado Road & Recreation Atlas*, p. 114
Colorado Atlas & Gazetteer, p. 81
The Roads of Colorado, pp. 143, 144

Route Directions

▼0.0	At the intersection of Colorado 69 and FR 559, zero trip meter and turn onto FR 559 at sign marked "National Forest Access, Medano Pass."
9.3▲	End at intersection with Colorado 69.
	GPS: N 37°50.19' W 105°18.44'

A warning sign with the massive sand dunes soaring in the background

Sandy trail with the massive sand dunes in the distance

▼0.3   SO   Cross over Muddy Creek.
9.0▲   SO   Cross over Muddy Creek.

▼6.8   SO   Cattle guard. Enter San Isabel
                National Forest.
2.5▲   SO   Cattle guard. Leave San Isabel
                National Forest.
                GPS: N 37°51.66′ W 105°24.09′

▼7.2   SO   Track on left.
2.1▲   SO   Track on right.

▼7.3   SO   Track on right.
2.0▲   SO   Track on left.

▼7.4   SO   FR 412 on right to South Muddy
                Creek.
1.9▲   SO   FR 412 on left to South Muddy Creek.

▼9.3   SO   Medano Pass. Leaving San Isabel
                National Forest and entering Great
                Sand Dunes National Preserve. Track
                on right; then gate. Zero trip meter.
0.0▲   Continue on main trail, now
                designated FR 559.

                GPS: N 37°51.37′ W 105°25.91′

▼0.0   Continue on main trail, now
                designated FR 235.
6.0▲   SO   Gate and track on left; then Medano
                Pass. Leave Great Sand Dunes
                National Preserve and enter San
                Isabel National Forest. Zero trip
                meter.

▼0.2   SO   Bridge over creek.
5.8▲   SO   Bridge over creek.

▼0.5   BL   Fork in track. Remain on 235. Turn
                right for some attractive backcountry
                campsites.
5.5▲   BR   Fork in track. Remain on 235. Turn left
                for some attractive backcountry
                campsites.

▼1.4   SO   Cross through creek.
4.6▲   SO   Cross through creek.

▼1.6   SO   Cross through creek.
4.4▲   SO   Cross through creek.

🌊 **Main Trail**

▼1.9 **SO** Track on right to cabin ruins; then cross through creek.
4.1▲ **SO** Cross through creek. Track on left to cabin ruins.

▼2.2 **SO** Cluster of cabin ruins.
3.8▲ **SO** Cluster of cabin ruins.
GPS: N 37°49.85′ W 105°26.76′

▼2.6 **SO** Cross through creek.
3.4▲ **SO** Cross through creek.

▼3.3 **SO** Cross through creek.

2.7▲ **SO** Cross through creek.

▼3.6 **SO** Small track on right.
2.4▲ **BR** Small track on left.

▼3.7 **SO** Cross through creek twice.
2.3▲ **SO** Cross through creek twice.

▼4.4 **SO** Cross through creek.
1.6▲ **SO** Cross through creek.

▼4.9 **SO** Cross through creek.
1.1▲ **SO** Cross through creek.

Medano Creek crossing

▼5.1	SO	Ruins (chimney) of old building.
0.9▲	SO	Ruins (chimney) of old building.
		GPS: N 37°48.47′ W 105°28.99′

▼5.2	SO	Cross through creek.
0.8▲	SO	Cross through creek.

▼5.6	SO	Cross through large creek.
0.4▲	SO	Cross through large creek.

▼5.8-5.9 SO	Tracks on left.
0.1-0.2▲ SO	Tracks on right.

▼ 6.0	SO	Leave Great Sand Dunes National Preserve and enter Great Sand Dunes National Park. Zero trip meter.
0.0▲		Cross through gate and proceed along FR 235.
		GPS: N 37°48.10′ W 105°29.85′

▼0.0		Cross through gate and proceed along FR 235.

4.8▲	SO	Leave Great Sand Dunes National Park and enter Great Sand Dunes National Preserve. Zero trip meter.

▼0.1	SO	Sand Creek Trail on right. Little Medano Trail on left.
4.7▲	SO	Little Medano Trail on right. Sand Creek Trail on left.

▼0.6	SO	Cross through creek; then picnic area, parking, and cabins.
4.2▲	SO	Cabins, parking, and picnic areas; then cross through creek.

▼2.4	SO	Gate and picnic spots.
2.4▲	SO	Picnic spots and gate.

▼4.8	TR	Pavement. Intersection with Colorado 150. (Note: Compressed air is available across the road.) Zero trip meter.
0.0▲		Proceed on Medano Pass Road (FR

235). Sign reads "Medano Pass Primitive Road."

GPS: N 37°44.66' W 105°30.39'

▼ 0.0   Proceed along Colorado 150.

1.5▲   **TL**   Opposite the National Parks building marked "private residence" and tire air station on right. Zero trip meter.

▼0.5   **SO**   Road on right to sand dunes and picnic area.

1.0▲   **SO**   Road on left to sand dunes and picnic area.

▼0.7   **SO**   Nature trail on left.

0.8▲   **SO**   Nature trail on right.

▼0.9   **SO**   Intersection. Visitor Center on the right.

0.6▲   **SO**   Visitor Center on the left. Intersection.

▼1.5   End at the tollbooth for Sand Dunes National Park.

0.0▲   At the tollbooth for Sand Dunes National Park, zero trip meter and proceed toward the dunes.

GPS: N 37°43.50' W 105°31.12'

Sand Creek meandering through the dunes

Selected Further Reading

Abbott, Carl, Stephen J. Leonard, and David Mc-Comb. *Colorado: A History of the Centennial State.* Niwot, Colo.: University Press of Colorado, 1994.

Bauer, Carolyn. *Colorado Ghost Towns—Colorado Traveler Guidebooks.* Frederick, Colo.: Renaissance House, 1987.

Boyd, Leanne C. and H. Glenn Carson. *Atlas of Colorado Ghost Towns.* Vols. 1 and 2. Deming, N.M.: Carson Enterprises, Ltd., 1984.

Bright, William. *Colorado Place Names.* Boulder, Colo.: Johnson Books, 1993.

Brown, Robert L. *Colorado Ghost Towns Past & Present.* Caldwell, Idaho: Caxton Printers, Ltd., 1972.

————. *Ghost Towns of the Colorado Rockies.* Caldwell, Idaho: Caxton Printers, Ltd., 1990.

Crutchfield, James A. *It Happened in Colorado.* Helena & Billings, Mo.: Falcon Press Publishing, 1993.

Dallas, Sandra. *Colorado Ghost Towns and Mining Camps.* Norman, Okla.: University of Oklahoma Press, 1985.

Eberhart, Perry. *Guide to the Colorado Ghost Towns and Mining Camps.* Chicago.: Swallow Press, 1995.

Green, Stewart M. *Bureau of Land Management Back Country Byways.* Helena, Mont.: Falcon Press, 1995.

Griffin, Wayne W. *Central Colorado 4-Wheeling Guidebook.* Aspen, Colo.: Who Press, 1994.

Heck, Larry E. *4-Wheel Drive Roads & Ghost Towns of the San Juans.* Aurora, Colo.: Pass Patrol, 1995.

————. *4-Wheel Drive Roads to Outback Colorado.* Aurora, Colo.: Pass Patrol, 1995.

————. *4-Wheel Drive Trails & Ghost Towns of Colorado.* Aurora, Colo.: Pass Patrol, 1995.

Helmuth, Ed, and Gloria Helmuth. *The Passes of Colorado.* Boulder, Colo.: Pruett, 1994.

Koch, Don. *The Colorado Pass Book.* Boulder, Colo.: Pruett, 1992.

McTighe, James. *Roadside History of Colorado.* Boulder, Colo.: Johnson Books, 1984.

Noel, Thomas J., Paul F. Mahoney, and Richard E. Stevens. *Historical Atlas of Colorado.* Norman, Okla.: University of Oklahoma Press, 1994.

Norton, Boyd, and Barbara Norton. *Backroads of Colorado.* Stillwater, Minn: Voyageur Press, 1995.

Ormes, Robert M. *Railroads and the Rockies.* Denver, Colo.: Sage Books, 1963.

Southworth, Dave. *Colorado Mining Camps.* Round Rock, Tx.: Wild Horse, 1997.

Swift, Kim. *Heart of the Rockies: A History of the Salida Area.* Boulder, Colo.: Johnson Books, 1996.

Ubbelohde, Carl, Maxine Benson, and Duane A. Smith. *A Colorado History.* Boulder, Colo.: Pruett Publishing, 1995.

Wilson, Ray D. *Colorado Historical Tour Guide.* Carpentersville, Ill.: Crossroads Communications, 1990.

Wolle, Muriel Sibelle. *The Bonanza Trail.* Chicago: The Swallow Press, 1953.

————. *Stampede to Timberline: The Ghost Towns and Mining Camps of Colorado.* Chicago.: Swallow Press and Ohio University Press, 1974.

Selected Internet Sources

Colorado Byways
www.coloradobyways.org

Colorado Historical Society
www.coloradohistory.org

Colorado State Parks
parks.state.co.us

GORP.com
gorp.away.com

Minerology Database
mindat.org

Mountain Studies Institute
mountainstudies.org

National Center for Disease Control: Hantavirus Pulmonary Syndrome
cdc.gov/ncidad/diseases/hanta/hps/

U.S. Bureau of Land Management, Colorado
blm.gov/co

U.S. Department of the Interior, Bureau of Reclamation
usbr.gov

U.S. Fish & Wildlife Service
fws.gov

U.S. Forest Service
www.fs.fed.us/r5/forests.html

Photo Credits

Unless otherwise indicated, all photographs are copyrighted by Adler Publishing, Inc., or by Peter Massey.

33 Denver Public Library Western History Collection; **80** Denver Public Library Western History Collection; **84** Denver Public Library Western History Collection; **91** Denver Public Library Western History Collection; **117** Denver Public Library Western History Collection; **184** Shutterstock; **198** Denver Public Library Western History Collection; **206** Denver Public Library Western History Collection; **208** Denver Public Library Western History Collection; **225** (upper) Colorado Historical Society; (lower) Denver Public Library Western History Collection; **226** Denver Public Library Western History Collection; **231** Denver Public Library Western History Collection; **256** Denver Public Library Western History Collection.

Acknowledgements

Many other people and organizations have made contributions to the research and production of this book. We owe them all special thanks for their assistance.

Trail map images from the Benchmark *Colorado Road & Recreation Atlas*. Produced by and copyright ©Benchmark Maps, Medford, Oregon. All rights reserved. Used with permission. Benchmarkmaps.com.

Adler Publishing Company, Inc.
Parker, CO 80138
Toll-free: 800-660-5107
Fax: 303-688-4388
AdlerPublishing.com

A D L E R
PUBLISHING

Trail Index

other colorado and utah trails

backroad & 4-wheel drive trail guides

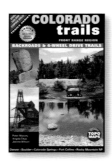

Colorado Trails-Southwest Region
48 of the region's best scenic backroads and four-wheel drive trails. It covers Silverton, Animas Forks, Ouray, Durango, Telluride, Lake City, and Creede. 336 pages.
ISBN: 978-1-930193-07-9; Price: $24.95

Colorado Trails–Front Range Region
42 scenic backroads and 4-wheel drive trails along the Front Range including trails near Fort Collins, Boulder, Idaho Springs, Denver, Colorado Springs, Cañon City, and Rocky Mountain National Park.
ISBN 978-1-930193-50-5; Price $24.95

Utah Trails–Northern
35 off-road routes near the towns of Vernal, Logan, Salt Lake City, Price, Wendover, Beaver, and Milford.
ISBN 978-1-930193-30-7; Price $19.95

Utah Trails–Central
34 trails near the towns of Green River, Richfield, Hanksville, Crescent Junction, and Castle Dale.
ISBN 978-1-930193-31-4; Price $19.95

Utah Trails–Moab
57 trails in and around Moab, Monticello, Canyonlands National Park, Arches National Park, Green River, Mexican Hat, Bluff, and Blanding.
ISBN 978-1-930193-09-3; Price $24.95

Utah Trails–Southwest
49 off-road routes in the Four Corners region and around the towns of Escalante, St. George, Kanab, Boulder, Bryce Canyon, Hurricane, and Ticaboo.
ISBN 978-1-930193-10-9; Price $24.95

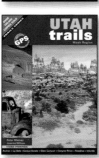
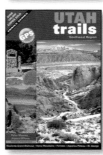

to order
call 800-660-5107 or
visit 4WDbooks.com

nevada and arizona trails
backroad & 4-wheel drive trail guides

Nevada Trails–Western Region
39 trails located near Reno, Carson City, Virginia City, Lake Tahoe, Tonopah, and Hawthorne.
ISBN 978-1-930193-15-4; Price $24.95

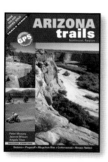
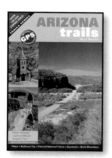

Arizona Trails–Northeast
47 trails located near the towns of Flagstaff, Williams, Prescott (northeast), Winslow, Fort Defiance and Window Rock.
ISBN 978-1-930193-02-4; Price $24.95

Arizona Trails–West
Descriptions for 33 trails located near the towns of Bullhead City, Lake Havasu City, Parker, Kingman, Prescott (west), and Quartzsite (north).
ISBN 978-1-930193-00-0; Price $24.95

Arizona Trails–Central
44 off-road routes located near the towns of Phoenix, Wickenburg, Quartzsite (south), Payson, Superior, Globe and Yuma (north).
ISBN 978-1-930193-01-7; Price $24.95

Arizona Trails–South
33 trails located near the towns of Tucson, Douglas, Mammoth, Reddington, Stafford, Yuma (southeast), Ajo and Nogales.
ISBN 978-1-930193-03-1; Price $24.95

to order
call 800-660-5107 or
visit 4WDbooks.com

california trails
backroad & 4-wheel drive trail guides

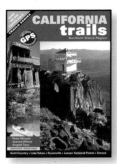
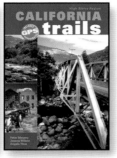

California Trails–Northern Sierra
55 off-road routes located near the towns of Sacramento (east), Red Bluff (east), Truckee, South Lake Tahoe, Sonora, Susanville, Chico, Oroville, Yuba City, Placerville, Stockton (east), Jackson, and Sonora.
ISBN 978-1-930193-23-9; Price $24.95

California Trails–High Sierra
50 trails located near the towns of Fresno (north), Oakhurst, Lone Pine, Bishop, Bridgeport, Coulterville, Mariposa, and Mammoth Lakes.
ISBN 978-1-930193-21-5; Price $19.95

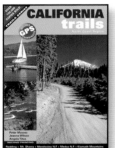

California Trails–North Coast
47 routes located near the towns of Sacramento, Redding (west), Red Bluff, Clear Lake, McCloud, Mount Shasta, Yreka, Crescent City, and Fort Bidwell.
ISBN 978-1-930193-22-2; Price $24.95

California Trails–Central Mountains
52 trails located near the towns of Big Sur, Fresno, San Luis Obispo, Santa Barbara, Bakersfield, Mojave, and Maricopa.
ISBN 978-1-930193-19-2; Price $24.95

California Trails–South Coast
50 trails located near the towns of Los Angeles, San Bernardino, San Diego, Salton Sea, Indio, Borrego Springs, Ocotillo and Palo Verde.
ISBN 978-1-930193-24-6; Price $24.95

California Trails–Desert
51 off-road routes located near the towns of Lone Pine (east), Panamint Springs, Death Valley area, Ridgecrest, Barstow, Baker and Blythe.
ISBN 978-1-930193-20-8; Price $24.95

to order
call 800-660-5107 or
visit 4WDbooks.com

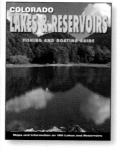
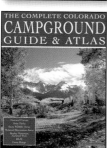